OKANAGAN COLLEGE LIBRARY

03579448

An Introduction to Kant's Aesthetics

D1617207

OKANAGAN COLLEGE
LIBHARY
BRITISH COLUMBIA

An Introduction to Kant's Aesthetics

Core Concepts and Problems

Christian Helmut Wenzel

Blackwell
Publishing

© 2005 by Christian Helmut Wenzel

BLACKWELL PUBLISHING
350 Main Street, Malden, MA 02148-5020, USA
9600 Garsington Road, Oxford OX4 2DQ, UK
550 Swanston Street, Carlton, Victoria 3053, Australia

The right of Christian Helmut Wenzel to be identified as the Author of this Work has been asserted in accordance with the UK Copyright, Designs, and Patents Act 1988.

All rights reserved. No part of this publication may be reproduced, stored in a retrieval system, or transmitted, in any form or by any means, electronic, mechanical, photocopying, recording or otherwise, except as permitted by the UK Copyright, Designs, and Patents Act 1988, without the prior permission of the publisher.

First published 2005 by Blackwell Publishing Ltd

1   2005

Library of Congress Cataloging-in-Publication Data

Wenzel, Christian Helmut.
    An introduction to Kant's aesthetics : core concepts and problems / Christian Helmut Wenzel.
        p.   cm.
    Includes bibliographical references and index.
    ISBN-13: 978-1-4051-3035-6 (hardcover : alk. paper)
    ISBN-10: 1-4051-3035-0 (hardcover : alk. paper)
    ISBN-13: 978-1-4051-3036-3 (pbk. : alk. paper)
    ISBN-10: 1-4051-3036-9 (pbk. : alk. paper)
    1. Kant, Immanuel, 1724–1804—Aesthetics.   2. Kant, Immanuel, 1724–1804. Kritik der Urteilskraft.   3. Aesthetics.   4. Judgment (Logic)   5. Judgment (Aesthetics)
6. Teleology.   7. Aesthetics, Modern—18th century.   I. Title.

    B2799.A4W46 2005
    111'.85—dc22   2005009258

A catalogue record for this title is available from the British Library.

Set in 10 on 12.5 pt Dante
by SNP Best-set Typesetter Ltd, Hong Kong
Printed and bound in India
by Replika Press, Pvt Ltd, Kundli

The publisher's policy is to use permanent paper from mills that operate a sustainable forestry policy, and which has been manufactured from pulp processed using acid-free and elementary chlorine-free practices. Furthermore, the publisher ensures that the text paper and cover board used have met acceptable environmental accreditation standards.

For further information on
Blackwell Publishing, visit our website:
www.blackwellpublishing.com

Contents

Correspondances

La Nature est un temple où de vivants piliers
Laissent parfois sortir de confuses paroles;
L'homme y passe à travers des forêts de symboles
Qui l'observent avec des regards familiers.

Comme des longs échos qui de loin se confondent
Dans une ténébreuse et profonde unité,
Vaste comme la nuit et comme la clarté,
Les parfums, les couleurs et les sons se répondent.

Il est des parfums frais comme des chairs d'enfants,
Doux comme les hautbois, verts comme les prairies,
— Et d'autres, corrompus, riches et triomphants,

Ayant l'expansion des choses infinies,
Comme l'ambre, le musc, le benjoin et l'encens,
Qui chantent les transports de l'esprit et des sens.

Charles Baudelaire

Correspondences

Nature is a temple whose living pillars
Utter at times confused words;
Man passes there through forests of symbols
That watch him with familiar eyes.

Like long echoes confounding distantly
Into oneness, unfathomable and dark,
Vast as the night, vast as light,
Scents, sounds and colors correspond.

Scents fresh as babies' skin,
Soft as oboes, as meadows green
— and others, broken, triumphant, rich,

Expansive as infinite things,
Amber, musk, incense and myrrh,
That sing the ecstasies of spirit and of sense.

(Translation by
Joseph Swann and C. H. Wenzel)

Foreword

It has been said that Kant probably never saw a great painting or piece of sculpture; indeed, this is quite likely, inasmuch as he spent his entire life in and around Königsberg in East Prussia. It is also clear that he had no great appreciation of music and that the only art form with which he had an extensive familiarity was literature. Nevertheless, this did not prevent him from producing what is generally regarded as one of the most important contributions to aesthetics in the history of modern thought. This is contained in the *Critique of the Aesthetic Power of Judgment*, which is the first part of the *Critique of the Power of Judgment* (or, in some English versions, the *Critique of Judgment*) of 1790. Unfortunately, however, this work is almost as forbidding to the uninitiated as it is rewarding to those able to penetrate its almost legendary obscurity.

There are a number of reasons for this obscurity, not least of which are the inherent difficulty of the issues involved and the unfamiliar technical terminology in which Kant expresses his views. The main reason, however, which also largely explains the terminological difficulties is that the *Critique of the Power of Judgment* is the capstone of an all-encompassing "critical system," which Kant developed in the 1780s. In fact, it is the third of three "Critiques," the first two being the *Critique of Pure Reason* (1781, second edition 1787) and the *Critique of Practical Reason* (1788), which is why it is often referred to simply as the "third Critique." Accordingly, much of what Kant has to say in this work cannot be understood without some grasp of the larger project of which it is an integral part.

In addition to contributing to the difficulty in understanding Kant's aesthetic theory, this theory's tight connection with his overall critical project is also directly responsible for two of its most distinctive features. First, as the title of the third *Critique* suggests, Kant's aesthetics is oriented more toward questions of aesthetic judgment, namely, the grounds and warrant for claiming that an object of nature or art is beautiful (or sublime), than toward questions of the nature of art. Although Kant did deal with the latter and, in the process, propounded a very influential theory of artistic creativity and genius, in his mind at least, this was secondary to the "critique of taste," which was the original title that Kant assigned to the work that was eventually to become the third *Critique*. In short, Kant's is more a "reception" than a "creation aesthetic."

Second, Kant's overall aesthetic theory is embedded in a set of questions regarding knowledge, morality, and even metaphysics. And, to complicate matters even further, it is combined with the *Critique of Teleological Power of Judgment*, which is the second part of the third *Critique*. All of this adds immeasurably to the richness and importance of Kant's account, but at the same time it reinforces the need for some guide to assist the reader who lacks sufficient knowledge of the intricacies of Kant's thought.

Although there has been no shortage of interpretive studies of Kant's aesthetics in the recent literature (including one by myself), there is really nothing of which I am aware that is both addressed to the reader with little or no prior knowledge of Kant's thought and thoroughly grounded in the texts. These are the main virtues of Christian Wenzel's brief work. His discussion is accessible, informed, and, given the modest size of the book, remarkably comprehensive. In fact, Wenzel has something useful to say about virtually every aspect of Kant's aesthetic theory. To be sure, in no case does he provide the last word – nor does he pretend to do so – but he does supply an excellent overview of this theory, as it is presented in the third *Critique*. Particularly notable in this regard are the glossary in which the key technical terms are explained and the reference to "further reading" following each section. Whereas the former will be of benefit to the reader who is confronting Kant for the first time, the latter will be of value to those who wish to pursue a particular topic or issue in greater depth.

Finally, it must be noted that, in spite of the modesty of its ambitions, Wenzel's book makes a significant contribution to the literature at two points. One is the topic of ugliness. Like most writers on aesthetics, at least those of his time, Kant's focus was on judgments of beauty (both natural and artistic) and he has very little to say about the ugly. The problem, however, is that it seems that a theory of aesthetic judgment *ought* to account for the possibility of judgments of ugliness as well as beauty. Wenzel tackles this issue head on, arguing that Kant's theory of taste can account for judgments of ugliness, as indeed it must.

The second topic on which Wenzel has something interesting to say concerns Kant's theory of genius. Notoriously, Kant claimed that genius is limited to the domain of art and, therefore, that great mathematicians and scientists – Leibniz and Newton are the paradigms – cannot truly be called geniuses because their discoveries were the result of the application of determinate rules, whereas the creation of a great work of art is not. Arguing as a mathematician (he has a doctorate in mathematics as well as in philosophy), Wenzel points out that something like the "free play" of the faculties, which for Kant is required for both the creation and assessment of beauty, is likewise operative in mathematical invention and even that mathematics has room for a genuinely aesthetic sense of beauty. Although Wenzel's treatment of both topics will no doubt prove to be controversial, it certainly serves to advance the discussion.

Henry E. Allison

Acknowledgments

Several people have contributed to this book and I would like to take this opportunity to thank them. My former teacher Manfred Baum spent much time, now already several years ago, reading and discussing Kant together with me. I still remember our meetings and lively disputes that usually went way past midnight. There are three people who contributed most directly to this book and made writing it much more enjoyable than it would otherwise have been. These are Joel Schickel, Robert Reynolds, and Jeff Dean. Joel Schickel and Robert Reynolds have carefully read through the whole manuscript, corrected my English (I am German), asked many good questions, and made many valuable suggestions, all of which improved the manuscript greatly. As we corresponded section by section while I was still in the process of writing, these exchanges were most stimulating and enjoyable. Jeff Dean, the philosophy editor from Blackwell, has been most supportive and helpful from the very beginning. He read through the manuscript more than once and at different stages, and he made many wise suggestions how to improve it. He, too, made the whole process of writing much more enjoyable for me. Danielle Descoteaux, also from Blackwell, carefully read through the final version and made many helpful comments. My thanks go to her as well. Five anonymous referees from Blackwell read through the manuscript at different stages and shared their detailed comments with me. At the final stages, Sarah Dancy, my copy editor and project manager, made many helpful suggestions, and Joseph Swann very kindly did the proofreading. Working with both of them was a source of great pleasure to me. I am also in debt to my students at Duke University and Chi Nan University, where I gave courses on Kant's aesthetics. I enjoyed the teaching and learned much from them. Also I would like to thank Henry Allison for kindly having written the foreword. Finally, I would like to thank my research assistant Wang Chun Ying for his help and the National Science Council of Taiwan for its financial support.

About This Book

This book is not intended primarily for Kant scholars. It is directed at a wider audience, including undergraduate and graduate students of philosophy and related fields such as art and literature. I want to lead the reader right into the middle of Kant's aesthetics and his third *Critique*. Accordingly, I have avoided any discussion of secondary literature in the main text of my book. Instead, at the end of every section within each chapter there is a list of suggested further reading that seemed to me most relevant to the topic of that section. These lists give first the English and then the German and French titles. Within each group I tried to arrange them according to relevance and accessibility. I also briefly comment on each item on the list, indicating what the main points of that paper or book are and what the reader may expect to find there.

As the title indicates, this book is about "core problems." It is more systematic than historical, and no knowledge of Kant is presupposed. Most sections can be read without any previous knowledge of Kant's first *Critique*, and in the few places where such knowledge is necessary I have tried to provide it. Of course, being familiar with Kant's first *Critique* is the best preparation for reading the third *Critique*. But the third *Critique* stands pretty much on its own feet and can be read by itself, at least if one gets a little help here and there. Such help I have tried to provide.

It is my aim to get to the heart of the matter as quickly as possible – that is, to show and to discuss the problems Kant himself was trying to solve. Of course this does not save the reader from the trouble of reading Kant's third *Critique*. On the contrary, my book follows Kant's text and asks the reader to take a close critical look at the text him- or herself. I have always found the third *Critique* a wonderful and inspiring book, difficult to understand, but very much worth the effort. I hope this book can pass on some of that feeling.

At the end of the book the reader will find a glossary, in which I give brief explanations of key terms in Kant that are technical or have an unusual meaning. These terms are usually emboldened when they occur for the first time in each chapter.

Note on the Translation

I have followed the translation provided by *The Cambridge Edition of the Works of Immanuel Kant*. In particular, I have used two volumes: the *Critique of the Power of Judgment*, translated by Paul Guyer and Eric Matthews (Cambridge University Press, 2000); and the *Critique of Pure Reason*, translated by Paul Guyer and Allen W. Wood (Cambridge University Press, 1998). Page references are given to the standard German edition of Kant's works, *Kants Gesammelte Schriften* (*Akademie Ausgabe*), the pagination of which is also indicated at the margins of the *Cambridge Edition*. References to the first *Critique* are given in the usual form, (A 820/B 848) referring to page 820 of the first and page 848 of the second edition. Translations from the recently published *Anthropologie Nachschriften*, volume XXV of the *Akademie Ausgabe*, are mine. Italics that occur in quotations from Kant are always mine, if not otherwise indicated.

Introduction

The Aesthetic Dimension Between Subject and Object

Imagine three people standing in front of a painting by Kandinsky or admiring the sun setting over the sea. Suppose that one of them finds pleasure in looking at what he or she sees and even calls it beautiful, whereas the second feels nothing special and says so, and the third even says that the painting, or the sunset, is downright ugly (which in the case of the sunset might be more difficult to imagine). Given this situation, is it possible that all three of them have taste? Can they all be justified in what they are saying? Can they all make "true" judgments of taste, judgments that are correct or true in some sense? Or is it the case that at most one of them can be right and the others must be wrong? Can we even find out who is right and who is wrong, either by examining the object or by engaging all three judges of beauty in a discussion of some kind?

If beauty is not an objective matter and also not merely subjective and a matter of personal opinion, then there may be room for some kind of *je ne sais quoi*, some kind of "I don't know what it is," the feeling that there is something objective about what one finds beautiful, or ugly, although one cannot spell out what it is.

Suppose (1) we want to argue that taste is not merely a subjective, personal matter, yet (2) we do not think taste is something that can be subjected to objective criteria, in the sense that there could be rules for what should count as beautiful and what should not. If we impose these two requirements and decline to reduce taste to either of the two extremes, the merely subjective and the purely objective, what then could taste possibly be? What could it be based upon? The task Kant sets for himself is to explain taste in a way that takes into account the intuition that some **aesthetic** judgments are right and others wrong, although no rules for assigning aesthetic values can be given. The task is thus to avoid the two extremes. Taste and beauty should be understood as being neither subjective nor objective, neither a mere matter of personal opinion or feeling, nor something that can be subjected to rules and objective criteria. Kant's aesthetics, as we will see, is written in such a way that it can accomplish this task. We will study his aesthetics in this light, and we will focus on his critical aesthetics, which is given in his book: *Critique of the Power of Judgment*, 1790. Much earlier he also wrote the essay *Observations on the Feeling of the Beautiful and Sublime*, 1764. These are his two works on aesthetics, of which the earlier one from 1764 is minor. We will concentrate on the later work of 1790, which offers Kant's mature, critical, and more influential aesthetics.

It is striking that Kant's aesthetics is not introduced under the heading "Aesthetics," or "Critique of Beauty," but appears under the title "Critique of the **Power of Judgment**." Compared with previous aesthetic theories, Kant's approach is marked by a certain *shift of focus*, a shift from the *object* to the judgment *about* the object. Instead of giving an account of the nature and quality of certain kinds of objects (the objects that we find beautiful), Kant analyzes a certain kind of judgment, namely the judgment of taste. This shift should not come as a surprise if we think of the central role the notion of **judgment** plays in Kant's first *Critique*, the *Critique of Pure Reason*. Furthermore, this shift is a fortunate one, especially in his aesthetics, because it enables him, as we shall see, to be in a better position to avoid both the subjective and the objective extremes described above.

If we concentrate on the act of judgment, instead of trying to figure out what it is about the object that makes us call it beautiful (or ugly), we have a wider perspective: we then have to take into account both the object and the subject, and we can study the *relation* between the object and the judging subject as a relation that is reflected in the judgment of taste itself, or in some act that underlies that judgment. In this way we will be able to avoid the two extremes, namely the subjective one, which construes taste as being mere feeling and personal opinion, and the objective one, which considers aesthetics to be a matter of rules and proofs.

We can say that, according to Kant, beauty is neither to be found in the object nor in the eye of the beholder. Contrary to what one might suppose, it is not just a relationship between the beholder and the object either. Rather, beauty has its roots in an act of contemplation that takes into account that relationship. The judgment of taste, as Kant develops it, is a sophisticated and reflecting judgment about our relationship to the object. This gives Kant a certain distance from the judging subject and the judged object, which allows him to take both of them into account and to keep a balance between two extreme perspectives. Furthermore, Kant argues that what on the part of the object is allowed to play a role in the judgment of taste is merely the "form" of the object, that is, its spatio-temporal structures. (Whether this includes colors will be discussed in chapter 3, in the section "Purposiveness and Form: Charm versus Euler." Leonard Euler was a famous Swiss mathematician who also wrote about colors, and Kant discusses his ideas.) But these objective structures alone, without the judging subject, are never sufficient to determine whether we should call the object beautiful or not.

Kant wants his aesthetics to be a part neither of psychology nor of the sciences. We will see that Kant sets out to discover new **a priori** justifying **grounds** for judgments of taste that do not belong to the domain of psychology or the sciences. These grounds are the so-called **principle** of "subjective **purposiveness**" and the contemplation of an object with respect to this principle in a so-called "free harmonious play" of our **cognitive** powers.

Kant wants to show us that judgments of taste are something special due to these (new) grounds, and he thinks that neither judgments of taste nor these grounds have been properly understood so far by any of his predecessors or contemporaries.

Kant tries to make room for an aesthetics that can stand on its own feet, an aesthetics that has an equal status with moral and theoretical philosophy. This new inquiry, an aesthetic theory in the form of a critique of the power of aesthetic judgment, should reveal something new and essential about us as human beings. A better understanding of these a priori grounds of judgments of taste will enable us to explain the phenomenon of the *je ne sais quoi*.

Further reading

Zammito, *The Genesis of Kant's "Critique of Judgment,"* has a nice section (pp. 17–45) vividly describing the philosophical mood of the time, the *Berliner Aufklärung*, Frederick II, cosmopolitan taste, Leibniz, Wolff, Baumgarten, Burke, Mendelssohn, Kant's problems with Hamann and Herder, and his hostility to *Sturm und Drang*.

Bäumler, *Das Irrationalitätsproblem in der Ästhetik und Logik des 18. Jahrhunderts bis zur "Kritik der Urteilskraft,"* offers a rich variety of insights into the historical background of the third *Critique*, from Spain, Italy, France, Switzerland, England, and Germany, especially on Wolff and Baumbarten (pp. 198–231). Bäumler sees the task of aesthetics (and of **teleology**) in explaining the individual and its irrationality and ineffability (*individuum est ineffablile*). He argues that this made the whole eighteenth century the "classical century of irrationality." Offers a wealth of sources and ideas, but should be read with a pinch of salt.

Kulenkampff, "The Objectivity of Taste: Hume and Kant," shows that the "task" we discussed in this section is specific to Kant and not to be found for instance in David Hume. Hume believed in standards and rules of taste (see his essay *Of the Standard of Taste*);

Kant did not. Hume nevertheless thought that judgments of taste ascribe only subjective values to their objects, whereas Kant, so Kulenkampff argues, thought of objective values, too. This article can serve as an introduction to the historical background of Kant's aesthetics in relation to Hume.

Daniel Dumouchel, *Kant et la genèse de la subjectivité esthétique*, analyzes the development of Kant's thoughts on aesthetics before the third *Critique*, from 1755 to 1779.

The Meaning of "Aesthetic"

Kant opens his aesthetics with a section entitled "The judgment of taste is aesthetic." This might sound odd. Why "judgment"? Is it not rather objects or attitudes that are aesthetic? The title should be read, I suggest, as saying at least two different things: first, stressing the expression "the judgment of taste" in that title: it is actually such a *judgment*, and not its object, that should be called "aesthetic." Not things out there, but our judgment of taste is "aesthetic." Second, stressing the word "aesthetic," the judgment of taste is specifically *aesthetic*, and never cognitive.

Regarding the first point, objects that are often called "aesthetic" have aesthetic value only insofar as they happen to be objects of judgments of taste. For Kant, it is the judgment of taste that is at the origin of whatever can justifiably be called "aesthetic" (and therefore we should analyze these judgments and not their objects). For the second point, Kant turns against the rationalist traditions of his time, as we shall see.

The title "The judgment of taste is aesthetic" can be read as Kant's response to, or reaction against, the mainstream understanding of "aesthetics" during that time. Alexander Baumgarten's book *Aesthetica* was published about 40 years earlier, in 1750, and Baumgarten's student G. F. Meier published a book with the title "Foundations of all Beautiful Sciences" (*Anfangsgründe aller schönen Wissenschaften*) two years before that, in 1748. Baumgarten had just begun a new philosophical discipline that we now call "aesthetics." In fact, the very word "aesthetics" was coined by Baumgarten.

Kant, however, opposes the main idea of Baumgarten's approach. According to Baumgarten, judgments of taste already express some kind of **cognition**; they are some kind of not yet fully developed judgments of cognition. Kant is opposed to this view of aesthetics and judgments of taste. He regards judgments of taste to be a completely different kind of judgment that is fundamentally different from judgments of cognition. According to Kant, and contrary to Baumgarten, judgments of taste are judgments in their own right. They should not be seen as forming a preliminary stage in a process of cognition, nor should they be understood as inferior to judgments of cognition. Rather, they should take a position of equal rank with judgments of cognition.

Baumgarten does not separate what Kant insists on keeping apart: beauty and cognition, or rather judgments of taste and judgments of cognition. Although Kant admits, and even with much effort develops, many connections between various elements, justifying grounds, and possible consequences of judgments of taste and judgments of cognition, still, for him a judgment can never be both at the same time. Whereas Baumgarten's *Aesthetica* addresses both beauty and cognition, Kant's aesthetics does not deal directly with cognition but only with beauty, the sublime, fine arts and aesthetic **ideas**. It deals with cognition only insofar as there are common underlying elements and possible later connections. Baumgarten believes that there can be rules of taste, rules for what should count as beautiful, and he believes that aesthetics can be a kind of science (*Wissenschaft*). Kant, however, thinks all this can never be, that there can never be rules of taste, and that there can never be an aesthetics of the sciences nor an aesthetics that is a science. Thus, it is not surprising that we see this opposition to Baumgarten's *Aesthetica* in the very title with which Kant opens the very first section of his own book on aesthetics: "The judgment of taste is aesthetic."

To set his own aesthetics apart from Baumgarten's, Kant makes a fundamental distinction between two meanings of the word *"Empfindung"* (**sensation**). The German word *"Empfindung,"* like the English word "sensation," can mean two different things: feeling (of pleasure and displeasure) and perception. Kant insists on keeping these two meanings strictly apart.

> Now here there is an immediate opportunity to reprove and draw attention to a quite common confusion of the double meaning that the word "sensation" [*Empfindung*] can have. (Section 3, 205)
> If a determination of the feeling of pleasure or displeasure is called sensation, then this expression means something entirely different than if I call the **representation** of a thing . . . sensation. For in the latter case the representation is related to the object, but in the first case it is related solely to the subject, and does not serve for any cognition at all . . . [I]n order not always to run the risk of being misinterpreted, we will call that which must always remain merely subjective and absolutely cannot constitute a representation of an object by the otherwise customary name of "feeling." (Section 3, 206)

Kant's aesthetics is concerned with feelings (*Gefühle*) of pleasure and displeasure, and not with sensation or perception as a form of cognition. Although Kant admits that perception is a first step towards cognition, he insists that a feeling never is. His aesthetics then is an investigation of a special kind of feeling, namely the "**satisfaction** in the beautiful" (*Wohlgefallen am Schönen*). According to Kant, such a feeling can never become cognition. The notion of a "satisfaction in the beautiful" is not to be understood as a composition of a satisfaction and something beautiful. Rather, the satisfaction in the beautiful is an elementary notion, and something is beautiful only through being the object of such a "satisfaction in the beautiful." This should be kept in mind when reading Kant's aesthetics.

The reader at this point might think that "sensation" usually means a feeling and not a perception, and that there is no reason to be worried about any confusion here. (The same applies to the German reader who meets the word "*Empfindung.*") But this is not so. In fact, there has been much discussion, and confusion, about the possibility of "sense data" in connection with sensation and perception (especially in the English traditions).

Kant, at the time of writing his first *Critique*, did not foresee that he would write an aesthetics as a "Critique of the Aesthetic Power of Judgment"; nevertheless, he was already clear about the strict distinction that would have to be drawn between beauty and cognition. In a footnote in the very first section of the first *Critique*, he writes:

> The Germans are the only ones who now employ the word "aesthetics" to designate that which others call the critique of taste. The ground for this is a failed hope, held by the excellent analyst Baumgarten, of bringing the critical estimation of the beautiful under principles of **reason**, and elevating its **rules** to a science. But this effort is futile. (*Critique of Pure Reason*, section 1, A 21/B 35)

This was written nine years before the third *Critique* appeared, and Kant did not change his mind regarding the need for such a strict distinction between taste and the sciences.

The contrast between Kant and Baumgarten, as far as their aesthetics are concerned, becomes apparent as soon as one compares the very first sentence of Kant's *Critique of the Power of Judgment* with the first sentence of Baumgarten's *Aesthetica*. Baumgarten begins as follows:

> Aesthetics (theory of the liberal arts, inferior cognition, art of beautiful thinking, art of reasoning by analogy) is the science of sensitive cognition. [*Aesthetica (theoria liberalium atrium, gnoseologia inferior, ars pulchre cogitandi, ars analogi rationis) est sciencia cognitionis sensitivae.*] (*Aesthetica*, section 1)

In his aesthetics, Kant opposes every one of these points. His *Critique of the Power of Judgment* does not teach us anything material about liberal arts. It is not a theory of inferior cognition, of beautiful thinking or of reasoning by analogy. It is never a science, and it does not involve sensitive cognition.

To make his aesthetics possible, Kant distinguishes between two reference points, so to speak, to which we can relate (*beziehen*) a representation (see quote below). When we have a representation of an object of the senses, be it a sunset or a painting, we can either refer this representation to ourselves, our mind (*Gemüt*), our feeling of our inner lives (*Lebensgefühl*), and our feeling of pleasure and displeasure; or we can relate it to the object in order to claim something objective about it. The former can give rise to a judgment of taste, the latter to a judgment of cognition. Kant makes this distinction clear in the very first sentence of the first section of his aesthetics:

> In order to decide whether or not something is beautiful, we do not relate the representation by means of **understanding** to the object for cognition, but rather relate it by means of the **imagination** (perhaps combined with the understanding) to the subject and its feeling of pleasure or displeasure. The judgment of taste is therefore not a **cognitive judgment**, hence not a logical one, but is rather aesthetic, by which is understood one whose determining ground cannot be other than subjective. (Section 1, 203)

In order for this to be true, Kant has to give much meaning and content to this kind of "relating a representation to the subject." In fact, much of the analysis of the judgment of taste will be an elaboration of exactly this notion. The notion of a free play of the faculties and the notion of the a priori principle of purposiveness will have to give meaning to this notion of our 'relating a representation to the subject'. Otherwise, Kant's aesthetics would not be able to stand on firm grounds.

Further reading

Zammito, *The Genesis of Kant's "Critique of Judgment"*: see above, p. 3.

Caygill, *Art of Judgment*, examines the "concealed sources" of the "aporia of judgment," reconstructing the traditions of taste and aesthetics against the intellectual and political backgrounds (pp. 11–187) and Kant's "interrogation" of these traditions in his third *Critique* (pp. 189–391).

Allison, *Kant's Theory of Taste*, pp. 68–71, shows that aesthetic judgments should be understood as being based on a special kind of feeling, the "feeling of life" (*Lebensgefühl*). He follows Dieter Henrich's suggestion to see Kant as applying a legal distinction of his time – the two questions: what is the case (*quid facti*), and whether a demand under examination is rightful (*quid juris*) – to arrive at the analysis–**deduction** distinction.

Crawford, *Kant's Aesthetic Theory*, has a nice introductory section (pp. 29–36) on the question of how we should understand the word "aesthetic," especially when we compare first and third *Critiques* and what "aesthetic" means in each, what the similarities and differences are.

Amoroso, *Kant et le nom de l'esthétique* is a short paper exactly on the topic of this section. Deals especially with Baumgarten and Kant. Mainly historical.

Parret, "De Baumgarten à Kant," claims that there is much continuity between Baumgarten and Kant. Mainly on Baumgarten, though. Expository, defending Baumgarten's originality.

Bäumler, *Das Irrationalitätsproblem in der Ästhetik und Logik des 18. Jahrhunderts bis zur "Kritik der Urteilskraft"* : see above, p. 3.

Juchem, *Die Entwicklung des Begriffs des Schönen bei Kant* is a study of the development of the concept of beauty up to Kant, with emphasis on beauty as "confused cognition," a conception from the Leibniz-Wolff-Baumgarten-Meier tradition that Kant was faced with and even grew up with.

Kulenkampff, *Kants Logik des ästhetischen Urteils*, pp. 67–73 (first edition: 57–63), argues that "aesthetic" is a technical term opposed to "logical," and that Kant introduces it to lead us to the judgment of taste as a judgment of a subject about itself. Although this kind of judgment is aesthetic, too, according to Kulenkampff, the prototype of aesthetic judgments is still the judgment about the agreeable, and Kant thus merely extends the category of aesthetic judgments by introducing his judgment of taste.

Categories as a Guide

Let us first give a brief overview of how Kant's third *Critique*, the so-called *Critique of the Power of Judgment*, is organized. It consists of two books, the first of which offers an aesthetics, the second a **teleology**. What unites them is their focus on our **power of judgment**, more specifically our power of **reflecting**, or **reflective,** judgment, by which Kant means our ability to reflect about a given object, whether in order to find out what exactly it is (teleology), or simply as a way of contemplating it for the sake of contemplation (aesthetics). What distinguishes the two books of the third *Critique* is that in aesthetic judgments our **feeling** of pleasure or displeasure plays a central role, whereas in teleological judgments this is not the case. The latter kind of judgment is more objective.

The first book, Kant's aesthetics, has two parts: one called "**Analytic** of the Aesthetic Power of Judgment," the other "**Dialectic** of the Aesthetic Power of Judgment." Of the two parts, we may say that the Analytic tends to be more down to earth, whereas the Dialectic deals with so-called "**ideas**" and the "supernatural" and is more metaphysical. It is the Analytic that forms the main part of Kant's aesthetics. (But we will of course deal with both parts, the Analytic and the Dialectic.) At the beginning of this Analytic, Kant gives an *analysis* of the judgment of taste. His method here is thus analytic, and not **synthetic** as was the case in the first *Critique*. Based on the results of this analysis, Kant then explains various related phenomena and issues. These include the *sensus communis*, the relationship between the beauty of art and the beauty of nature, the nature of **genius**, and the notion of "beauty as a symbol of morality." What Kant has to say here should be construed as being based on the results of his analysis of the judgment of taste. The analysis of the judgment of taste is thus placed at the very beginning of his aesthetics, both literally and as a matter of method.

In this analysis of the judgment of taste, Kant proceeds according to themes he was very much concerned with in the *Critique of Pure Reason*, namely the "logical function of the understanding in judgments" and the so-called "**categories**," or "**concepts** of pure understanding." Kant has introduced these categories of the understanding in the first *Critique*, and he uses them now as a *guiding thread* of analysis in the third *Critique*. Keeping this in mind of course makes sense only if in a judgment of taste, which we will see is *not* a cognitive judgment, we still find elements, or features, of cognition and understanding that would justify this type of analysis, i.e. an analysis that is guided by glances back to the first *Critique*.

The two main discoveries that Kant makes by analyzing the judgment of taste in this way are the following: First, there is the so-called "free play of our cognitive powers," imagination and understanding. This is a pleasant (or unpleasant) interplay within or of our mind, with perceptions that we have of something we see or otherwise perceive through our senses and that we judge to be beautiful (or ugly). According to Kant, when we look at a painting, it is our imagination (*Einbildungskraft*), or "power of imagination," that intuitively takes up, goes through, recollects and recalls what we see; and it is our understanding that tries to grasp and decide what is depicted or what it all means. In aesthetic contemplation this is primarily enjoyable by itself and not a way of gaining knowledge. It is a "free play." (We will explain this notion further in later sections. See, for example, the last section of chapter 2: "How to Read Section 9.") Nevertheless, this play is not without relation to cognition. It is related to what Kant calls "**cognition in general**" (*Erkenntnis überhaupt*).

The second discovery goes deeper. It reveals something that allows us to see this free play in a wider perspective, as something based on our relationship to the environment, a relationship not just within our mind, but one between ourselves, our mind or inner nature, and the outer nature that surrounds us. Kant here discovers an a priori principle that is new in his philosophical system, an a priori principle that belongs to our power of judgment. According to Kant, we base our judgment of taste on some kind of "purposiveness" [*Zweckmässigkeit*] of the object in relation to our aesthetic contemplation of it. We simply find the object *suitable* for an aesthetic contemplation in the form of a free and joyful play of our powers of cognition. We cannot exactly point out what it is that accounts for this purposiveness, or suitability. There is no objective criterion. We have to give the play a try, so to speak. We have to try the object out. And basically anybody can do this. Kant's aesthetics therefore does not stress on connoisseurship or even favor elitism, and as we shall see later on, Kant even points out some

advantages of beauty of nature over beauty of art. The positive side of this
absence of any objective rules for beauty is that there remains open room for the
possibility of the *je ne sais quoi*, the phenomenon that we cannot say what exactly
accounts for our feeling and our playful enjoyment. We simply happen to find
the object suitable and purposive for such enjoyment. There are no rules or concepts that could serve as criteria for deciding what is beautiful and what is not.
Kant therefore speaks of "purposiveness without a concept," or "purposiveness
without a purpose."

The entire analysis of the judgment of taste discloses four so-called
"**moments**" (*Momente*) of the judgment of taste. How to understand the notion
of "moments" is central but unfortunately very difficult. "Moments" are not
moments of time (at least not just that). Rather, they are categorial aspects that
are related to the twelve categories from the first *Critique*. Consideration of the
Latin root of momentum, *movere* (to move), and the notion of momentum in
physics are helpful here. These moments are more than mere external aspects of
the judgment of taste. They give it its essential *force* and *life*. These moments are
related to the "logical function of the understanding in judgments" in general
(introduced in the first *Critique*) and can be discovered, Kant suggests, if we pay
close attention to the role certain "logical functions" (section 1, 203) play in a
judgment of taste. Accordingly, he takes these logical functions as a *guide* for
analysis, reveals the four moments of taste, and then works out his aesthetics as
a whole by making use of these moments.

In the first *Critique*, Kant sets up a table of twelve categories and divides these
categories into four groups, each having a so-called "title." These are: quality,
quantity, relation, and modality. It is a general claim in the first *Critique* that any
judgment, at least a judgment of cognition, is intrinsically related to exactly one
category from each of these four groups. Accordingly, Kant thinks, there must
be four "moments" of a judgment of taste (because it is has some relation to
cognition), one for each title. Schematically, the correspondences (title: moment)
are:

Quality: disinterestedness   (1st moment)
Quantity: universality   (2nd moment)
Relation: purposiveness   (3rd moment)
Modality: necessity   (4th moment)

Roughly speaking, these moments are then the following. The first is (or is
related to) a certain kind of **disinterestedness**. My liking, or satisfaction (*Wohlgefallen*) is without any personal or moral interest, that is, it is neither a "satisfaction in the agreeable" nor a "satisfaction in the good." What this should have to
do with "quality" is questionable though, and it is hard to avoid finding the cor-

relation "quality-disinterestedness" artificial and forced, the result of what is called "forced by the system" (*Systemzwang*) in German, something Kant is often accused of. We will return to this in the chapter on disinterestedness. The second moment is (or makes possible) a **universality** expressed in the claim that everybody should agree with my judgment of taste whenever I make one, a claim which further analysis discloses to be based on the free play described above. Some Kant scholars consider this second moment to be the central point in Kant's aesthetics. Unlike the first moment, the correlation "quantity-universality" does not seem artificial and forced. It comes naturally. The third moment is the moment of purposiveness. I find the object suitable (purposive) for aesthetic contemplation, and this kind of contemplation again involves various features of purposiveness. The fourth moment is that of *necessity*. Whenever the conditions one to three are satisfied, I cannot but judge the object to be beautiful. The second and the third moment are certainly the essential ones. They constitute the main result of Kant's analysis.

Kant takes it as a fact that whenever we make a judgment of taste, we think, or at least could justifiably think, that *everyone* should agree with us. This fact expresses some kind of universality, because every single human being, whoever he or she may be, without exception, should (this is part of my claim) agree with my judgment of taste. This subjective universality serves as a point of departure for the entire *Critique of the Power of Judgment* as part of Kant's **transcendental** philosophy, because such a claim to universality requires, according to Kant, a priori grounds, and it is the task of the *Critique of the Power of Judgment* to reveal such grounds.

The universality of a judgment of taste, the claim that everyone should agree with my judgment, is somehow based on the pleasure or displeasure that I feel when looking, or otherwise perceiving the object. It has no purely objective basis. It cannot be inferred from any rules of taste or properties of the object. There is nothing in the object that I could point out, such that everyone must agree with what I claim. We can call it a "subjective universality," where the word "subjective" has a double meaning: (a) the justifying *grounds* are subjective (a feeling), and (b) the *domain* of universality is the domain of all possible judging subjects (the domain of all human beings, not to be confused with any domain of objects that are being judged).

On the one hand, the pleasure involved in a judgment of taste cannot be completely subjective. Otherwise, the claim that everyone should agree could never be justified; such a claim would not even arise and there would not be any quarrels in matters of taste. On the other hand, the grounds for pleasure in aesthetic contemplation cannot be completely objective either, because then quarrels in matters of taste could be settled in a scientific fashion (as in physics). There has to be room for the *je ne sais quoi*.

This apparent dilemma calls for grounds of the judgment of taste that are neither merely subjective nor purely objective. To find such grounds is the task of explaining and justifying the peculiar nature of the subjective universality of a judgment of taste. This task is worth our effort, for, as Kant remarks in section eight of the *Critique of the Power of Judgment*:

> [The] particular determination of the universality of an aesthetic judgment that can be found in a judgment of taste is something remarkable, not indeed for the logician, but certainly for the transcendental philosopher, the discovery of the *origin* of which calls for no little effort on his part, but which also reveals a property of our **faculty** of cognition that without this *analysis* would have remained unknown. (Section 8, 213)

This "analysis" is the essence of Kant's approach. It is an analysis of the judgment of taste as a judgment that claims *universality* (intersubjective universal validity) and must therefore be viewed as an a priori judgment, a judgment with non-empirical "origin" (see quote above); and it is then the task of this analysis to reveal this a priori origin (mainly the second and the third moment of the judgment of taste). All that follows in the *Critique of the Power of Judgment* – Kant's discussions of the *sensus communis,* the beauty of art and the beauty of nature, genius, beauty as a symbol of morality, aesthetic ideas, the supersensible, the sublime, and the quest for God – should be seen as based on this approach.

Further reading

Allison, *Kant's Theory of Taste,* pp. 72–8, defends the reading that the moments build on each other progressively (p. 77) and that they are indeed organized according to the table from the first *Critique*; in particular, he defends (pp. 78–82) this reading against claims made by Guyer in *Kant and the Claims of Taste.*
Guyer, "Kant's Distinction between the Beautiful and the Sublime," discusses, especially in the beginning of this article, the problem of what exactly the meanings, functions, and roles of "moments" and "definitions" (*Erklärungen*) are. Guyer explicates logical and epistemological versus psychological and phenomenological aspects.
Kulenkampff, *Kants Logik des Ästhetischen Urteils,* pp. 23–8 (1st edtion: 12–18) gives an overview of Kant's analysis, questioning the relevance of the schematic table of logical functions from the first *Critique* (*Äusserlichkeit des Schemas der Urteilstafel für die Analytik des Schönen*).
More on the table of judgments, reflection, and the logical functions from the first *Critique* can be found in Brandt, *The Table of Judgments*; Longuenesse, *Kant and the Capacity to Judge*; and Wolff, *Die Vollständigkeit der kantischen Urteilstafel,* discussing on pp. 9–32 the logical functions of judging. But these go far beyond an introduction to the issues here.

The "Moments" of a Judgment of Taste

This is going to be a difficult section. It is, like the previous one, a section about Kant's method, in particular about where he begins and what guides him. This is a fundamental question and the reader should therefore be at least aware of it as soon a possible. The reader who wants to meet this challenge might want to read this section straight away. He or she will then get a flavor of how difficult a small passage in Kant can be. He or she may also choose to skip this section and to come back to it later. In any case one should not be discouraged. Specialists have their problems here, too.

To give a rough overview, let me briefly say what I will be doing here. I will (1) comment on the word "moment" and its roots in physics; (2) comment on a footnote that Kant introduces at the very beginning, in which he says what "guides" his investigation; (3) discuss the definition of the beautiful, a definition that is "derived" from the first moment; and (4) return to the footnote and discuss "reflection," the "logical functions of judging," and the role of the understanding. All this leads (5) to a problem of methodological circularity, and (6) I point out one more problem in the footnote, a problem about the moment of quality. Finally, (7), I make a suggestion as to how to understand "moments" in this context, namely that they have two sides, or allow for two different aspects, and that this helps avoiding the problem of methodological circularity.

(1) Before we get started, a brief comment on the word "moment." In German there are two words: *"der Moment"* (masc.) and *"das Moment"* (neuter), and they differ in meaning. *"Der Moment"* has a temporal meaning, referring to an instant, a minute portion or point of time. *"Das Moment,"* on the other hand, has a very different meaning. It refers to a decisive circumstance, a mark, or an aspect, and it is this word that is also used in physics, as in *das Drehmoment* (torque). In Latin, *momentum*, there are two meanings as well, and Kant was often thinking in Latin (he wrote his dissertation in Latin): first, movement, change, instant, minute portion of time; and, second, weight, pressure, push, influence. Now the second meaning, or set of meanings, is what Kant primarily has in mind. He often thinks of moments as *causal* activities. For instance, he says that a change does not consist of moments (as in the first category), but is *produced* by moments (as in the second category), and is their effect (A 208/B 254). He thinks of moments as causes, for instance as moments of gravity (A 168/B 210). Also the English word "moment" can be used to express a 'tendency or measure of tendency to produce motion, especially about a point or axis'. This is the meaning from physics, and this is not what usually comes to today's readers' minds, especially in the context of beauty and taste. Nonetheless, this is actually close to what Kant had in mind when he wrote of "moments of the under-

standing," or of "logical moments of judgments," or "moments of taste." Kant
thus writes *"das Geschmacksmoment,"* or *"das Moment des Geschmacks,"* but not:
"der Moment des Geschmacks." He uses the neutral (*das Moment*), and this is closer
to the meaning in physics, as we pointed out above. Keeping this in mind should
help us to understand better what follows – not only in this section, but also
regarding the whole analysis of judgments of taste.

(2) The footnote and the guide. The question of where to start is often a difficult one, especially in philosophy. Kant in some sense begins his aesthetics with
a footnote. At the very beginning of the "Analytic of the Beautiful," in the title
"First Moment of the judgment of taste, concerning its quality," he inserts a footnote in which he indicates his method and even gives a brief justification of it.
The footnote reads as follows.

> The definition of taste that is the basis here is that it is the faculty for the judging
> of the beautiful. But what is required for calling an object beautiful must be dis-
> covered by the analysis of judgments of taste. In seeking the *moments* to which this
> power of judgment attends in its reflection, I have been guided by the *logical func-*
> *tions for judging* (for a relation to the understanding is always contained even in the
> judgment of taste). I have considered the *moment* of quality first, since the aesthetic
> judgment on the beautiful takes notice of this first. (Section 1, 203)

Kant does not spend much time developing a definition of taste. He simply
states one at the beginning, in a footnote, and then uses it as a basis for something he seems to be more interested in, namely an analysis of the judgment
of taste. He wants to discover "what is required for calling an object beautiful."
This may seem vague and ambiguous. Is it something in the object, which is
"required" for calling the object beautiful? Or is it something in us, some ability
or state of mind, by means of which we call the object beautiful? At this early
stage of his investigation Kant leaves the question open.

Kant is "seeking the *moments* to which this power of judgment attends in its
reflection." But what exactly does he mean by such "moments"? And in what
sense does the power of judgment attend to them?

The "Analytic of the Beautiful" consists of four chapters that are entitled "First
[Second, Third, Fourth] Moment of the judgment of taste, concerning . . ."
(*erstes, zweites, drittes, viertes Moment* – notice *"das Moment"*, not *"der Moment"*).
The whole "Analytic of the Beautiful" consists of nothing but discussions of these
four "moments." What these discussions reveal is fairly clear, but just what the
four moments exactly are is not so obvious. They seem to be something hidden
in the background, something in a black box, invisible forces like gravitational
forces. We will try to cast some light on them.

(3) The definition of the beautiful. The first discussion is entitled "First
Moment of the judgment of taste, concerning its quality" and extends over five

sections that lead to the "Definition of the beautiful *derived from the first moment*." This definition reads as follows:

> Taste is the faculty for judging an object or a kind of representation through a satisfaction or dissatisfaction without any interest. The object of such a satisfaction is called beautiful. (Section 5, 211)

One often reads in the secondary literature that the first moment of a judgment of taste *is* disinterested satisfaction (or enjoyment, or pleasure). But this cannot be quite correct, because the "definition of the beautiful" is directly concerned with disinterested satisfaction and can be "*derived* from the first moment." If disinterestedness can be "derived" from the first moment, it cannot be this moment itself. What Kant means by "moment" here seems to be something different, something that lies deeper and is more fundamental. It must be something from which the "definition of the beautiful" and the role of disinterested satisfaction can be *derived*.

(4) Reflection and the understanding. We now return to the footnote quoted above. Kant there writes: "In seeking the moments to which this power of judgment attends in its reflection, I have been guided by the logical functions for judging." But what are these "logical functions for judging"? They are the object of study in section nine of the *Critique of Pure Reason*. This section is entitled "The Logical Function of the Understanding in Judgments." An examination of this section should help us see what the moments of a judgment of taste are. Kant writes: "the function of thinking in . . . [a judgment] can be brought under four titles, each of which contains under itself three *moments*" (*Critique of Pure Reason*, A 70/B 95). The second of these titles is: "quality of a judgment," and it "contains" the three moments: "affirmative," "negative," and "infinite." Could it be these moments, or something related to them, that Kant had in mind when he wrote at the beginning of his aesthetics about "*the moments* to which this power of judgment attends in its reflection" (203; see Kant's footnote quoted above)?

Thinking of these moments of "affirmation" and "negation" under the heading of "quality" from the first *Critique*, as I have indicated above, one might then naturally want to interpret the footnote in the following way: What "the power of judgment attends [to] in its reflection" is the question whether we find the object beautiful or not, i.e., whether our judgment of taste should be an "affirmative" or a "negative" one. Although this makes sense, it cannot be quite right, or at least it cannot be the whole story, for the following reason. Kant writes that he is still "*seeking* the moments to which this power of judgment attends in its reflection." He wants to *find* the moments and does not have them yet. Hence they cannot simply be "affirmation" or "negation." Instead, they must be the justifying *grounds* for such affirmation or negation. The "satisfaction or dissatisfaction without any interest" Kant talks about in the "Definition of the beautiful derived from the first moment" would offer such grounds. Interpreters of Kant thus usually take the satisfaction and dissatisfaction to be the moments. But, as we have already pointed out, Kant himself says that the definition, which talks about this satisfaction and dissatisfaction, is *derived from* the first moment, and thus the definition cannot at the same time *give* the first moment (without getting us into some kind of circularity). Certainly, the five sections that Kant offers under the title "First Moment of the judgment of taste, concerning its quality" lead essentially to the notion of a "satisfaction or dissatisfaction without any interest." But simply identifying this notion with the "first moment" might be an oversimplification. We have to say more about "moments" and the power of judgment in general.

The *Critique of Pure Reason* is concerned with cognitive judgments and not with judgments of taste. So how can Kant be justified in his approach to judgments of taste (relying on what he says about judgments of cognition in the first *Critique*) if taste is not to be confused with cognition? Aesthetics is not a kind of epistemology, and judgments of taste are not cognitive judgments. How can Kant base his analysis of judgments of taste on "moments" of judgments of cognition from the first *Critique*? Judgments of cognition are based on concepts. Judgments of taste are not. There are no (objective) **rules** for applying the predicate "beautiful." Judgments of taste, so Kant claims later on, also do not add to our understanding of the object under consideration. If Kant's method can be justified at all, if he is not looking in the wrong place when he says: "In seeking the moments to which this power of judgment attends in its reflection, I have been guided by the logical functions for judging," then taste must have *something* to do with understanding. It is for this very reason that Kant, in his footnote quoted above, adds a parenthetical remark: "a *relation* to the understanding is *always* contained even in the judgment of taste." The nature of this "relation to the understanding" is nevertheless still unclear at this point. It will become clear later, during the discussions of the second and fourth moments. There this "relation" will be understood as depending on the so-called "free play of the faculties of cognition," a play of imagination and understanding in which we engage in aesthetic contemplation (second moment). Furthermore, this "relation to the understanding" will be seen to depend also on what Kant calls "cognition in general" and on some kind of purposiveness that serves as an a priori principle for the power of judgment, a principle to be used when applying this power. All this will be discussed later. But there is a problem here about what can be discussed *later* and what can be presupposed *now*. To this problem we will now turn.

(5) The circularity problem. We face the following *methodological problem*. Kant tacitly *presupposes* some knowledge of the result of his analysis in the third

Critique in order to justify the *beginning* of this very analysis. We are only justified in using the "logical functions of judging" as a guiding thread for analyzing the judgment of taste if we know from the very beginning that they are somehow involved in the judgment of taste. But that they are indeed somehow involved is something we see only after we have done the analysis. So how shall we ever get started? Do we have to read Kant backwards?

All this may seem *circular*. Of course, we may assume that Kant *anticipated* the results of his investigation when he set out to write the book. But still, it remains somewhat problematic to assume the results of an investigation in order to justify how to proceed in it. One may have the impression that Kant takes the reader by the hand and says: "Trust me for the moment and simply follow me! Later on you will see that it all makes sense." This is a problem one often encounters when reading Kant and more or less with any philosopher who offers a somewhat holistic philosophical system.

(6) Quality, and the footnote again. Before returning to the problem of methodological circularity, I want to point out one more problem concerning the "moments" mentioned in the footnote quoted above. The last sentence in that footnote mentions "moments" again, but this time in the *singular*. Kant writes that he has "considered *the* moment of quality first, since the aesthetic judgment on the beautiful takes notice of this first." This raises several questions. According to the first *Critique*, there are three moments of quality. Which one is he referring to? Or does he think of quality itself as a moment? And why is it that the judgment "takes notice of this *first*"? According to the *Critique of Pure Reason*, it is quantity, and *not* quality, that is listed first in the tables of the categories. Hence what the judgment of taste "takes notice" of first must be something special, something that can only be found in the specific nature of a judgment of taste and not in any judgment in general. Kant cannot derive it from the table of judgments in general that can be found in the *Critique of Pure Reason*. He must look into the specific nature of the judgment of taste. And indeed, we will see that the discussion of the first moment involves *psychological* and *phenomenological* elements that reveal features that are specific to the judgment of taste. Thus, on the one hand Kant says he is "seeking the moments," but on the other he claims already at the very beginning that a judgment of taste "takes notice of this [the moment of quality] first." He simply states this without providing any further justification for this claim.

(7) The two sides of a moment. Finally, I would like to suggest that we should understand the "moments" as having *two aspects* here, a general one and a particular one: The general aspect has its roots in the general features of judgments, essentially the categories, as presented in the *Critique of Pure Reason*. The particular aspect depends on the particular features of the judgment of taste that arise whenever we make a judgment of taste. These features are, as we will see

later: a satisfaction that is disinterested, a claim to universality based on a free
play of the faculties, and the *a priori* principle of purposiveness.

It is the *union* of these *two aspects* of the moments of a judgment of taste, the
general aspect *together* with the particular one, which, I would suggest, justifies
Kant's method. The general aspect justifies Kant's reference to the table of judgments from the first *Critique* as a guiding thread. The particular one allows us to
take the judgment of taste as an empirically given fact that we can analyze. The
analysis of judgments of taste therefore has two features as well: one stems from
the transcendental logic of the first *Critique*, the other depends on the specific
nature of the judgment of taste and has empirical, phenomenological, and
psychological features.

One more note about how the power of judgment "attends" to the moments
(*acht haben* may also be "to pay attention to," "to apply itself to," "to heed," "to
serve"), as Kant writes in the footnote. We should not think of these moments
as being merely formal. Rather, we should also think of them as real *forces* that
can cause movements or actions and reactions (in the mind, within the process
of making the judgment). We should think of the Latin root *movere* and the
expression *momentum* (as used in physics). The power of judgment "attends" to
some kind of force. This attention is not an attention to something external, but
an attention that is a reflection about and a reflection *through* such a force. Kant
is not explicit about this, but I think this is how we should understand him. The
moments should be seen as *living forces* within the structure that I have suggested
above, i.e. within the structure of the two aspects of the moments in a judgment
of taste, the general one and the specific one.

Further reading

Allison, *Kant's Theory of Taste*, pp. 73–6, discusses the footnote and in general defends
    Kant's organization of the moments according to the logical functions from the first
    Critique.
Brandt, *The Table of Judgments*, (translated from the German) explains the table of judg-
    ments and its systematic unity from the first *Critique*. It focuses on the question of com-
    pleteness of this table and gives a good overview of the German scholarship on this
    issue. This is not at all about aesthetics, but useful if one wants to know more about
    the "transcendental table of all *moments* of thought in judgments," what Kant's idea of
    a judgment was, and why he was looking for *four* moments of taste, and not for ten,
    or twenty.

1

Disinterestedness: First Moment

Disinterestedness as a Subjective Criterion

The first criterion that Kant's analysis provides for a judgment of taste is that of "disinterestedness": an object is beautiful if I like it without any interest. I should be free from any kind of desire, aim, or purpose, or any social, moral, or intellectual considerations. (Kant wants to exclude personal as well as non-personal interests – which correspond to the agreeable and the good, as we shall see later.) Only then can my contemplation of the object be "pure," as Kant says. It should be pure in a double sense of the word – a negative and a positive one: pure because it is not contaminated by such considerations and interests, and pure because it is based, instead, on the free play of the **faculties** and the **a priori principle** of **purposiveness**. Thus, if my judgment is based on some interest that I have in the object, then my judgment of taste will not be free and pure. In that case, according to Kant, this is (strictly speaking) not really a judgment of taste. Put more generously, an aesthetic judgment is a judgment of taste *insofar as* it is based on satisfaction (pleasure) that is free from any considerations involving interest.

Now Kant defines **satisfaction** as "interested" if it depends on any care or concern for the "existence" of the object. Kant writes rather abstractly: "The satisfaction that we combine with the **representation** of the existence of an object is called interest" (section 2, 204). In the case of the agreeable, I might hope that the object will last and continue to give me pleasure; in the case of the morally good, I might even feel pressure to bring the object, in this case an act, into existence. But in pure contemplation I am free from any such worries or pressures. I just enjoy looking at the rose and find it beautiful. I do not need to possess, understand, or bring into existence the object of my contemplation. Rather, "what matters is what I make of this representation in myself, not how I depend on the existence of the object" (section 2, 205). Disinterestedness is thus a mark of some kind of self-containedness on my, the perceiver's, part. It allows me to rely more on myself and my own powers.

If I see a sunset or a painting, then of course the object needs to exist in some way or other. But it might also merely be an object in a dream or a movie. Regardless of which is the case, I should be free from considerations regarding the existence of the object, that is, my satisfaction should not depend on them. I should not be disappointed when I realize that it was all only a dream. If I were disappointed, I would have had other considerations underlying my satisfaction, maybe the wish that the sunset might last so that I can forget myself and my worries, or the fantasy that I am the proud possessor of the painting. Forgetting oneself goes well with contemplation and appreciation. But even this should not be the purpose of my contemplation, at least not a purpose I am conscious of. (Anyway, forgetting yourself does not work if you have to try too hard.)

Sometimes, in particular cases, it is difficult to draw the line between a free, pure, and disinterested satisfaction on the one hand, and a satisfaction into which some interest is mixed, on the other. Do you like this woman, or this man, without any interest? Are you sure that your liking of her or him does not depend on imagining what you would gain from being at the side of this person? Are you free from any considerations of what others would say or what your future would look like? Such considerations may of course accompany satisfaction in the beautiful, but they should not be the ground or reason for it. The line between accompanying satisfaction and being the reason for it is often difficult to draw. We may even wonder whether we are ever without interest, whether there can be satisfaction without interest, or whether it is only an ideal and something to strive after. But in any case, you have to decide for yourself where the line should be drawn, if you ask yourself during (or after) an act of aesthetic contemplation whether you were "truly" disinterested. Nobody can tell this from "the outside." Disinterestedness is in that sense a *subjective* criterion; if one *applies* it, one applies it to *one's own* state of mind. But in another sense, it is an "objectively" (or better "logically") necessary condition for making a judgment of taste in the sense that it applies to everybody and every judgment of taste. That is, there is no objective criterion or rule available that one could apply to anyone. Instead, one can only apply it to oneself. But still, everyone can do so. That *everyone* can do this follows from the criterion being an objectively necessary one; that everyone can only apply it *to himself* follows from the subjective nature of our feelings.

We have seen that disinterestedness is a necessary condition for a satisfaction to be a satisfaction in the beautiful. Accordingly an object can justifiably be called "beautiful" only if it happens to be the object of such a (subjectively felt) "satisfaction in the beautiful." Thus there is another "subjective" aspect in Kant's aesthetics: the starting point of analysis is the judging subject and his feeling; beauty is (philosophically) seen from the perspective of our *actually* judging it to be beautiful. But we have to be very careful not to misconstrue the meaning of "subjective" here. In the end, we will see that this "subjective" **feeling**, the satisfaction in the beautiful, is based on universal elements and intersubjective aspects.

Being without interest requires a certain distance from the object as well as from oneself. One's satisfaction should not depend on considerations of the object in its social contexts, nor should it depend on one's personal needs and desires. "One must not be in the least biased in favor of the existence of the thing, but must be entirely indifferent in this respect in order to play the judge in matters of taste" (section 2, 205). Here one might wonder whether there could possibly be anything left that could serve as a positive ground for such satisfaction. What is left when the self and the object are crossed out? What could there be besides, or between, the subject and the object? But these questions are much too coarse. We must come to a finer understanding of what a "subject" is; develop a much finer-grained picture of the subject who makes such a judgment of taste. Kant's notion of the free play of the **cognitive** faculties will allow us to obtain such a picture. In particular, it will allow us to distinguish between a personal self whose desires are affected by the object, and some kind of universal self that is defined by the cognitive faculties.

When Kant explicates interested satisfaction as one that "always has . . . a relation to the faculty of desire" (section 2, 204), he already has in mind the two other kinds of satisfaction he is going to discuss in the following sections, namely "satisfaction in the agreeable" and "satisfaction in the good." Interested satisfaction can have a "relation to the faculty of desire" in two different ways, "either as its determining ground or else as necessarily interconnected with its determining ground" (section 2, 204). Interested satisfaction is the "determining ground" of a desire, if it is satisfaction in the agreeable, and it is "necessarily interconnected" with a desire if it is satisfaction in the good. In the first case, we like what is agreeable and therefore desire it. In the second case, we desire the morally good and this, in connection with rational insights, makes us like it. In both cases there is a desire, a consideration of aims and purposes, and an interest in the object's existence, which prevent the satisfaction from being free, pure, and self-contained.

I will not discuss here how Kant's notion of disinterestedness relates to those we find already in the writings of Shaftesbury and Hutcheson at the beginning of the eighteenth century and what Kant might have taken over from them, except to note that this idea – that judgments of taste should be disinterested – was not shared by everyone in Kant's time, and Kant certainly had his own way of incorporating it.

Still, some further questions remain. How can we be unconcerned about the existence of the object, if we wish to linger in our contemplation of it? And when it comes to the beauty of art, the question of whether our satisfaction can be disinterested becomes particularly pressing. Don't we depend on the existence of objects of art when we want to go to a museum? Does the artist not have purposes in mind when he creates a piece of art? If we want to appreciate art as such, don't we need to know many things about the history of art? Doesn't this then spoil our disinterestedness or even make it impossible? On the other hand, can't there be an intellectual interest in the beautiful, especially the beauty of art? We will turn to these questions in the later sections on art, genius, and aesthetic ideas in chapter 5.

Further reading

Crawford, *Kant's Aesthetic Theory*, pp. 37–54, discusses disinterestedness in various lights and asks whether a "purely aesthetic interest" is possible at all. A good introduction to this topic, detailed, sympathetic, and clear.

Guyer, "Disinterestedness and Desire in Kant's Aesthetics," shows that Kant's notion of disinterested satisfaction is compatible with our ordinary beliefs about interest in beauty. His *Kant and the Claims of Taste*, pp. 148–83 (2nd edition), stays close to the text and at places tries to set Kant's arguments right; *Kant and the Experience of Freedom*, pp. 48–130, includes two essays, "The dialectic of disinterestedness," I and II; these are more historical (eighteenth century) and of wider scope, discussing Shaftsbury, Hutcheson, Hume, Burke, Kames, Baumgarten, Mendelssohn, and others. The second essay is devoted to Schiller. Guyer offers many rich and detailed accounts and arguments.

Allison, *Kant's Theory of Taste*, pp. 85–97, explains the notion of "interest" in Kant's moral theory and argues that it is compatible with the new role it plays in the third *Critique*.

McCloskey, *Kant's Aesthetic*, pp. 29–49, not only discusses the moment of disinterestedness within Kant's third *Critique*, but also confronts it with more contemporary disputes, put forward, for instance, by George Dickie and Marshall Cohen, about aesthetic attitude theories.

Basch, *Essai critique*, pp. 25–107, offers rich and original discussions, systematic as well as historical, about the relationships between feeling and desire and feeling and knowledge. Basch also develops a theory of feeling of his own, a theory, he argues, that Kant should have provided himself in the context of his aesthetics. Only available in French, quite old, but still very good and too much ignored.

Dörflinger, *Die Realität des Schönen in Kants Theorie rein ästhetischer Urteilskraft*, pp. 91–139, discusses the moment of disinterestedness in the light of the question whether Kant's theory of taste allows for, or even includes, a positive and new and wider account of (our experience of) objectivity.

Prauss, "Kants Theorie der ästhetischen Einstellung" makes the interesting and unusual claim that in order to reach an aesthetic attitude we have to "overcome" (*überwinden*) the interests and intentionality we find in theoretical attitudes. He stresses *Liebe, Bewunderung, Gunst, Beifall*, and speaks of "increased freedom" (*potenzierte Freiheit*).

Wenzel, *Das Problem der Subjektiven Allgemeingültigkeit des Geschmacksurteils bei Kant*, pp. 72–83.

Three Kinds of Satisfaction: Agreeable, Beautiful, Good

Kant distinguishes between three kinds of "satisfaction" (*Wohlgefallen*). These are satisfaction in the agreeable, the beautiful, and the good. The Kantian expression "*Wohlgefallen*" can also be translated as "enjoyment" or "pleasure." The term "satisfaction" might not be the happiest choice, but I will follow the new English translation from the now standard *Cambridge Edition*. Kant's classification of satisfaction into three kinds is fundamental to his aesthetics and he makes ample use of it throughout the "Critique of the Aesthetic Power of Judgment" (the first part of the third *Critique*). Kant also thinks of the three kinds of satisfaction in terms of representations: "The agreeable, the beautiful, and the good . . . designate three different relations of representations to the feeling of pleasure and displeasure, in relation to which we distinguish objects or kinds of representations from each other" (section 5, 209–10). When he investigates these representations and our feelings of pleasure and displeasure, Kant often considers them under specific circumstances and then argues that in such and such a situation it cannot possibly be a satisfaction in the agreeable, nor a satisfaction in the good, and must therefore be a satisfaction in the beautiful. We should be aware that this sort of argumentation presupposes that there are exactly these three kinds of "satisfaction" and no more.

The "satisfaction in the beautiful" should not be understood as something that is in some way "composed" of the beautiful and some kind of satisfaction. It is not the case that something is beautiful in itself and that enjoyment of it is then, in some derived way, called "satisfaction in the beautiful." On the contrary, something is called "beautiful" because we feel a "satisfaction in the beautiful." Much depends therefore on this specific kind of satisfaction and what goes into it, and it is quite deliberate that Kant begins his analysis not with an analysis of the beautiful but with an analysis of the "satisfaction in the beautiful." The relevance of this should become apparent in the course of the following sections, especially when we discuss paragraph nine of Kant's aesthetics.

When we enjoy something agreeable or something good, that is, when there is a case of "satisfaction in the agreeable" or a case of "satisfaction in the good," Kant argues that our enjoyment relates to specific *interests* and considerations of those interests. Satisfaction in the beautiful, on the other hand, must be free of such considerations. In fact, it is the only kind of satisfaction among the three that is truly "disinterested." Disinterestedness is the specific mark of satisfaction in the beautiful.

Compared with the other two kinds of satisfaction, satisfaction in the beautiful can be thought of as being "in between" the other two in the following way. Think of an ascending chain of beings, with animals at the bottom, humans in the middle, and spirits on the top. Now, humans have some features in common with animals and some (other) features in common with spirits – in particular: animals *and* humans have the capacity for satisfaction in the agreeable; and spirits *and* humans have the capacity for satisfaction in the good. Thus humans have both capacities, and because it is only they who have both, they can be thought of as being in between animals and spirits. Furthermore, there is one capacity that only humans have: the capacity for satisfaction in the beautiful.

> Agreeableness is also valid for nonrational animals; beauty is valid only for human beings, i.e., animal but also rational beings, but not merely as the latter (e.g., spirits), rather as beings who are at the same time animal; the good, however, is valid for every rational being in general. (Section 5, 210)

The ability to find something beautiful is part of our human nature. The German playwright Schiller read Kant's third *Critique* and was much influenced by it. He was familiar with Kant's analysis of the satisfaction in the beautiful and also with his notion of free play of our faculties, **imagination** and **understanding**, which Kant offered as a result of his analysis and as the justifying ground for this (particularly human) satisfaction in the beautiful. Unlike Kant, Schiller was not a philosopher. He did not write about deep or abstract things such as our free play of faculties. Instead, he wrote about our ability to play, in the everyday sense of the word, as we use it when we say that children are playing. And, as with Kant's satisfaction in the beautiful, he saw this ability as central to our human nature, writing in his *About the Aesthetic Education of Mankind in a Series of Letters* that "man only plays whenever he is human in the full sense of the word 'human', and he is only fully human whenever he plays" (*Der Mensch spielt nur, wo er in voller Bedeutung des Wortes Mensch ist, und er ist nur da ganz Mensch, wo er spielt*, Letter 15).

"The Agreeable," Kant explains, "is that which pleases the senses in **sensation**" (section 3, 205). What we like in sensation determines an inclination and a desire, and therefore we are not free in such a state of mind. We depend on the existence of the object and on the fact that it produces in us such a sensation, which then is a satisfaction in the agreeable. In the case of the satisfaction in the good, we are not free either. In fact, there are two ways in which something might please us as being good. Something can be good for something else or good in itself. Both kinds presuppose an understanding of the object and a concept, purpose, or aim, and, therefore, neither is free. But beauty does not require any of this:

> Flowers, free designs, lines aimlessly intertwined in each other under the name of foliage, signify nothing [*bedeuten nichts*], do not depend on any determinate concept, and yet please. (Section 4, 207)

In order to appreciate them as aesthetic objects, we do not need to own such flowers or free designs, nor do we need to understand or do anything with them. We are free of such interests.

When Kant writes in his aesthetics about "the good," he is mainly concerned with the morally good. According to him, satisfaction in the morally good has to be fundamentally distinguished from satisfaction in the beautiful or the agreeable. Although we often find these kinds of satisfaction occurring together in us, we should see them as three different (ideal) kinds that have their own and specific **grounds**.

Satisfaction in the morally good is not free but interested, because once we understand what is morally good, Kant argues, our will to realize it is **determined** by this understanding. Satisfaction in the good depends on concepts, purposes, values, and our interests in bringing the object or the act into existence. None of this is the case with respect to the beautiful.

Kant later argues that beauty can be a symbol of morality (section 59). It is not easy to understand exactly what he means by this. It can easily be understood as implying that beauty depends on morality. But we will see, later, in a separate section on this topic, why this cannot be correct, and we will discuss in some detail what Kant has in mind when he says that beauty can be a "symbol of morality," in fact *the* symbol of morality.

Kant wants to make the distinction between the agreeable and the good very strong, and he uses this occasion to argue against Epicureanism, or some vulgar version thereof that was prominent at his time. Happiness (*eudaimonia, Glückseligkeit*) as the greatest possible sum total of agreeableness in one's life can never be the highest good in Kant's view, because reason "can never be persuaded" to accept this as the final goal in our lives (section 4, 208).

It is important to keep in mind that Kant now has two different, though very closely related, criteria for the "satisfaction in the beautiful" (and thus for the beautiful) at his disposal: (a) satisfaction in the beautiful meets the criterion of *disinterestedness*; (b) satisfaction in the beautiful is *neither* satisfaction in the good, *nor* satisfaction in the agreeable. Kant uses both of these criteria in his arguments throughout his aesthetics. When he considers pleasure or displeasure under specific circumstances or in certain respects, he sometimes argues that there cannot be any interest involved and therefore, according to (a), it must be satisfaction in the beautiful; sometimes he argues case by case that it is neither satisfaction in the agreeable nor satisfaction in the good, and therefore, according to (b), it must be satisfaction in the beautiful, because it is the only one that is left of the three kinds of satisfaction. This kind of argumentation often seems rather schematic, but at least it brings formal clarity into his arguments. We should also keep in mind that both criteria for the satisfaction in the beautiful are merely *negative criteria*. Both tell us only what satisfaction in the beautiful is *not*: it is not interested, and it is satisfaction neither in the good nor in the agreeable. Kant thus still has to offer some *positive* grounds for satisfaction in the beautiful. He has to say what it is based upon. He will do this later, when unfolding the notion of free play and the *a priori* principle of subjective purposiveness.

Further reading

Allison, *Kant's Theory of Taste*, pp. 90–4, argues (drawing on Kant's moral philosophy) that the agreeable and the good exhaust all kinds of interest, and that we therefore have indeed exactly three kinds of satisfaction of which one is without interest.

Fricke, *Kants Theorie des reinen Geschmacksurteils*, pp. 14–29, discusses the three kinds of satisfaction. It is mainly expository and stays close to the text, but at places also refers to Kant's moral philosophy.

2

Universality: Second Moment

The Argument from Self-Reflection: Private, Public, Universal

Kant takes it as a matter of fact that a judgment of taste is always accompanied by a certain claim to **universality**. If I find something beautiful, I claim that everyone should agree. I do not need to make this claim explicitly, but I could do so and would be *justified* in doing so. At least this is what Kant tries to establish. If we find something beautiful, we cannot but think that the object itself is beautiful and that therefore everyone should find it so. But because beauty is not something objective, because there are no proofs and **rules** in matters of taste, I cannot by way of argument force anyone to agree. All that remains is my claim that anyone would agree if only he or she had a look at what I see (or hear or otherwise perceive). The universality of a judgment of taste thus cannot be inferred from anything objective. Rather, it is part of my **representation** of, and my **satisfaction** in, the object.

Kant begins his discussion of the second moment with section 6, which is entitled "The beautiful is that which, without concepts, is represented as the object of a universal satisfaction." That the object is an object of universal satisfaction is not something extrinsic or additional to the judgment of taste. Rather, it is an essential and intrinsic part of it. The universality is part of the representation itself. This is the point of section 9 of the *Critique of the Power of Judgment*.

Although Kant does not say so, he gives two different arguments for this kind of universality, one in section 6 and the other in section 9. At the end of the discussion of the second moment, after section 9, we find the *"definition* of the beautiful drawn from the second **moment**," which reads as follows: "That is beautiful which pleases universally without a **concept**." But it seems that this has already been established in section 6, because this section has been entitled: "The beautiful is that which, without concepts, is represented as the object of a universal satisfaction." So, if section 6 lives up to its title, then Kant could have skipped sections 7, 8, and 9 and could have given the "definition" right after section 6.

But there is an essential difference between sections 6 and 9. Section 6 argues for the universality of judgments of taste by way of inference from the first moment, **disinterestedness**, whereas section 9 offers new and independent **grounds**, namely the notion of free play of the **faculties**. Furthermore, the criterion of disinterestedness is merely negative, whereas the notion of free play allows a positive account.

A particular feature of the argument in section 6 is its psychological and phenomenological character. It is based on an introspection engaged in by someone who makes a judgment of taste. Kant here makes the reader take two roles at the same time, one being the role of the philosopher, who argues, so to speak, "from the outside," and the other being the role of the person who actually makes a judgment of taste. This is actually rather complex, and when one tries to follow Kant's arguments, one should be very careful to distinguish between these two levels (outside-inside) and to be aware of the level on which an argument takes place: the logical-philosophical one (from the outside) or the psychological-phenomenological one (from the inside).

"The beautiful is that which, without concepts, is represented as the object of a universal satisfaction," and this, Kant asserts, can be "deduced from the previous explanation of it as an object of satisfaction without any interest" (section 6, 211). Kant argues for this inference by asserting: "one cannot judge that about which he is aware that the satisfaction in it is without any interest in his own case in any way except that it must contain a ground of satisfaction for everyone" (section 6, 211). That is, if one is "aware" of one's own disinterestedness, one thinks it "must" contain a universal ground. The inference ("it must") is logical, whereas one's introspection ("he is aware") is a psychological matter.

But there are several problems with this inference. First of all, it is not obvious how we can infer the existence of a universal ground (to be found in, or valid for, all human beings) from the non-existence of a personal (individual) ground. To make this inference, we need to be sure that there are no other options between these two extremes: the personal and the universal.

If the grounds we are looking for are not personal ones, why should we have to go so far as to demand grounds that are valid for everyone? Why should it not be possible that there be grounds that apply just to a particular group of people? After all, in the first *Critique*, in the table of judgments regarding quantity, we already find that Kant admits not only singular and universal judgments, but also particular ones:

singular (one) – particular (some) – universal (all)

But we have to be careful not to get confused here about objects and subjects judging objects. In the first *Critique*, Kant is thinking of the objects a judgment is about (one tree, some trees, all trees), and for him the judgment of taste is of course always a singular judgment, a judgment about a single object that is given to our senses (this rose). So there is no question about particularity here. But if we reflect on the possible grounds of our judgment of taste, we make ourselves the object of **reflection**, asking whether the ground is one found only in us or also in others, and at this point I want to bring up the threefold distinction, singular–particular–universal, from the first *Critique*. I want to apply this distinction to the grounds and the subjects that have them (me and the others), not to the object the judgment of taste is about (this rose); and this makes sense, because the reflection here in section 6 is about these grounds, whether they are to be found only in me or also in others. This reflection is implicit in the judgment of taste.

Now we can ask (hopefully without getting confused): why not allow for particular judgments here (implicit in the judgment of taste)? If the grounds of my satisfaction are not my personal ones, maybe they are grounds for others as well, for a particular group of people, people of a particular nationality or race, or just for people with a particular interest that they have in common? Is it not obvious that one cannot infer "for all" if we are just given "not only for me," that we cannot jump so quickly from the denial of singularity to the assertion of universality?

The only answer I have to offer in defense of Kant here is that such particular (even if only implicit) judgments would move the whole discussion into the empirical realm and out of the **transcendental** one. It seems to me that there is no place for considerations of particular groups of people in Kant's transcendental philosophy. Either you think of yourself as an individual with personal interests, or you think of yourself as a representative of humanity in general. Within the framework of transcendental philosophy, there is nothing in between: you cannot think of yourself as a member of a particular group, because the characteristics of such a group would be empirical and never **a priori**. What distinguishes particular communities, societies, races, or cultures are always empirical and never a priori characteristics. Thus, particular groups fall outside the scope of Kant's transcendental philosophy. (They would be a legitimate topic for his anthropology instead.) We may find this unsatisfying, but Kant's aesthetics, as far as it is part of his transcendental system, simply cannot deal with such phenomena as cultures and communities. You are an individual and you are also part of humanity in general. Transcendentally speaking, there is nothing in between. We simply have to accept this point. Even if we do not accept this, we do not need to reject Kant's aesthetics. We simply have to see this analysis as being part of transcendental philosophy, and we can still learn much from it.

A second problem with the above inference is whether it is really necessary that the person be "aware that the satisfaction in [the object] is without any interest in his own case" (section 6, 211). Similarly, Kant, at the end of the section, writes: "there must be attached to the judgment of taste, with the *consciousness* of an abstraction in it from all interest, a claim to validity for everyone" (section 6, 212). It seems to me that such a "consciousness," although possible, is not really required. If you really make a judgment of taste and if, on top of this, you ask yourself what the grounds for your satisfaction actually are, then you necessarily will (or at least should) find that you are not interested in the object's existence, that you are free of desire, and that there are no personal or rational (conceptual) grounds for the satisfaction you happen to have. It is not necessary that you really ask yourself whether these conditions are satisfied. But it is necessary that *if* you were to introspect, you would not find any interest underlying your satisfaction.

Whether your satisfaction is really disinterested or not is something that only you yourself can determine, through introspection. Introspection is a psychological, personal, and empirical matter, whereas the inference to universality is a logical one, at least within the framework of transcendental logic: not private, hence universal! It is an argument the philosopher can make. He does so in theory, from the outside, so to speak. But Kant here wants the reader to do both – to imagine him- or herself making a judgment of taste, and to be the philosopher following Kant's arguments.

The empirical side has its problems: maybe you are never sure whether you are really disinterested, as you are never sure whether what you did was really morally good. (Are you sure that what you just did and what you think was done selflessly was not at bottom done out of selfish motives, deep down, maybe unknown to yourself? This is a question that troubled Schiller.) In a particular case, when you are really involved, it is difficult to know the workings of your mind and all your hidden motives. But these are empirical questions, not theoretical and transcendental ones. They are empirical questions about finding out and about certainty. Kant is not interested in such considerations here. He does transcendental philosophy, not what he would call "anthropology." To understand Kant, we have to keep transcendental considerations apart from empirical ones. We have to distinguish between considerations about what we can do in principle and under ideal circumstances and those that concern empirical facts and our finding out about them, especially, as is the case here, if we can easily be mistaken.

Further reading

Allison, *Kant's Theory of Taste*, pp. 99–103 offers a defense against Guyer's claim that Kant's inference of the second moment (universality) from the first (disinterestedness) is not valid.

Peter, *Das transzendentale Prinzip der Urteilskraft*, pp. 106–8, argues, distinguishing between phenomenological, logical, and transcendental points of view, that the "continuity of transition" from disinterestedness to subjective universality in section 6 is not justified.

Subjective Universality

When making a judgment, we often do not expect others to agree with us. We may not be sure whether what we claim is correct. We may also think of our judgment as a merely private or personal one that is based on a momentary feeling, such as the feeling of agreeableness. In these cases we usually do not expect others to agree. On the other hand, sometimes when we make judgments, we expect others to agree with us, but we usually don't bother demanding their agreement, because we take it for granted. Mathematical judgments are of the latter kind. There are proofs in mathematics, and we could always refer to such proofs to convince others of the truth of what we say. We could force them to agree with us, it seems, by making them follow a mathematical proof step by step. But when doing mathematics, we usually do not think about this. We do not try to convince others that the square root of 2 is an irrational number. Either we know a proof of this, or we don't. In either case we don't bother claiming that others should agree. If we have a proof, we are content. We feel assured that we could convince anyone of the truth of the statement. If we do not have a proof but yet believe it to be true, we think that there is a proof and that by means of it everyone, including ourselves, could be led to see the truth of the statement. Universality of agreement seems not to be a problem in mathematics, where intersubjectivity is guaranteed by the nature of the rules that establish the truth of mathematical statements. In mathematics, intersubjectivity comes for free, so to speak.

But not all objective **judgments** are mathematical. There are also empirical objective judgments such as "This tree is taller than that one" or "This chair is brown and not green." There may be problems of perspective, or perception of color, but we usually assume that such problems can be solved, that things are objectively as we claim them to be, and that everyone would agree with us when we make such judgments under normal circumstances (provided the judgments are true). My judgment and yours should not contradict each other, because they are about the same thing. The object forces the judgments to agree with each other by serving as a third element that mediates between them. In the first *Critique* (A 820/B 848), Kant uses the Latin phrase *"consentientia uni tertio, consentiunt inter se"* (agreeing with a third thing, they agree among themselves) to characterize intersubjective agreement in the case of objective judgments. Based on this small piece of logic, agreement between objective judgments comes for free and poses no problem. (This is the case at least in an ideal situation. In particular situations it is sometimes not clear what objectivity is and whether, for instance, a judgment is true or not.)

Judgments of taste, on the other hand, are not objective, and the principle *"consentientia uni tertio, consentiunt inter se"* cannot be applied. Therefore the claim that others should agree becomes problematic. Kant writes in section 19 of the *Prolegomena* (1783) that "objectivity" and "universality" (or "universal assent," "universal agreement," and "intersubjectivity") are "interchangeable concepts" (*Wechselbegriffe*) because each of them can be deduced from the other. Objectivity implies intersubjectivity, and, conversely, universal assent implies objectivity.

Although a judgment of taste is of course based on experience, because I must see or otherwise perceive the flower to find it beautiful, Kant nevertheless says that the judgment of taste is a judgment "a priori" (i.e. prior to experience). So what exactly is "prior to experience" here? To understand this, we have to see what is at issue here: the judgment's claim to *universality*, "Everyone should find this rose beautiful." Universality is something very different from mere generality. A statement of the form "All S judge so and so" is universal if its truth can be derived from higher principles, whereas it is merely general if its truth is based on a case-by-case investigation. We can imagine an exception to a general statement, but not to a universal one. For example, the statement expressing the fact that all children of a certain village at a certain time happened to have red hair would be a general statement. We can imagine that there could have been a child with blond hair. With universal statements, by contrast, no exception is thought to be possible. A typical universal statement is: "All humans are mortal." Such a statement applies even to those human beings who are not yet born. We certainly cannot check this statement in a case-by-case fashion. Even in a single case it can be problematic. For how do we know that someone is mortal and not immortal? Do we have to wait until he or she dies? What if we keep waiting and waiting and that person keeps on living? Furthermore, if we somehow conclude that this person is immortal, we might have to change our very concept of what a human being is. We see that when it comes to universality we must be prepared to offer conceptual grounds. I must think, for instance, that mortality is part of our human nature as such. A simple example from geometry would be the statement "All triangles have three sides." An example from algebra would be: "All polynomials with real coefficients and of degree two have at most two zeros." That is, given any polynomial of the form $x^2 + ax + b$ with a and b real numbers, there are at most two solutions to the equation $x^2 + ax + b = 0$. Now, there are infinitely many, even uncountably many, real numbers, and hence there are infinitely many different polynomials of this form. We certainly cannot go through all such polynomials in a one-by-one fashion (as we cannot look at each possible triangle in the previous example). Instead, we must derive the truth of the general statement in a logical and deductive way from other statements. (Of course there are also axioms and problems of how to get started in mathematics. But that is another issue.)

Kant assumes that by making a judgment of taste one's judgment includes the claim that everyone (that is, all human beings) should agree. But we do not have an objective basis to make this claim to universality. In the judgment "All humans are mortal," mortality is thought of as an objective and essential feature of human beings as such. But in judgments such as "All human beings should agree to my judgment of taste" and "All human beings should find this beautiful," there is an irreducibly *normative* element involved that refers to *acts* (the judgment and the agreement) which are not objective properties like that of mortality. Thus, if there are grounds for this claim to universality in a judgment of taste, these grounds must be very different in nature from those we find in objective judgments.

When Kant wrote his first *Critique* (1781) and the *Prolegomena* (1783), he was concerned with cognitive judgments and not with aesthetic ones. Objectivity therefore seemed to be the only possible basis for universality. In the third *Critique*, though, a new kind of judgment comes into focus. The subjective universality of a judgment of taste cannot be inferred from the judgment's being true of its object. There is no such thing, so this kind of universality does not come for free. It cannot be guaranteed in advance, i.e., before a judgment of taste is actually made. Rather, it is part of the very act of such a judgment.

At the end of section 6, Kant writes: "There must be attached to the judgment of taste . . . a claim to validity for everyone without the universality that pertains to objects, i.e., it must be combined with a claim to *subjective* universality" (section 6, 212). The universality of the judgment of taste is not an objective but a "subjective universality," because, Kant argues, it is not based on concepts. Concepts give rules and are applied to objects (such as roses or sunsets), but judging subjects are not objects in that sense, they are not subjected to rules, and it is such judging subjects that are in question here. We should add here that the "subjective universality" is *subjective* in two senses of the word "subjective." A judgment of taste is subjective (a) because it *refers to* all judging *subjects*. If I make a judgment of taste, I claim that everyone should agree. A judgment of taste is subjective (b) because it is *based on* subjective *grounds* (**feeling**, taste, some-thing you have to try yourself, something that you have to make happen your-self). Now, there must be a *link* between the subjective ground of a judgment of taste (b) and the range of subjects who should agree to that judgment (a). The object must play a role too, but it alone does not provide the link.

Kant must thus offer a new element that can take the place of the "third" element we find connecting two objective judgments, the object these two judg-ments are about (*consentientia uni tertio, consentiunt inter se*). In a judgment of taste the object is, in a certain sense, *bracketed*. It is not the object that guarantees some kind of intersubjective validity of judgments of taste. In place of it, Kant offers the "free play of the faculties" and the "**principle** of **purposiveness**." We have to engage ourselves in this free play and the object must be suitable (purposive) for it. That is, the object must be one that we find to be suitable for such a free play of the faculties. Furthermore, when we make a judgment of taste, we not only refer to the object, we also refer to ourselves, insofar as we judge the object in relation to us. It is for these reasons that we may say the object is "bracketed" in a judgment of taste as compared with a judgment of **cognition**.

There are no rules in matters of taste. The truth of the judgment "This chair is red" is in a certain sense predetermined by the concept of redness. If you have that concept (leaving aside blind or colorblind people), then you will have a rule for applying it and you will have no choice in how to do so, at least as far as the truth of the statement "This chair is red" is concerned. But the concept of beauty does not function like this. It differs from the concept of redness insofar as it is a subjective rather than an objective concept; therefore, a judgment of taste is not "true" in the sense that it corresponds to its object in the right way. (If you think redness is not completely objective, take "weighs five kilograms," or "is made of wood" instead.) Kant, interestingly, never mentions the problem of truth with regard to judgments of taste, and there are good reasons for this. He takes it for granted that "truth" means the agreement between knowledge and its object (*Critique of Pure Reason*, A 58/B 82). Judgments of taste do not express knowledge of an object. Instead, we may say, we have to make something happen ourselves, namely the free play, in order to see whether this chair is beautiful or not. We have to engage in the free play of **imagination** and **understanding** to see whether contemplating the object is pleasurable or not. We cannot predict whether such a harmonious free play will happen. Nobody can. You have to try it out for yourself. There is an important element of *openness* and *autonomy* here. You have to be creative. You do not follow rules. Instead, it is almost as if you create new ones. (When we discuss fine art, we will see that geniuses in a certain sense create new rules.)

The free play of our faculties and the feeling of pleasure or displeasure that is involved in this play are the subjective elements of a judgment of taste. It is crucial to notice that according to Kant these subjective elements are themselves universal, because they are accessible to every human being. You can engage in free play as well as I can. This is reflected upon in a judgment of taste itself (we will explain this when we discuss Kant's section 9 in the final section of this chapter), and based on this reflection the claim to universal subjective validity has a justifying ground.

Further reading

Subjective universality is also central to the following three sections in this book. The reader might want to have a look there as well and see the suggested readings for those sections.

For the alleged interchangeability of objectivity and intersubjectivity in the context of judgments of perception, see Kant's *Prolegomena*, sections 18–22.

Ginsborg, *The Role of Taste in Kant's Theory of Cognition*, especially chapter 3, makes the central claim that intersubjectivity precedes objectivity and that Kant accordingly wrote the third *Critique* in order to fill a gap he left in the first. Highly suggestive writing. For criticisms, see Wenzel, *Das Problem*, 57–70, and Allison, *Kant's Theory*, pp. 113–18.

Ameriks, "Kant and the Objectivity of Taste," argues that the moment of subjective universality is indeed the crucial element requiring the "deduction," but that this deduction in the end fails and that "a Kantian ought to acknowledge the objectivity of taste." Offers a comparison with the judgment "This rose is fragrant" (p. 8). This is a clear, but sweeping and challenging article.

Wenzel, *Das Problem*, pp. 155–67, and "Kann aus einem Urteil," offer comparisons between judgments of taste and judgments of perception and their justifying grounds for inter-subjective validity.

A Case of Transcendental Logic

This section is somewhat of a side issue, especially for anyone who is more interested in art, literature, or aesthetics in general. But for Kant the problem discussed here is important, especially in the light of the first *Critique*.

Section 8 of the *Critique of the Power of Judgment* is entitled: "The universality of the satisfaction is represented in a judgment of taste only as subjective." Kant begins to explain the nature of this subjective universality and the way it is "represented" in a judgment of taste as follows:

> This particular determination of the universality of an aesthetic judgment that can be found in a judgment of taste is something remarkable, not indeed for the logician, but certainly for the transcendental philosopher, the discovery of the origin

of which calls for no little effort on his part, but which also reveals a property of our faculty of cognition that without this analysis would have remained unknown. (Section 8, 213)

The transcendental philosopher has to make *"no little effort"* to discover "the origin" of the "determination of the universality" of the judgment of taste, not because he is less capable than the logician, but because he takes a wider perspective, he sees more and asks for more. He asks for justifying grounds that cannot be established by methods of formal logic alone. For instance, the transcendental philosopher may bring into the discussion considerations of morality and justice, which the formal logician does not.

In the first *Critique*, Kant made it clear that his transcendental logic is not only concerned with the possible relations between one judgment and another, as is formal logic. Rather, the transcendental philosopher is also concerned with the relations between a single judgment, a perception, and the object being judged. The transcendental philosopher is concerned with the faculty of imagination and how our understanding is related to objects by way of **intuition** and perception. The question of how a judgment such as "This tree is green" is related to the visual image we have of the tree is a problem for the transcendental philosopher and not for the formal logician, simply because the latter just does not worry about such issues. We may say that the formal logician is concerned with propositions, not with (the act of making) judgments. He is not concerned with the judging subject and the subjective elements that are necessary for making a judgment.

In the *Critique of Pure Reason*, Kant distinguishes between general and transcendental logic: "General logic abstracts . . . from all content of cognition, i.e. from any relation of it to the object, and considers only the logical form in the relation of cognitions to one another, i.e., the form of thinking in general" (A 55/B 79). In opposition to this, he wanted his own and new "transcendental logic" *not* to abstract from all content. He wanted it to be sensitive to a priori aspects of intuition as they are reflected in his categories.

What Kant in this passage calls "general logic" is today called by the name "formal logic." Such formal logic "abstracts from all content of cognition." If all humans are mortal and if Socrates is human, then Socrates is mortal. You know this without having to know what exactly it means to be human, to be mortal, or to be Socrates. You know the conclusion for formal reasons: if all h are m and if S is h, then S must be m. A consequence of this is that a formal logician regards a judgment, for instance a singular one like "Socrates is mortal," in a way that is fundamentally different from the way a transcendental philosopher looks at it. The formal logician does not worry about the application of such a judgment to its object and therefore thinks of a singular judgment as behaving similarly to a universal one in the following sense: the judgment "This tree is green" is similar to "All trees are green" in that whatever falls under the subject-term ("this tree" or "tree") is said to be green. Kant makes this point clear several pages later:

> The logicians rightly say that in the use of judgments in syllogisms [i.e. when judgments are used in syllogisms] singular judgments can be treated like universal ones. For just because they have no domain at all [there is only *one* object that is meant by "this tree"], their predicate is not merely related to some of what is contained under the concept of the subject while being excluded from another part of it. . . . [L]ogic . . . is limited only to the use of judgments *with respect to each other*. (A 71/B 96–7)

In the first *Critique*, Kant was interested in showing that beside singular and universal judgments, there is a third kind of judgment, which he called "particular judgments," judgments like "Some trees are green." This need not interest us here. But what we can learn from this passage is that he thought of the "general" (formal) logic of his time as being insufficient. This becomes apparent, if we again consider the syllogism "All humans are mortal, Socrates is human, and therefore Socrates is mortal." This syllogism is formal because I do not have to pay attention to Socrates as an actual being and an individual. I just pay attention to the predicate "human," cancel through it, and substitute "Socrates" for "All humans." Such quasi-mechanical procedures of canceling and substitution are formal. It does not matter what "Socrates" really is. "Socrates" could refer to anything as long as it is human. In opposition to this, Kant introduced in the first *Critique* the notions of intuition (*Anschauung*), **categories**, and schematism. Logicians, Kant thought, did not pay sufficient attention to these notions and the actual applications of judgments to objects of intuition, and all this has reverberations here in the third *Critique*, as we shall see.

Kant's treatment of logic is not just concerned with the relations between judgments but also with such (somewhat psychological) elements as intuition, imagination, perception, and the application of concepts to appearances. Kant calls his own and new logic a "transcendental" one, "transcendental" referring to the safe and solid basis for the application and limitation of our concepts, a basis we actually have (to be distinguished from "transcendent," which refers to what goes beyond our abilities). Now this approach to logic from the first *Critique* creates a special background for analyzing judgments of taste and makes Kant's aesthetics a special and unique one, too.

Returning to the title of section 8 and to the quote given at the beginning of this section, we should now be in a better position to understand the concept of subjective universality and the "effort" it requires on the part of the transcendental philosopher. As a transcendental philosopher, one focuses on the role that both concepts and intuitions play in a judgment, and it is from this perspective that we make our "discovery of the origin" of the "particular determination" of the subjective universality in question. We shall see what that origin and that determination are.

The universality of a judgment of taste is "subjective" not only in the sense (a) of referring to the sphere of all judging subjects, but also in the sense (b) of having its origin in the judging subject. It is the latter sense that is overlooked by the ordinary logician and that is relevant here. In the next section of his aesthetics, section 9, Kant introduces the notion of a free play of our faculties of cognition, imagination, and understanding, and it turns out that this is the "origin" that we will "discover" – at least it is part of that origin. In a second step we will discover the a priori principle of subjective purposiveness underlying that free play of our faculties of cognition. These two discoveries will be the "compensation" for our "effort," and they are discoveries of transcendental philosophy, not of psychology or logic.

Several years before the third Critique was written, Kant himself did not know about this kind of "origin" of the judgment of taste's claim to universal assent. He even thought that an aesthetics as part of his transcendental philosophy was utterly impossible. In the first Critique (1781) and in the Prolegomena (1783) he was concerned with cognitive judgments and he thought that a claim to everyone's assent must be based on objectivity. In section 19 of the Prolegomena, for instance, he wrote that objective validity and validity for everyone were "interchangeable concepts" (Wechselbegriffe). There, any kind of subjective universality seemed utterly impossible. In that work, he did not think of the possibility of a kind of universal validity that could be based on anything but objectivity. Nevertheless, in the third Critique he argues that we find exactly such subjective universal validity in a judgment of taste. For Kant this was really a "discovery."

Now we must see that the singularity of a judgment of taste has to be of a very special kind, or must have very special grounds, to allow for the claim to (intersubjective) universal validity. In a judgment of taste, the representation of an object, for instance a tree when we look at it, must play a new kind of role, a role that is not to be found in cognitive judgments. On the one hand, judgments of taste involve less than judgments of cognition, because they lack objectivity; but on the other hand, they must involve more, because a new element is needed, an element that cannot be found in judgments of cognition and that can take the place of objectivity, so to speak, in order to justify the claim to universality. This new element must be found in the grounds of this singular judgment, and we will see that especially the singularity in some sense allows for these grounds. The particular relatedness of this singularity (one object, but an object of the senses that is represented in our mind in a special way) and universality (all judging subjects – with their representational powers) will be discussed in the next section.

What I wanted to show here is that, for Kant, to look for justifying grounds for a judgment that claims intersubjective universal validity although it is not objective, makes sense only from a *transcendental* point of view, because only in that view does an analysis of a judgment also involve an analysis of our cognitive faculties (understanding and imagination) and the roles they play in such a judgment. This becomes especially relevant, as we will see in the next section, in a judgment that is just about a single object that is given in perception. From a general logical point of view, there would not be much to say. But even if one is not a mere general logician but a transcendental one and has read the first *Critique*, the idea of an intersubjective universality that is not based on objectivity is somewhat paradoxical. Section 8 of the third *Critique* is devoted to pointing this out.

Further reading

Cohen, "Three Problems in Kant's Aesthetics," and Rind, "Kant's Beautiful Roses," discuss various possibilities of how to relate the two judgments "This rose is beautiful" and "Roses in general are beautiful." They ask what Kant could possibly have meant by saying that the latter is "an aesthetically grounded logical judgment," because the predicate "beautiful" is never a logical one. Although they do not discuss the relevance of transcendental logic, which I focus on, they still bring out the fact that the predicate "beautiful" is not a logical one and the problems this creates.
Kulenkampff, *Kants Logik*, pp. 80–7 (1st edition: 70–7), tries to make sense of Kant's difficult section 8 and the various kinds of "quantity," logical and aesthetic, which Kant introduces therein. Similarly Wenzel, *Das Problem*, pp. 142–55.

Singular "but" Universal

Kant at several places in the third *Critique* expresses the idea that judgments of taste are singular "but" universal. This raises at least two questions. First, why should judgments of taste have to be singular, that is, about a single object? Why should, for example, a judgment like "All roses are beautiful" not be a judgment of taste? Secondly, saying that judgments of taste are singular "but" universal gives the impression that it is somehow "difficult" for a singular judgment to be universal. This is astonishing, because judgments like "This rose is the longest" or "The number 5 is a prime number" are singular, too, and there is no problem with their being valid for everyone. If they are true, they are true for you as well as for me and anyone else.

These are the questions we will focus on in this section. I will quote and explain several passages from the third *Critique* that express the idea of a judgment of taste being singular but universal. We will see that a judgment of taste is singular in a special way.

In section 23, Kant observes the following about the satisfaction in the beautiful or sublime:

> [This satisfaction] does not depend on a **sensation**, like that in the agreeable, nor on a determinate concept, like the satisfaction in the good; but it is nevertheless still related to concepts, although it is indeterminate which, *hence* the satisfaction is connected to the mere presentation or to the faculty for that, through which the faculty of presentation or the imagination is considered, in the case of a given intuition, to be in accord with the faculty of concepts of the understanding [in case of the beautiful] or of **reason** [in case of the sublime], as promoting the latter. *Hence* both sorts of judgments are also *singular*, [emphasis Kant's] and yet judgments that profess to be universally valid in regard to *every subject*, although they lay claim merely to the feeling of pleasure and not to any cognition of the object. (Section 23, 244)

We will focus on the two conclusions expressed by the phrases "hence . . ." and "Hence. . . ." We will explain what they presuppose and how they have to be understood.

As Kant often does, he first eliminates certain possibilities and then focuses on what is left. The satisfaction in question does not depend on sensation or on a determinate concept and hence, according to the classification of the three kinds of satisfaction from section 3, it must be the satisfaction in the beautiful. This kind of satisfaction presupposes reflection (to be explained in section 9) and is "still related to concepts, although it is indeterminate which" (section 23, 244). When I look at a flower and find it beautiful, I might say all kinds of things about it. I might subsume it under a variety of concepts, such as that of a flower or that of a rose. I may say that it is red here and green there, or that the red of this petal changes slightly in the sunlight when the wind blows gently. I might say all these things, but I do not need to do so. Similarly, when I look at something that I find sublime, a huge wave for instance, I will be overwhelmed and moved by its size and force. I could say many things about the wave, too, or about my feelings and the ideas this spectacle brings forth in me. But again, I do not need to spell out any of this. I could leave it all open and express my feelings and thoughts in a gesture or a poem. Nevertheless, concepts play a role in such contemplation, not as **determining** concepts, but as concepts that I could apply if I wanted to express my feelings and thoughts in judgments of cognition. This is, I would suggest, what Kant means by saying that "it is indeterminate" to which concepts the satisfaction in the beautiful is "related."

Instead of subsuming the object under a concept (rose) in order to predicate something of it (its redness), I leave this open and I play with the possibilities of what properties the object could possibly have, or what it could mean to me, and I enjoy the pleasure this play brings to me. My feelings of pleasure and displeasure are involved in such a play with possibilities of (predicate) concepts, and this is so not only in the case of the beautiful but also in case of the ugly or the sublime: The ugly can be fascinating and intriguing in many ways that are connected to concepts and purposes that are allowed to vary and to change; and the sublime is related to moral concepts. But still, in all these cases the relations to concepts should not be determining ones. The judgments must be aesthetic judgments. It is the mere possibility of application of such concepts and the open horizon of such concepts that matters here. (We will see later that this horizon of possibilities creates room for freedom and autonomy.)

In aesthetic reflection we do not have just one or two concepts but a whole range of possible concepts at our disposal. It is the "faculty of concepts" (*Vermögen der Begriffe*) that takes the place of (determinate) concepts in judgments of taste. Whereas in judgments of cognition it is intuitions and concepts that determine the judgment and its object, in judgments about the beautiful or the sublime it is the faculties themselves, the faculties of intuitions and concepts, which, as it were, "take over." My perception of the object is of course still necessary. It is still the flower or the wave that I see. I still have an intuition (*Anschauung*) of it, and I still make a judgment. I judge the flower or the wave to be beautiful or sublime, but no particular concept plays any decisive role in this judgment of taste. The flower is not beautiful *as* a flower and the wave is not sublime *as* a wave, in the sense that although we usually of course know that this is a flower, or a wave, this kind of knowledge should not matter in our judging it to be beautiful, or sublime.

In aesthetic contemplation the object provides an open range of possibilities of what we could say and how I could look at it. My satisfaction in the beautiful is a pleasure in the act of reflecting about, and by means of, this open range of possibilities. My satisfaction is not confined by any determinate concept, neither the subject concept (rose) nor any predicate concept (redness). Rather, it is playfully connected with a whole range of possibilities of concepts (of shapes, shades, figures, gestures, and all kinds of memories and association) that are at our disposal, concepts that we have already in a more or less clear fashion and that we can make more determinate or possibly even create in a conceptualizing process based on what happens to be perceptually given to us. We avail ourselves of this entire range of possible concepts whenever we allow the imagination and the understanding to engage with one another in a "free play," that is, whenever we contemplate an object and find it beautiful. It is for this reason that Kant can write that "the satisfaction is connected to the mere presentation or to the faculty for that, through which the faculty of presentation or the imagination is considered, in the case of a given intuition, to be in accord with the faculty of concepts of the understanding" (section 23, 244, see quote above). The "accord" is manifest subjectively in the pleasure I feel and quasi-objectively, we may say, in the range of possibilities.

Even the subject concept (rose, human being, horse, church: see below) should not really matter in a judgment of taste, because it might downgrade beauty to mere adherent beauty: "But the beauty of a human being (and in this species that of a man, a woman, or a child), the beauty of a horse, of a building (such as a church, a palace, an arsenal, or a garden-house) presuppose a concept of the end that determines what the thing should be, hence a concept of its perfection, and is thus merely adherent beauty" (section 16, 230). Thus in a judgment about the beautiful or the sublime, the intuition is isolated and, so to speak, "totally singular," because although it is subsumed under a subject concept (I know it is a rose), this should not matter: the subject concept is not used in any (objective) connection (*Verknüpfung*) with a predicate concept, which would further determine the object. Instead of determinate subject and predicate concepts, such an intuition faces the whole faculty of concepts and a range of possible concepts and their possible applications. We should keep this in mind when trying to understand the nature of the singularity of a judgment of taste and the fact that "both sorts of judgments [about the beautiful or the sublime] are also *singular*, and *yet* [they are] judgments that profess to be universally valid in regard to *every subject*, although they lay claim merely to the feeling of pleasure and not to any cognition of the object" (section 23, 244, see quote above).

The judgment of taste is thus "singular" not only because it is about a single object, but also, and more importantly, for additional reasons. The judgment is based on the relationship between the faculties *themselves*, part of which is that in a judgment of taste we refer to the object without any determinate concept playing a decisive role. This *open* relationship between the faculties that play with the object, or rather that play with our intuition of it, does not really, or at least not fully, determine the object (the flower or the wave), because nothing at all is objectively predicated about the object, such as its color or size. Even the subject concept does not come to serve a cognitive role, which it would find only through combination (*Verknüpfung*, some kind of "tying with knots" or "knitting together") with other concepts. In the cognitive judgment "This rose is red," the subject concept "rose" would be combined with the predicate concept "red," while both would be applied to the object. Not only is the rose subsumed under the subject concept "rose" and the predicate concept "red," so that these two concepts get determined (by the rose), but at the same time the given manifold of intuition of the rose (given in perception) is ordered and structured by these very concepts and their connection. The rose determines the concepts, and the concepts determine (the perception of) the rose and each other. Furthermore, it is I who do all this. In fact, the four "elements" – the **manifold** of intuition, the subject concept, the predicate concept, and, on top of all, **apperception** – are all *interwoven* with each other in a judgment of cognition – and with the (objective) predicate concept missing (beauty not being an objective predicate) the whole structure collapses! If we think of this structure as constituting objectivity, the object *as such*, then we might even say that in a judgment of taste the object is not even cognized as an object.

A further reason for saying that the judgment of taste and the judgment about the sublime are singular in a particular way is the fact that what becomes relevant in these judgments is our state of mind and that we become conscious of this state merely through our feeling of pleasure and displeasure. Roughly speaking, subjective features (although, as Kant takes great pain to show, intersubjectively universal features) take the place of objective ones. It is for these reasons, the *collapsing* or at least absence of the cognitive structure and the relevance of our state of mind as *felt*, that such judgments are *singular* in a very special way. Accordingly the word "singular," when applied to judgments of taste or judgments about the sublime, should be understood in the light of these particular reasons.

There are several other passages in which Kant writes about aesthetic judgments being singular "but" universal and which we are now in a much better position to understand. Such passages can be found in sections 8, 31, 33, 37, and 57. We will now briefly discuss these passages.

In section 8, Kant writes that the universality of a judgment of taste is "subjective," that it is "aesthetic," and that it "must also be of a special kind":

[F]rom a *subjectively universal validity*, i.e., from aesthetic universal validity, which does not rest on any concept, there cannot be any inference at all to logical universal validity; because the first kind of judgment does not pertain to the object at all. For that very reason, however, the aesthetic universality that is ascribed to a judgment must also be of a *special kind*, since the predicate of beauty is not connected with the concept of the *object* considered in its entire logical sphere, and yet it extends it over the whole sphere of *those who judge*. (section 8, 215; emphasis Kant's)

In the judgment "This rose is beautiful" it does not matter that the rose is a rose. This judgment "does not pertain to the object at all." We do not connect the predicate "beautiful" with the rose as a rose, i.e., as subsumed under the concept of a rose. Nor do we connect it with any other concept, like that of a flower or a plant; we do not even think of the rose as an object (as such) at all. Hence the "predicate of beauty is not connected with the concept of the *object* considered in its entire logical sphere." That is, it plays no role what kind of object it is or possibly could be, or how it could be related to other objects or concepts. It is for this reason that the claim to universality in a judgment of taste comes as a surprise. If the concepts of subject and predicate were connected in a judgment of taste, and if there were rules for how to do this, it would be less surprising that such a judgment "extends it [the predicate] over the whole sphere of those who judge" (see quote above).

Kant calls it a "peculiarity" that a judgment of taste has "universal validity a priori, yet not a logical universality in accordance with concepts, *but* the universality of a *singular* judgment" (section 31, 281). The universality is not based on concepts; it is based neither on the concept of the subject (rose), nor on the concept of the predicate (beauty), nor on the concept of the object in general (*Gegenstand überhaupt*). The universality is not a logical one. Rather, it rests on the satisfaction in the beautiful, which may seem as isolated and, so to speak, "singular," as is the intuition of the object in a judgment of taste.

In matters of taste, one cannot rely on the opinions of other people, nor can one rely on concepts and rules. Rather, we must try something out (that is, engage in the free play) ourselves and we must be quasi-autonomous (engage ourselves in a free play and reflect about its universality). The universality that one claims must "rest on an autonomy of the subject judging about the feeling of pleasure in the given representation, i.e., on his own taste" (31, 281).

The singularity of a judgment of taste has to be seen in the light of this kind of autonomy and also in the light of the requirement of "having a taste," so to speak, of the object oneself. Kant says that in matters of taste I cannot rely on what others say but that "I try the dish with *my* [emphasis Kant's] tongue and *my* palate, and on that basis (not on the basis of general principles) do I make my judgment" (section 33, 285); and he goes on to say: "In fact, the judgment of taste is always made as a *singular* judgment about the object" (section 33, 285). Strange though it may seem, the singularity of a judgment of taste can, in this case, be seen as reflected in the singularity of "*my* tongue."

The special nature of the singularity and universality of the judgment of taste will play a role again in the **Dialectic**, in connection with "the transcendental concept of reason of the **supersensible**" (section 57, 339). What is the "supersensible"? And how is it connected with the judgment of taste's singularity? We will discuss the supersensible in more detail in a separate section later on, but we can make some preliminary remarks about the connection now.

In a judgment of taste the judging subject and the object being judged are in a certain sense, as we have seen above, both isolated and singular. A judgment of taste demands that everyone should agree, but we do not base this demand on determinate concepts (of, for example, the rose). Is there something else that we can rely on, or at least something toward which this demand for agreement points? It is here that the supersensible comes into play. The supersensible is something that cannot be sensed, that transcends our abilities of sensibility and understanding but nevertheless is not meaningless. The supersensible in question here is the idea of something underlying our relation to outer nature in general, in particular to outer nature's systematicity that the natural sciences try to reveal. Reason demands that there be something that explains why we fit into such an organized nature, a nature that we can understand and contemplate with pleasure. We can distinguish two steps here. In a first step, Kant will establish the a priori "subjective principle of purposiveness" (third moment) as underlying the judgment of taste. This is a principle of our power of judgment. In a second step, he will point out a possible further ground for this principle. This comes down to answering (although in a merely speculative way) the question why we fit into nature.

In the Dialectic, Kant works this out: in the judgment of taste, we relate ourselves, as well as the object, to "a general ground for the subjective purposiveness of nature for the power of judgment" (section 57, 340). This ground might be, Kant suggests, the idea of the "supersensible substratum of humanity" (57, 340). This widens the perspective. A new view beyond cognition and toward a higher and more speculative realm opens up. Maybe it is here that the judgment of taste's demand for universal agreement can find a new explanation and makes sense in another way, namely with connection to morality and our idea of humanity. For Kant, it is through the principle of purposiveness that "the judgment of taste doubtlessly contains an *enlarged* relation of the representation of the object (and at the same time of the subject), on which we base an *extension* of this kind of judgment, as necessary for everyone" (section 57, 339). I and the object, or rather the representation of myself and the object and the relation of this representation (*Beziehung der Vorstellung*), are "enlarged" (*erweitert*); and based on this speculative "enlargement," we can ground the "extension" (*Ausdehnung*) of the validity of the judgment of taste to everyone. This speculation is made possible, not *despite*, but *because* the judgment of taste is "a singular judgment immediately accompanying the intuition" (section 57, 340). First, because the conceptual determination is absent, there is room and freedom for some kind of "enlargement" (of the judging subject and the object) that otherwise would not be possible; and due to the judgment of taste's demand for agreement, this room should be filled. Secondly, this "enlargement" can be seen as a new possible (although speculative) ground for the "extension" (of my judgment of taste from a private to a universal one). We will return to this in a later and separate section on the supersensible.

Further reading

Dörflinger, *Die Realität des Schönen in Kants Theorie rein ästhetischer Urteilskraft*, has a section on the singularity of judgments of taste in connection with their subjective universality (pp. 142–60). He argues that Kant extended (*Erweiterung*) his concept of objectivity from the first *Critique* to include the very individuality of objects (*individuelle Gegenständlichkeit*). This is part of Dörflinger's general claim that Kant did not "subjectivize" (*Subjektivierung*) aesthetic experiences but saw them as "augmented experiences of objects" (*gesteigerte gegenständliche Erfahrung*).

In general, it seems to me that, apart from Dörflinger's book, not much has been made out of the "but" in the "singular but universal," although one can find several variations of it in Kant's aesthetics.

How to Read Section 9

Section 9 of Kant's "Analytic of the Beautiful" is one of the most important in his aesthetics. Kant himself calls the problem he addresses in this section the "key to the critique of taste." The problem he is concerned with is already given in the title of the section: "Investigation of the question: whether in the judgment of taste the feeling of pleasure precedes the judging [*Beurteilung*] of the object or the latter precedes the former." Kant begins this section by saying that "the solution [*Auflösung*] of this problem is the *key* to the critique of taste, and hence worthy of full attention." I suggest that we think of this "problem" as being similar to a geometrical problem – that is, we have to solve it in a *constructive* manner as we solve a geometrical problem constructively with ruler and compass. This implies that the correct "solution" must consist not only in giving the correct answer (to the question whether the feeling precedes the judging or the judging the pleasure), but it must also show us *how* we arrive at this answer. Only this kind of solution can be a useful "key," as Kant says, to his critique of taste: a key that allows us to open the door to an aesthetics that is not an empirical investigation but a transcendental critique. Such a critique has to reveal to us the a priori elements that make the phenomenon of taste possible at all, whereas an empirical investigation would show us, for instance, how to evaluate a theater performance.

Just as a constructive solution to a geometrical problem avails itself of certain accepted methods and gives us a better understanding of the problem itself, so the solution to the question here should be done in a way that sets up new perspectives giving us a better understanding of what the problem actually is, i.e., how exactly we should understand the "judging" involved in a judgment of taste and how this judging is related to pleasure (the satisfaction in the beautiful). The tools we are allowed to use to arrive at the solution are limited. In geometry we may use only compass and ruler. In Kant's aesthetics, we are restricted to the notions of the faculties and their functions as they have been introduced in the first *Critique*.

The answer to the question posed in the title is not fully given until the sixth paragraph of section 9. Although Kant has already told us in the second paragraph that the pleasure cannot come first, he there compares pleasure with communicability and not with the "judging" which is actually at issue in the title. Communicability is closely related to judging, as we shall see, but it is not the same thing. Because the full solution comes so late in section 9, the reader must be patient.

Section 9 is supposed to provide the *"key* to the critique of taste." It establishes the universality of the judgment of taste and thereby opens the door, so to speak, to the possibility and need for a discussion of the third and most important categorical aspect (moment), in which the a priori principle of subjective purposiveness is going to be discovered.

The question posed in the title is a question about a certain priority. It asks whether it is "the feeling of pleasure" or "the judging of the object" that comes first. It is the logical, not the temporal, order that is intended here. After all, we are concerned with justifying a claim to universality, and for such a justification we need to know the logical order, and not the temporal, psychological, or empirical order, which might be merely accidental. If the pleasure that is specific for a judgment of taste implies a certain kind of judging, because such a judging makes that specific kind of pleasure possible at all, then that judging logically "precedes" the pleasure. We will see that this is the case here.

Kant does not address himself directly, and right away, to the question posed in the title. Instead of investigating directly the relationship between pleasure and the "judging of the object" that he thinks takes place in a judgment of taste, he focuses on pleasure in relationship to various kinds of "universal communicability." Here, for the sake of argument, the notion of communicability takes the place, so to speak, of "the judging of the object." (The expression "judging of the object" may sound clumsy to the English reader. It sounds more natural in German: *Beurteilung;* but this also can be deceiving to the German reader, because this expression is used as a technical term here.) The notion of communicability, be it the communicability of a pleasure or of the whole mental state, serves as an intermediate stepping stone and criterion in Kant's argumentation. If pleasure came first, without any further specifications as to its origin – if it were, so to speak, "mere pleasure" – there would be, Kant argues, no hope of ever justifying any claim to universality based on such a pleasure, and, as a consequence, aesthetics would have no place in his transcendental philosophy: "If the pleasure in the given object came first, and only its universal communicability were to be attributed in the judgment of taste to the representation of the object, then such a procedure would be self-contradictory" (section 9, 217).

The pleasure in judgments of taste thus must be a very peculiar one. It must be based on grounds that allow us to communicate our judgment to others. The grounds of this pleasure must make some kind of universal communicability possible and must also account for this pleasure's being a satisfaction in the beautiful. That the pleasure is a satisfaction in the beautiful, and not a satisfaction in the agreeable, must be a logical consequence of the nature of such grounds: "It is the universal capacity for the communication [*allgemeine Mitteilungsfähigkeit*] of the state of mind in the given representation which, as the subjective condition of the judgment of taste, must serve as its ground and have the pleasure [as a satisfaction in the beautiful] in the object as a consequence" (section 9, 217). This sentence is problematic. First, to avoid a possible confusion in the English translation, note that Kant here talks about the "universal capacity for the communication" of a "state of mind," and not about the "universal capacity" for the "communication of a state of mind." (There is a single word for "capacity for communication" in German: *Mitteilungsfähigkeit*.) Second, there is an ambiguity in the German here, and the English translation might give the wrong impression. How should we read the word *"des"* (of) in *"die allgemeine Mitteilungsfähigkeit des Gemütszustandes"* (the universal capacity for the communication *of* the state of mind)? There are two ways of reading this. First, there is a capacity for communication, which is a capacity held by the state of mind, and, second, there is a capacity for communicating a state of mind. (For those who are more familiar with the German: the word *"des"* can function as, respectively, subjective genitive, *genetivus subjectivus*, or as objective genitive, *genetivus objectivus*.) Later we will see – and it might come as a surprise – that there are good reasons for choosing the second option, i.e. for saying that it is the state of mind which is communicated (objective genitive). But in any case, we must note that it is the "universal capacity for the communication of the state of mind" (however we read this), that (logically) makes the pleasure into a satisfaction in the beautiful and saves it from merely being a satisfaction in the agreeable.

The notion of communicability here serves as a *criterion* in Kant's investigation. It allows us to find the right kind of grounds for the pleasure we are interested in (the satisfaction in the beautiful). Whatever underlies judgments of taste and the special kind of pleasure we feel in making such judgments, it must be something that is universally communicable. Kant, at this point, refers to it, still in rather broad and vague terms, as the "mental state, in the given representation." It is the "mental state" (*Gemütszustand*) in the act of reflecting about the representation. (The German word *"Gemüt"* not only means mind, but also feeling.) This rather broad concept of a mental state allows for various kinds of purposiveness to play a role in this state of mind and its communicability, an idea that Kant will develop immediately after section 9.

In order to have a better understanding of the role of universal communicability, we turn for a moment to judgments of cognition. With respect to such judgments, the object that is being judged serves as a common ground and reference point for communicability. A judgment of cognition is true if it corresponds to the facts. And if these facts are accessible to everyone, everyone will have to agree with the judgment. But such a *common reference point* is missing here. In the first *Critique*, with respect to judgments of cognition, Kant wrote: "Truth . . . rests upon *agreement with the object*, with regard to which, consequently, the judgments of every understanding must agree (*consentientia uni tertio, consentiunt inter se*) [agreeing each with a third, they agree with each other]. The *touchstone* of whether taking something to be true is conviction or mere persuasion is therefore, externally, the possibility of *communicating* it and finding it to be valid for the reason of every human being" (*Critique of Pure Reason*, A 820/B 848). Although judgments of taste are not judgments of cognition, Kant makes use of the notion of communicability in the third *Critique* as a certain "touchstone," so that we may find the right kind of grounds for satisfaction in the beautiful.

However, beauty is not an objective property, and a judgment of taste is not a statement about objective facts. Instead, the judgment of taste requires a certain activity on our side, namely the "judging" (*Beurteilung*) of the object, which is mentioned in the title of section 9 (see above). And although the judgment of taste does not have the object (the rose) as an objective reference point that would guarantee that everyone has to agree with us, there is still something that can serve as a universal reference point, namely, "the mental state, in the given representation." This is not just my personal mental state. Rather, there is something universal about it, something that applies to you and me. And is must also involve the "given representation" of the object, though not in a determinate way.

Kant goes on to specify this representation, first still rather vaguely, as being a "representation insofar as it belongs [*gehört*] to cognition." It is through this relation to cognition that the mental state acquires its universality. But what kind of relation is it? We find it in "the state of mind that is encountered in the relation of the powers of representation [imagination and understanding] *to each other* insofar as they relate a given representation to cognition in general [*Erkenntnis überhaupt*]" (section 9, 217). The cognition in question here is not a determinate one. No determinate concept is involved that would determine the object and at the same time "the relation of the powers of representation to each other." Instead, their relation remains indeterminate. Understanding does not, by means of a determinate concept, guide, determine, and fix imagination. Imagination remains free. The "cognition in general," which is cognition as such, cognition universally conceived, does not specify anything about the rose, such as its color or its size.

This relation to "cognition in general" is of a very special form. It is based on what Kant famously calls a "free play" between the powers of representation (imagination and understanding). But what is this "free play"? How should we understand this metaphor? And how should we understand Kant, when he says that the powers of representation are in a free play *"so far as* they agree with each other as is requisite for a cognition in general" (section 9, 218)? Let me try to illustrate this by giving an analogy. Imagine children playing. They do not follow strict rules. They play "freely." Their behavior is creative and not determined by rules. Nevertheless, their behavior is not chaotic, but *makes sense*. It literally *creates* meaning and sense. The children "make up the rules as they go along," we might say with Wittgenstein. The powers of representation – imagination and understanding – are a little like these children engaged in a play. Their relation is free but still makes sense, *"so far as* they agree with each other as is requisite for a cognition in general." It is here that universality comes in: this "free play" between imagination and understanding is not just a personal one, because it engages capacities that we all share (imagination and understanding) and it happens with respect to cognition in general. These are intersubjectively universal elements and not personal ones. We will return to the expression "so far as" later on and say more about it. The expression "for *a* cognition in general" quoted above, *zum Erkenntnisse überhaupt*, should not be understood as referring to this or that "cognition in general", as if there were many "cognitions in general." The German *"zum"* in *"zum Erkenntnisse überhaupt"* can be read *"zu einem"* (for *a* cognition in general) or as *"zu dem"* (for *the* cognition in general). But however we read it, there is only *one* "cognition in general."

This "state of mind," the "kind of representation" (*Vorstellungsart*), the "free play of the imagination and the understanding," and our being "conscious that this subjective relation [the free play of imagination and understanding] suited to cognition in general must be valid for everyone" (section 9, 218): all these elements and features give content to the expression "judging of the object," which Kant mentioned at the beginning, in the title of section 9, and which he claimed must "precede" the pleasure. This becomes apparent in the following sentence, through the word "this," which refers to "the judging of the object" *as well as* to these elements and features: "Now *this* merely subjective (aesthetic) judging [*diese Beurteilung*] of the object, or of the representation through which the object is given, *precedes* the pleasure in it, and is the ground of this pleasure" (section 9, 218). Notice that this "judging of the object" is not to be confused with the judgment of taste itself. Rather, it is its justifying ground.

It is only now, in the sixth paragraph of section 9, that the question posed in the section's title has been answered and that the "solution" of the problem has been given. What has been revealed in the process of solving the problem is a state of mind which is a certain free play of the faculties.

Kant seems to say that this "state of mind in the free play" is "requisite for a cognition in general" (section 9, 218). But it should certainly not be the case that every judgment of cognition presupposes such a free play, because this would turn every judgment of cognition into a judgment of taste. Therefore, we have to realize that although a judgment of cognition presupposes a harmonious relation between the faculties, this is a *determinate* harmonious relation, a relation by which the representation of the object is determined by concepts. Such a determinate harmonious relation is different from the *free* harmonious relation underlying a judgment of taste. It is not a relation where imagination is free from conceptual constraint, and it is not accompanied by pleasure. And indeed, Kant writes more carefully (than I quoted him above), that what matters is the "state of mind in the free play of the imagination and the understanding . . . *so far as they agree* with each other as is requisite for a cognition in general." So it is not the whole state of mind in free play that is requisite for cognition, but merely so far as the *agreement* between the faculties in this state of mind is concerned.

The agreement is not necessarily the agreement in the free play. It must be understood more generally here. That is, we must think of a more general notion of a (harmonious) relation between imagination and understanding, a notion that can be used to describe the grounds of judgments of taste *as well as* the grounds of judgments of cognition. That is, this notion must be indeterminate regarding the two possibilities of the relation between imagination and understanding being a *harmonious free* play (in a judgment of taste) *or* being a *harmonious determinate* relation (in judgments of cognition). It is by means of such a relation of imagination and understanding, a relation *thus generally conceived*, that a judgment of taste makes a claim to universal communicability. Otherwise, the claim to universal validity could not be justified, or a judgment of taste would turn into a judgment of cognition and vice versa.

To make sure that I am not misunderstood, I want to add that it is of course possible that cognition be accompanied by pleasure in various ways. When I see something in front of me and don't quite know what it is, I might try to find out, using my imagination and understanding in various ways to reflect about the object. Finally, I suddenly recognize what it is and feel pleasure. But is this pleasure then satisfaction in the beautiful? Were imagination and understanding engaged in a free play? I would say: no, because there was a purpose involved. I engaged in reflection in order to know what kind of thing the object was, and the pleasure was a pleasure of success. Thus the relation between imagination and understanding was not free. One might go so far as to call their relation "play," but it was certainly not free play. On the other hand, to make things more complicated (and possibly more realistic), I might *at moments* indeed engage in a free play, contemplate the object, and feel pleasure (or displeasure, if I find it ugly), which then would be satisfaction in the beautiful (or the ugly). In such moments I must have forgotten my purpose (the purpose of cognizing the object) and simply enjoyed my contemplation of it. Such moments might come and go, they might come in degrees, they might be mixed with other moments of purposeful reflection, and in reality it might be difficult to draw the line between the two. But that does not prevent us from claiming that there is a clear theoretical difference between the two (ideal) cases.

Further reading

Budd, "The Pure Judgment of Taste as an Aesthetic Reflective Judgment," explains the power of judgment when exercised reflectively, in free play, schematizing without concept. Introductory, not technical.

Guyer, in *Kant and the Claims of Taste*, chapter 3 (2nd edition), and in particular "Pleasure and Society in Kant's Theory of Taste," offers a two-step account of the judgment of taste, which he argues Kant had held earlier and later got confused about. According to this account, there must be a two-step process of reflection: the first leading to pleasure, and the second, reflecting about the first, leading to intersubjective validity.

For a detailed criticisms of Guyer's account and interpretation of section 9, see Baum, "Subjektivität, Allgemeingültigkeit und Apriorität," pp. 277–82; Wenzel, *Das Problem der Subjektiven Allgemeingültigkeit*, pp. 33–46 and 169–78; and Allison, "Pleasure and Harmony in Kant's Theory of Taste: A Critique of the Causal Reading," and his *Kant's Theory of Taste*, p. 112.

Opposed to Guyer's interpretation there is also Ginsborg, *The Role of Taste in Kant's Theory of Cognition*, and in particular "On the Key to Kant's Critique of Taste." The latter focuses on section 9. She sees the judgment of taste not as a two-step process but as a single judgment that is essentially self-referential, claiming its own universal validity. More fundamentally, she argues that universal communicability is the basis of objectivity (and not the other way around), and that the third *Critique* should therefore be seen as filling a gap that exists in the first.

For a criticism of Ginsborg's highly suggestive views, see Wenzel, *Das Problem*, pp. 57–70; Allison, *Kant's Theory*, pp. 113–18; and Kulenkampff, *Kants Logik*, pp. 178–82 (only in the 2nd edition).

Savile, *Aesthetic Reconstructions*, pp. 99–129, discusses Kant's arguments about the relation between taste and cognition. Reconstructive, analytic in style and relatively independent of Kantian terminology.

Falk, "The Communicability of feeling," compares aesthetic feelings with feeling such as pain, gives a sketch of Kant's theory in section 9, and then applies Kant's "strategy," his theory of "examplariness" and the self, to argue for the communicability of a common feeling like pity.

The power of imagination is central in section 9 and thus the reader might want to learn more about this power and its mediating functions from Mörchen, *Die Einbildungskraft bei Kant*, Gibbons, *Kant's Theory of Imagination*, and Makkreel, *Imagination and Interpretation in Kant*; the last two lead from the first to the third *Critique*, the latter beginning even with the precritical Kant and pointing, in a somewhat hermeneutical way, toward a "reflective interpretation" of the world; Mörchen offers separate treatments of imagination from the first and third *Critiques*, pp. 42–129 and 130–78 respectively.

Kulenkampff, *Kants Logik des Ästhetischen Urteils*, pp. 87–106 (1st edition: 77–97), is devoted to section 9. He critically points out the problems and discusses them very well in a reconstructive way. He brings in also the transcendental dimensions, especially of imagination from the first *Critique*. Detailed, clear and subtle.

Dörflinger, *Die Realität des Schönen in Kants Theorie rein ästhetischer Urteilskraft*, pp. 178–200, focuses on the conditions of possibility of cognition in general that we become aware of through the free play of our faculties. He sees this as an "aesthetic understanding" of ourselves.

Fricke, *Kants Theorie*, has a chapter (pp. 38–71) on section 9 and the difference between judgment and judging (*Beurteilung*).

Heidemann, *Der Begriff des Spiels*, offers a general ontology and epistemology of the concept of play. Part of this is a chapter on Kant: *Der Spielbegriff bei Kant*, pp. 125–216, in which she does not focus on Kant's theory of free play from section 9 but draws on other sources from Kant to discuss the general relevance of play for science, experience, happening, spontaneity, favor, concept, and thought. There is also a long chapter on the concept of play in Heidegger (pp. 278–372). All this puts Kant's concept of free play from section 9 in a much wider and more general philosophical context.

3

Purposiveness: Third Moment

Purpose without Will, Purposiveness without Purpose

Among the four **moments** of the judgment of taste, Kant's discussion of the third moment is the longest. This should not come as a surprise for at least two reasons. First, the discussion of the third moment is supposed to reveal the **a priori principle** underlying judgments of taste. Second, already in the first *Critique*, the group of categories under the third title, "relation," is the most fundamental of the four groups of **categories**.

The title of the discussion of the third moment is: "Third Moment of judgments of taste, concerning the *relation of the ends* that are taken into consideration in them." The relation in question here must, as the title asserts, be a relation of ends, or **purposes**. There has to be a relation of some kind that we take into consideration when making a judgment of taste, because of what Kant has already promised at the very beginning of his aesthetics in the footnote to the title of the first section, where he said that he would discover certain "moments" that a judgment of taste "attends" to: "In seeking the moments to which this power of judgment *attends* in its reflection, I have been guided by the logical functions for judging." Now, according to the first *Critique*, the third group of logical functions is that of relation. Thus, there must be a logical function of *relation*, or several such functions, that a judgment of taste "attends to," and we must be able to see that this function somehow leads us to the "relations of ends." To realize this transition from relations in *general* (among the logical functions and categories underlying any cognitive judgment, from the first *Critique*) to relations of *ends* (underlying judgment of taste in particular, in the third *Critique*), it is helpful to be aware of the following two facts. First, the most important category of relation from the first *Critique* is the category of causality, and, second, there are traditionally two kinds of causality, namely ***causa efficiens*** and ***causa*** *finalis*: the *causa efficiens* is a moving cause, for instance the builder of a house; and the *causa finalis* is a purpose or end, for instance the shelter the house provides. It will be the latter one, the *causa finalis*, i.e. the causality of ends, which Kant sees as being essential for the judgment of taste.

Kant starts out, in section 10, with a general discussion of the causality of ends, the results of which he then applies to the judgment of taste. He first gives a rather abstract definition of what an end, or purpose (*Zweck*) is: "An end is the object of a **concept** insofar as the latter is regarded as the cause of the former (the real ground of its possibility)" (section 10, 220). This is not only rather abstract, but it also sounds strange: a concept is the cause of its object. But how can a concept be a cause of anything? Is it not something abstract rather than physical? How can the concept of a house, say, be the cause of a house?

Usually, we think that an end, or purpose, presupposes an intention or a will. The purpose of a roof, for instance, is to provide shelter against rain. The roof was intended for this purpose and designed and built accordingly. Hence someone's intention and plan preceded the construction of such a roof. We wanted shelter and then we built such a roof. Applying Kant's definition, we should say that the concept of the roof, as an end, "caused" the roof to come into existence. At least we "regard" (see quote above) the concept of a roof as a cause. But this is not so strange as it might at first appear. If the object in question is an object of nature, like the wings of a fly, we often imagine that God has created those wings with a certain purpose in mind, for instance that they enable the insect to fly. Even when we explain the existence of the wings (and the fly) not by referring to God's or someone else's will but by referring to natural selection, it is often still useful to think in terms of purposes and ends in order to explain what a wing is (something that enables the insect to fly) and to guide our further investigation. (In any case, we think about the object in terms of *functionality* and **purposiveness**, and it seems to me to be a non-trivial question whether the concept of functionality can be explained by, or even reduced to, that of natural selection. Is it not the other way around? After all, what survives in certain circumstances is what functions better in those circumstances, so that evolution seems to presuppose functionality.)

When thinking of a purpose (shelter) we usually think of a thing (a roof) or an act (opening your umbrella) that can serve this purpose, and of someone who has such a purpose in mind when producing the thing (the architect of the house) or who acts in a certain way (your friend who opens the umbrella for you). We think of someone having an intention and a will that cause the thing and the act to come into existence or to be carried out. But Kant's abstract definition of a purpose does not require us to do so. According to his definition, the concept of an object is regarded as the cause of that object, and this does not say what exactly the causal relation between the concept and its object is, nor how this relation is brought about. It does not require the existence of a *will* that grounds this rela-tion between concept and object: my having the concept in mind (my thinking of shelter and the roof) *and* my willpower to realize it (to make the roof). Instead, Kant here merely alludes to the representation of the object: "The representa-tion of the effect [*Vorstellung der Wirkung*] is here the determining ground of its cause, and precedes the latter" (section 10, 220). I imagine a house and then build it accordingly. Imagining the effect is the ground for its realization. Again, this is rather abstract. But in order to establish an a priori principle, we do not need an empirical, but rather a **transcendental** understanding of ends, and we should not be surprised that such an understanding turns out to be rather general and abstract.

Now what does all this have to do with taste? This will come in several steps. First, according to Kant, it is through one's consciousness of a feeling of pleas-ure (or displeasure) that such a relation between a **representation** and its effect becomes concrete and causally effective: "The consciousness of the causality of a representation with respect to the state of the subject, for maintaining it in that state, can here designate in general what is called pleasure" (section 10, 220). The representation seems to cause our pleasure, and our becoming aware of this seems to be the cause for our wanting to remain in this state. But this would all look more like *causa efficiens* than *causa finalis*. We will have to take a step back, and we will do so in the following paragraphs and in the next section. The causal-ity involved here is that of an "animation of . . . cognitive powers." Imagination and understanding are activated and become alive. They are "animated" in the process of my representing and contemplating the object. (Here one begins to see connections with the second part of the third *Critique*, Kant's teleology, which is concerned with living organisms and "animated" nature.) Kant calls this ani-mation of our cognitive powers an "inner causality" (section 12, 222) – "inner," because it takes place in our mind and because we are conscious of it through our feeling of pleasure.

This is a very special kind of pleasure, a self-producing and self-perpetuating pleasure in the mind that is, as we shall see, related to cognition or, rather, to what Kant calls "cognition in general." (*Erkenntnis überhaupt* may be better trans-lated as "cognition as such," or "cognition universally conceived," not a general-ization of instances of cognition, but cognition transcendentally conceived.) Although this pleasure is felt and is therefore something empirical, there is also an a priori basis for it, namely the principle of purposiveness, as we shall see, and that of course makes this kind of pleasure even more special.

This pleasurable self-animating state of mind cannot be intended and willfully forced. If we want to call it a purpose at all, we should think of it as a purpose in itself. Cause and effect are the same: free play. We want the play to last, whenever it occurs. It is a *present*, a *gift*, something given to us. Of course we can prepare ourselves for it. We can go to a concert or to a museum with the intention of feeling aesthetic pleasure. But what then actually happens when I hear the music or see the painting cannot be planned and willfully forced. Once I am really in such a state of mind, when it is an ideal situation, when my enjoyment of the music is at its best, I have forgotten all about my intentions and deliberations.

Now we will step back a little and move to the notion of purposiveness. Imagine someone a thousand years ago finding a watch lying on the ground. He or she picks it up, opens it, studies it, and admires it. He sees how its parts fit nicely together and interact in various ways, but the general idea of what the thing and its purpose might be escapes him. Now this would be a case of purposiveness (of the parts to each other). But at some point he might discover, or just be told, what the purpose is. So this would then not be a case of "purposiveness without purpose." For Kant, there is no *objective* purposiveness without a purpose. But if the subject and its feelings are involved, as is the case in judgments of taste, we will see that Kant believes and argues that there is some kind of purposiveness *without* purpose, which is then a *"subjective* purposivenes without purpose."* Briefly put: our feelings and our faculties cannot be studied the way outer nature can (through concepts of the understanding), and therefore a purpose, which always involves a concept, cannot be found.

The various ingredients underlying a judgment of taste – for instance the relation between the object and my representation of it, and the relation between the mental powers of imagination and understanding when representing it – are all purposive (*zweckmässig*) in various respects, which we become aware of through our feelings of pleasure and displeasure. The purposiveness underlying these phenomena felt within ourselves is therefore a subjective one, a purposiveness in our minds, or in relation to our minds, which we simply feel and encounter. We need not, and cannot, derive this purposiveness from anything else. There is no reductive explanation for it. For Kant, it is (an instance of) a primitive and fundamental element: the principle of subjective purposiveness, which is an a priori principle of our power of judgment. In particular, it is not necessary that we presuppose a will and the existence of a higher being that had a purpose in mind and created things according to that purpose so that we have the feelings we have. Rather, it suffices that we realize the possibility of what Kant calls a "purposiveness without a purpose," or a "purposiveness without an end" (*Zweckmässigkeit ohne Zweck*).

One may ask why the notion of causality (*causa efficiens*), which is essential in the first *Critique*, is dropped here, and why the notion of purposiveness (finality, *causa finalis*) takes its place. Why should we not try to find causal connections between the object and our liking of it? We have to see that this would run counter to a fundamental assumption that Kant makes, or takes as a given fact, namely that there are no **rules** governing our judgments in matters of taste. Instead, we are *autonomous* in *making* judgments of taste, that is, in each instance of making one it is as if we set the rules (for others and ourselves to follow).

We also find autonomy in morality, and there Kant did indeed allow causality to play a role, namely as a "causality of freedom": Through my free will I can start a causal chain in the outer physical world. But this kind of causality involves free will and reflection about *a priori* rules (reflecting about moral rules in order to decide what I should do). In matters of taste, on the other hand, although there is an *a priori* basis as well, we merely feel and experience purposiveness without a purpose and do not rationally reflect about this as a principle. This purposiveness cannot serve as a rule, and that is the point here. When making a judgment of taste, we do not rationally reflect as we do when making a moral judgment. Morality is accessible to rationality. Beauty is not. Kant stresses a difference between beauty and morality in section 12, saying that in morality "we could also step beyond the bounds of experience and appeal to a causality that rests on a supersensible property of the subject, namely that of freedom" (section 12, 222; see the section "The Analytic, the Dialectic, and the Supersensible" in chapter 6). But beauty is more down to earth, so to speak. Although the supersensible, as we learn in the "**Dialectic** of Aesthetic **Power of Judgment**," also plays a role in relation to judgments of taste, it does so only by solving an **antinomy** of **reason** and not by justifying the judgment of taste itself. The supersensible there is more metaphysical: it operates more on a meta-level than on the level of the powers of cognition themselves, as we shall see later in the section dealing explicitly with the analytic, the Dialectic, and the supersensible in chapter 6.

The notion of purposiveness without a purpose does not presuppose the supersensible, and in this point taste is different from morality. There is no causality of freedom underlying judgments of taste. And the notion of an outer causality would make the matter an empirical one, a case of "causal relation[s], which (among objects of experience) can only ever be cognized a posteriori" (section 12, 221–2). But this of course leaves us with the question of how to interpret the "inner causality" and the "animation" of our cognitive powers of which Kant speaks (222). Are there deeper connections with his philosophy of biology from the second part of the third *Critique*? Would Kant allow for causal or **teleological** accounts of our faculties? This would lead us into deep waters: questions about the relations between transcendental philosophy, psychology, and biology.

Positively speaking, the notion of purposiveness without a purpose and that of the free play of the faculties both leave, or even create, *room* for the (phenomenon of the) *je ne sais quoi*. If there were a determinate purpose in an aesthetic experience, we would ask who it is that had this purpose in mind, and how and why this higher being arranged things the way they are. Instead, all we have to do is to be content to notice that there are such things as taste – how lucky we are, *felix aestheticus*! – and that they simply happen to be purposive in certain respects. It may seem to us as if there must be a purpose behind our ability to experience beauty, or a thing appearing beautiful to us, but we need not suppose so. When we make a judgment of taste, we often have the feeling that we belong and fit into nature, but at the same time this feeling comes with a feeling of surprise, as if it were all an unexpected present from nature. There are good reasons for such feelings. There is the principle of purposiveness at the level of the understanding and there is the idea of the supersensible at the level of reason (as we shall see in the Dialectic). Each of them explains the judgment of taste in some respects and leaves it indeterminate in other respects. This combination of explanation and indeterminacy in turn explains both our feeling of belonging and fitting into nature and our feeling of surprise.

More on the nature of purposiveness and its various specific appearances in the free play of the faculties can be found in the next section.

Further reading

Allison, *Kant's Theory of Taste*, pp. 120–5, gives section 10 a sympathetic reading, trying to make it fit into the wider context of Kant's goals, "a daunting, if not hopeless, task."

Guyer, *Kant and the Claims of Taste*, from p. 188 onwards (2nd edition) argues, less sympathetically, that Kant's definition of "end" in section 10 is misleading. There is a whole chapter on finality.

Dickie, *The Century of Taste: The Philosophical Odyssey of Taste in the Eighteenth Century*, puts Kant's aesthetics in the historical context of Hutcheson, Gerard, Alison, and Hume (the hero in the end), and does not see much good in Kant. He offers severe criticisms in a separate chapter on Kant, "Taste and Purpose," pp. 85–122, arguing that Kant should have placed his teleology first and his aesthetics second, that many things would otherwise be "impossible to understand," that some conclusions are "baffling" and reasons "obscure," and that there is much "redundancy" and a continuously "repeated starting over." This brings at least some fresh wind into the discussion.

Marc-Wogau, *Vier Studien*, has a very long chapter (the second *Studie*) on purposiveness (pp. 44–213), with a section on "inner purposiveness" (pp. 44–69) discussing aspects such as the general and the particular, the inner and the outer, aspects of system, harmony, perfection, and organization (see especially pp. 57 and 64). Creative, detailed, and clear; old (1938), but still good and inspiring.

——'s account is criticized by Tonelli ("Von den verschiedenen Bedeutungen des Wortes 'Zweckmässigkeit' in der Kritik der Urteilskraft") for its "artificial generalization." Tonelli prefers to track the development of the various concepts of purposiveness according to the temporal sequence and contexts in which they were produced (the temporal order of writing is not always what the book suggests, sometimes earlier chapters were written later). Has useful tables indicating many different distinctions of purposiveness (useful also if one does not read German). Written with great historical insight.

Fricke, *Kants Theorie des reinen Geschmacksurteils*, offers three chapters on the power of reflective judgment, one of which (chapter 4) focuses on purposiveness (from section 10). She puts forward a theory of "hypothetical purposiveness," placing the judgment of taste in a wider context. In "Explaining the Inexplicable," she offers a similar discussion in English, discussing section 10 in the first part of the paper.

Wohlfart, *Metakritik der Ästhetischen Urteilskraft*, is a study of Kant's theory of the power of judgment, starting "from above," from transcendental purposiveness and ideas, and going down to aesthetic purposiveness and reflective judgment, and to imagination and free play.

Jeng, *Natur und Freiheit*, is a study of Kant's third *Critique* as a whole and draws also from the first and the second *Critiques*. The last chapter, "Aesthetic Representation of Natural Purposiveness" (pp. 225–304), gives a thorough exposition of the notions of free play, purpose, and purposiveness.

Prauss, "Kant's Theorie der ästhetischen Einstellung," argues, somewhat unconventionally, that aesthetic attitudes require purposeful intentionality as we find it in theoretical attitudes to be "overcome" (*überwinden*). He sees this as a moment of spontaneity and freedom (*potenzierte Freiheit*) based on love, favor, and admiration.

For more on Kant's "purposiveness," see the list of further reading that accompanies the next section.

Purposiveness and Form: Charm versus Euler

After having introduced the general notion of "purposiveness without purpose," Kant makes ample use of it in his subsequent discussion of the third moment of a judgment of taste. What underlies a judgment of taste is not charm (*Reiz*) or emotion (*Rührung*), nor perfection, but purposiveness without purpose. But what exactly are "charm" and "emotion"? Kant spends little time explaining what he means by "emotion": it is "a **sensation** in which agreeableness is produced only by means of a momentary inhibition followed by a stronger outpouring of the vital force" (section 14, 226). We have this kind of sensation when we feel touched by something. It often has moral elements and is similar to the feeling of the sublime. Kant quickly dismisses it here, probably because he thinks he will be dealing with the sublime in detail later. Charm, on the other hand, is a sensation Kant spends much time discussing in sections 13 and 14. He gives two examples: color and tone – which, however, later turn out to be very problematic – "a mere color, e.g., the green of a lawn, a mere tone (as distinct from sound and noise), say that of a violin" (section 14, 224). Kant first says that they are "mere sensations" and "only agreeable" and thus should not be called beautiful. What they lack is *structure* and *composition*. They can be added, but they should not distract from what is essential: "The charm of colors [in paintings] or of the agreeable tones of instruments can be added, but drawing in the former and composition in the latter constitute the proper object of the pure judgment of taste" (section 14, 225). Also ornaments or a gilt frame of a painting can add to beauty, but they should not distract. To make the distinction between charm and beauty more prominent, theoretically and not just by giving some examples, Kant uses the classical distinction between matter and form. He associates beauty with various aspects of form (drawing, shape, composition) and charm with matter. This will turn out to be highly problematic. For instance, what exactly can "matter" be when we consider a color or a tone? And how can we be sure that they do not have formal structures of some kind? Kant is well aware of these problems and discusses them in section 14, drawing on theories by the Swiss mathematician Leonard Euler (1707–83), as we shall see.

As it is the **formal** and not the material aspects of states of mind that are traditionally associated with what is communicable, the justifying **grounds** of a judgment of taste must somehow be formal and not material. Charm on the other hand should be seen as material. Charm is more of a direct result of our being affected by the object and involves to a lesser degree, if at all, any acts of reflection on our side. It belongs to the sphere of mere sensation and is less communicable than our feeling for the beautiful, because the latter involves **reflection** in connection with cognition, and cognition is communicable. As is the case with emotion, charm in the end hinders the impartiality that is required for a judgment of taste. "Taste is always still barbaric when it needs the addition of charms and emotions for **satisfaction**, let alone if it makes these into the standard for its approval" (section 13, 223). Charm and emotion thus do not qualify as grounds of a judgment of taste. They would only make it impure. If we want to find the true grounds of judgments of taste, we have to abstract all charm and emotion from our act of contemplating an aesthetic object.

Since the judgment of taste claims universal communicability, and since it is formal aspects that are thought to be communicable, Kant addresses himself to various kinds of **form** that are relevant to a judgment of taste. He focuses on "form of purposiveness," "formal purposiveness," and "purposiveness of form." In section 14 alone, the word "form" appears as many as eleven times. Purposiveness without a purpose, subjective purposiveness, formal purposiveness, and form of purposiveness in the end all mean the same thing – at least roughly, and taking into account specific differences in specific contexts (which we will point out in what follows). But purposiveness of form, which is not in the above list, is something different. Here, the form is not a form of some kind of purposiveness but the form of the object itself, such as its spatial and temporal shape and structure. Nevertheless, Kant tries, and this is the main point here, to establish a connection between these two very different kinds of form, between forms of purposiveness (underlying the judgment of taste) and forms of objects. He argues that it is only the form of an object, its spatial and temporal structures, that can possibly play a role in a judgment of taste.

I suggest that at this point we distinguish between three different kinds of relation involved in a judgment of taste, and that we see each of them as having a particular kind of purposiveness, so that we obtain a threefold structure of purposive relations, or three stages of purposiveness – let us call them P1, P2, and P3 – that underlie a judgment of taste.

An object of a judgment of taste must be suitable, or purposive (P1), for the free play of our **faculties** of **cognition**: **imagination** and **understanding**. Furthermore, in this free play of the faculties, imagination and understanding complement and strengthen each other. As such, they are purposive (P2) for each other regarding their respective functions of "apprehension" and "comprehension," i.e. regarding the function of the imagination to apprehend (take up) what is perceptually given, and regarding the function of the understanding to subsume under concepts that which has been apprehended. Finally, all of this is purposive (P3) for "cognition in general" (*Erkenntnis überhaupt*; cognition as such). Although cognition is not intended in such free play, our capacity for cognition is strengthened by it. This threefold structure is shown in the following diagram:

$$
\begin{array}{ccccc}
 & & \text{understanding} & & \\
 & P_1 & & P_3 & \\
\text{object} & \longrightarrow & \updownarrow \quad P_2 & \longrightarrow & \text{cognition in general} \\
 & & \text{imagination} & &
\end{array}
$$

In the light of this analysis we arrive at a better understanding of what Kant refers to as purposiveness without a purpose, formal purposiveness, or form of purposiveness. The relations are described in terms of (general) functions and independently of the particular object and content of representation. But all this still seems to have nothing to do with the form of the object, its temporal and spatial aspects, its design and composition. It all seems to be on the side of the judging subject. Thus, how can we make a connection between the subject and the object with its spatio-temporal properties, such as "design" and "composition" as we find them in "shape" or "play," "mimetic art," or "dance" (section 14, 225)? And why should we have to make such a connection at all?

Kant argues for purposiveness without purpose as an a priori principle of judgments of taste. This principle has to be such that the claim for the universality of a judgment of taste can be based on it. Whatever it might be about the object that we find beautiful, it cannot be brought under any objective rules. Nevertheless, the reason we find an object beautiful should not be merely subjective, as charm and emotion are. Locke's distinction between primary and secondary qualities may be helpful at this point with regard to understanding the notion of purposiveness without a purpose. Secondary qualities include colors, flavors, smells, sounds, and sensations such as warmth or cold. Primary qualities are physical properties, which are essentially structures in time and space. Since the secondary qualities are less formal and less communicable, it is the primary ones that seem to be more relevant for judgments of taste than the secondary ones. We might think that it is these primary qualities that we reflect about when making judgments of taste; however, to say this would be too simplistic.

The now much-debated problems of qualia (what it is like to have certain sensations and perceptions, how coffee smells, the way turquoise looks) are related to these issues, and we should not expect an easy solution. Are we sure that colors, tastes, smells, sounds, warmth, and cold cannot somehow be reduced to spatio-temporal structures? Furthermore, it is not clear that these secondary qualities are coextensive with charm and emotion; therefore, it is not clear that abstracting the latter from the judgment of taste will have the result of abstracting all of the secondary qualities from it. Thus, we cannot be sure that abstracting from charm and emotion leaves us with only the primary qualities, the ones Kant would seem to care about under this interpretation. Certainly, the form of the object, i.e. its spatio-temporal structures, appears, in the light of the a priori nature of time and space, to be a most suitable anchorage for an a priori principle underlying the judgment of taste. But unfortunately this suggested connection is not at all clear-cut.

Kant is aware of the fact that there are qualities that seem to be secondary and that are often asserted to be objects of judgments of taste: "A mere color, e.g., the green of a lawn, a mere tone (in distinction from sound and noise), say that of a violin, is declared by most people to be beautiful in itself, although both seem to have as their ground merely the matter of the representations, namely mere sensation" (section 14, 224). To accommodate such cases in his theory, in which objects qualify as objects of judgments of taste only due to their primary qualities, Kant has to give some additional explanations. It suffices here, and Kant is aware of this, to point out that there may be ways of showing that what seem to be secondary qualities are sometimes in the end found to be primary ones. At this point he refers to Euler, who suggested the possibility that "colors are vibrations (*pulsus*) of the aether [*Äther*: the English translation here says "air" instead of "aether"; the latter seems to me a better translation] immediately following one another, just as tones are vibrations of the air" (section 14, 224). Such vibrations are formal, mathematical, and spatio-temporal in nature. Viewed in the light of this explanation, colors and tones are not secondary but primary qualities, which would explain how even colors and tones can be regarded as objects of judgments of taste. Euler might be wrong about the physical basis for secondary qualities, but Kant can still make his point as long as there is the possibility of another model that reduces colors and tones to primary qualities. After all, even today we do not have a clear picture of what light really is.

The spatio-temporal structure of an object, its "form" in a wider sense of the word, is a structure that is rich and suitable for reflection. Both imagination and understanding find many ways of apprehending and combining the spatio-temporal manifold of objective data that is associated with a certain object. This manifold provides a material that is suitable for the free play of the faculties to exhibit purposiveness without purpose at the three different levels (P1, P2, and P3) described above. As we all have the same faculties of imagination and understanding, we are all a priori capable of such a free play. If you like a "mere tone" based solely on its spatio-temporal structures, and if your pleasure is based on your reflecting on this structure such that you are justified in your demand that everyone else should be able to do what you are doing, then the pleasure you feel is not one of mere sensation but a pleasure (satisfaction) in the beautiful. Thus we have found an appropriate basis for judgments of taste. The demand for universality cannot be based on sensations, because "we cannot assume that in all subjects the sensations themselves agree in quality" (section 14, 224).

We have seen how Kant makes use of the classical distinctions between matter and form and between primary and secondary qualities. It is useful to keep these distinctions in mind. The following diagram, rough and schematic as it is, should be helpful in this regard.

	Sensation	Object perceived
Form	Satisfaction in the beautiful	Primary qualities, design and composition
Matter	qualia (?)	Secondary qualities

Further reading

See my comments on Marc-Wogau, Fricke, and Dickie in the further reading that accompanies the previous section.

Gregor, "Aesthetic Form and Sensory Content," compares Kant's aesthetic formalism with modern formalisms put forward by art critics Eduard Hanslick and Clive Bell. She discusses sensations, intensive and extensive magnitudes, and the significance of spatio-temporal and mathematical aspects.

Ginsborg, "Reflective Judgment and Taste," is not on subjective purposiveness proper, but on the power of reflective judgment in general and its connections with taste and purposiveness, subjective and objective. This gives a wider perspective. She stresses perception and nature's systematicity, and their relations to intersubjectivity within reflective judgments broadly conceived, and thus including judgments of taste.

Tonelli, "Von den verschiedenen Bedeutungen," offers nine tables that sketch different distinctions of purposiveness. Tonelli follows the different contexts and temporal sequences of Kant's actual writing (Kant, for instance, wrote the First Introduction after the Dialectic and the Second Introduction, which then became the one that was actually printed, after he had written everything else). These tables give a good overview and can serve as a guide for further investigation. Also useful because they pay attention to the Introductions, which I did not discuss here. Tonelli argues that it would be wrong to try to create a single synthesis of all the different conceptions of purposiveness that Kant developed at different times and in different contexts. Such a synthesis would be artificial and not do justice to Kant. Tonelli already explained the historical development of the third *Critique* in his earlier paper, "La formazione del testo." Both papers show great historical competence and knowledge.

Of "Greatest Importance": Beauty and Perfection

When we find something beautiful, we often think of it as being "perfect" in some way or another. Even though it may sound a little odd to say that a sunset is perfect, or that a red rose is perfect, we often say such things with regard to artifacts or works of art without this sounding odd at all. A painter sometimes calls a painting he just finished a "perfect" painting, and so do those who see the painting displayed in an exhibition. We talk of a "perfect symphony" and even of "perfect beauty." We often think of such objects as being "ideal" and the "utmost" or "best possible." But Kant sees a problem with the role of perfection here. He writes that "it is of the greatest importance in a critique of taste to decide whether beauty is really reducible to the concept of perfection" (section 15, 227). His main idea here is that various concepts of perfection may very well accompany a judgment of taste, but that they should never be its justifying grounds.

According to Kant, beauty can never be reduced to the concept of perfection. This should not come as a surprise, because perfection tends to be an objective criterion based on (objective) knowledge. If such a reduction were possible, beauty would belong to the realm of cognition, and Kant then could not have

written his third *Critique* at all, at least not the first part of it, the "Critique of the
Aesthetic Power of Judgment." Kant therefore takes great pains to show that
there must be a *"specific* difference" (section 15, 228, Kant's emphasis) between
beauty and the good (the morally good or the useful). For him, "an aesthetic
judgment is of a unique kind" (ibid.) that is specifically different from judgments
of cognition. He wants to make sure that he gets this point across to the reader
and therefore calls the question of the reducibility of beauty one of "greatest
importance," devoting an entire section to it: section 15. If we do not properly
decide the issue of whether or not "beauty is really reducible to the concept of
perfection," i.e. if we cannot show that beauty is indeed irreducible to perfection, then there might not be any aesthetics in its own right. Aesthetics then
might be merely a part of epistemology. It is for this reason that the issue is of
"greatest importance."

Kant addresses himself to Baumgarten and those who belong to the rationalist tradition of Leibniz and Wolff, or those who are at least familiar with that
tradition, when he writes that perfection has been "held to be identical with
beauty even by philosophers of repute" (section 15, 227). That these "philosophers of repute" softened the identification they made between beauty and perfection by adding the proviso that beauty is perfection "thought confusedly"
(*verworren gedacht*, ibid) does not really help the matter in Kant's eyes. If there
are hidden criteria of perfection deciding about beauty that we are aware of only
in a confused and not in a clear and distinct way, then maybe one day we could
bring these criteria to the surface and make them clear and distinct to ourselves.
Then beauty would become something objective. That is, if the "confusion"
could be cleared, aesthetics would in the end be part of epistemology, or even
disappear altogether. Kant wants to avoid this from the very start and therefore
argues against any attempt to see beauty as perfection "thought confusedly."

With respect to the question of the reducibility of beauty to perfection, Kant's
distinction between subjective and objective **purposiveness** becomes crucial. In
response to the rationalists, who argue for perfection as a possible ground for
beauty, Kant points to his own distinction between subjective and objective purposiveness: beauty is a matter of subjective but not objective purposiveness, and
because perfection belongs to the latter, where there are rules and objective criteria of functionality that undermine the freedom necessary for aesthetic contemplation, these philosophers tend to eliminate the phenomenon of beauty as
a basic experiential reality.

The perfection and the objective purposiveness of an object presuppose
"the concept of what sort of thing it is supposed to be," whereas in matters of
taste one does not need to know what the object is meant to be, Kant argues.
(See the section above in chapter 2, "Singular 'but' Universal.") If we were to
allow the concept of perfection to play a role in deciding what is beautiful and

what is not, we would run into the danger of deriving explicit and objective rules
that allow us to decide what should and what should not count as beautiful. But
the existence of such rules would contradict Kant's basic assumption that there
are no rules of taste. Baumgarten tried to point out such rules, but Kant
dismisses them.

Kant distinguishes between two kinds of perfection: qualitative and quantita-
tive. Given the concept of an object, the former lies in the "agreement of the
manifold in the thing with this concept," the latter in the "completeness" of
the "thing in its own kind" (section 15, 227). Thus knowledge of the concept of
the object and even a way of measuring completeness are required. But if we
drop this requirement, we are free to find another basis for beauty, a basis that
does not depend on the object's perfection. Instead of perfection, Kant suggests
the following:

> What is formal in the representation of a thing, i.e., the agreement of the mani-
> fold with a unity (leaving undetermined what it is supposed to be), does not by
> itself allow any cognition of objective purposiveness at all, because since abstrac-
> tion is made from this unity, as an end (what the thing is supposed to be), nothing
> remains but the subjective purposiveness of representations in the mind [*im
> Gemüte*] of the beholder, which indicates a certain purposiveness of the represen-
> tational state of the subject [*des Vorstellungszustandes im Subjekt*], and in this an ease
> in apprehending a given form in the imagination, but not the perfection of any
> object, which is here not conceived through any concept of an end. (Section 15,
> 227)

Instead of the object having to live up, so to speak, to some specific and conceptually determined unity (for example, the unity of a rose, a unity that is determined by the concept of a rose), Kant merely asks for an undetermined formal
unity and "subjective purposiveness."

Regarding his idea of formal unity, Kant probably draws on the first *Critique*
and the fundamental and general a priori roles and functions of imagination and
understanding described there (the categories and schematism). These underlie
the formation and application of all empirical concepts but are not specific
enough to determine any particular empirical concept (like that of a rose) or to
determine any perceptually given manifold (my sense impressions of a rose) in
accordance with such a concept (by applying the concept of a rose to that manifold of impressions, that is, by guiding our imagination and understanding in
apprehending, reproducing, and recognizing it).

What matters instead of any such specific concepts is "the subjective purposiveness of representations in the mind of the beholder." This purposiveness is
subjective, because it is a purposiveness *in* the free play of the faculties and a
"purposiveness of the representational state of the subject". The purposiveness

lies not in the object but both in its relation to us and in our free play with the representation of the object. We feel this purposiveness as an "ease in apprehending" the object. Here it is useful to look again at the diagram we introduced in the previous section (reproduced below):

$$\begin{array}{ccccc} & & \text{understanding} & & \\ & P_1 & & P_3 & \\ \text{object} & \longrightarrow & \updownarrow \quad P_2 & \longrightarrow & \text{cognition in general} \\ & & \text{imagination} & & \end{array}$$

No concept of the object is supposed to play a **determining** role here. Regarding the justifying grounds for subjective purposiveness, the role a concept of the object is allowed to play is very limited. The closest Kant comes to assigning such a role to the concept of the object is in giving it the role of specifying "what is formal in the representation of a thing, i.e., the agreement of the manifold with a unity (leaving undetermined what it is supposed to be)" (see quote above). But such a role, or aspect, of the concept of the object should be a very general one. I suggest it is essentially the categories, a priori concepts of the understanding, that Kant is thinking of here. They underlie all empirical concepts and make their application possible. They are therefore necessary and can be thought of as aspects of such concepts as their application.

Kant gives the following example: "If I encounter in the forest a plot of grass around which the trees stand in a circle, and I do not represent a purpose for it, say that it is to serve for country dancing, then not the slightest concept of perfection is given through the mere form" (section 15, 227–8). If we were to say that it is the circular form that matters here and that the perfection of this form is what makes the plot beautiful, Kant would probably say that this leans too far toward the objective side, i.e., that the circular form and its perfection alone cannot explain the beauty we find in the plot of grass. (Nevertheless, concepts and perfection play a special and more essential role in mathematics, and Kant's account therefore becomes problematic regarding the possibility of beauty of mathematical objects. This will be discussed later in the section "Can there be Beauty and Genius in Mathematics?" in chapter 7.)

We should not have too much trouble following Kant's general direction of argument, which is to cancel the criterion of perfection and to introduce the principle of subjective purposiveness in its place. But the intuitive link between beauty and perfection that we often feel in ourselves or witness in others should make us hesitant to disregard perfection as radically as Kant asks us to do. Might it not be possible that there is some kind of perfection *post factum*, a perfection that we become aware of only after it came into existence by means of our free play and that is a unique phenomenon which does not follow any preconceptions but rather creates new concepts and sets new standards? Kant later develops the idea of "exemplary necessity" (see the separate section on this in chapter 4 below). Could we not similarly think of what I would like to call "exemplary perfection"? – a perfecting that creates and introduces new concepts and is not bound by already existing ones?

There might be a further problem, a problem with respect to what Kant calls "dependent" or "adherent" beauty, because in such cases he explicitly allows perfection to play a role, and we have to see whether he can prevent this from affecting the general arguments against perfection that he makes in section 15.

Further reading

Allison, *Kant's Theory*, pp. 139–43 defends the compatibility of beauty without perfection and dependent beauty with perfection.

Guyer, *Kant and the Claims*, pp. 212–14 comments less favorably on Kant's treatment of perfection. In *Kant and the Experience*, he has a chapter on perfection and art in Kant and his contemporaries Mendelssohn and Moritz (pp. 131–60).

Menzer, *Kants Ästhetik in ihrer Entwicklung*, pp. 23–5, shows in great detail how Kant was influenced by Baumgarten and his student Meier by pointing out many passages from Meier's textbook which Kant used for many years in his logic lectures. Baumgarten and Meier saw aesthetics as integrated into logic, which had a great impact on Kant. Menzer discusses the notion of "perfection" (pp. 32–5, 55–8). This book gives many primary sources that are otherwise hard to find.

Fricke, *Kants Theorie*, shows how Kant's idea of an "agreement of the manifold with a unity" (see above) fits into the picture of his theory of cognition from the first *Critique* (pp. 57–64).

Model, *Metaphysik und reflektierende Urteilskraft bei Kant*, pp. 258–76, discusses purposiveness in relation to perfection and morality. Explains the notion of perfection in taste in Leibniz, Gottsched, and Wolff, and shows how Kant turns against this notion.

Beauty: Free, Dependent, and Ideal

When looking at a house, we often think of its functions. And when we see functionality achieved in an optimal and perfect way, we are often inclined to call the building beautiful. But according to Kant, in that case we do not make a judgment of taste, at least not a pure one. At best, we make an impure judgment of taste, one that is spoiled by conceptual deliberations. To make a pure judgment of taste we have to abstract from concepts, purposes, and functions as determining grounds of beauty. But because conceptual aspects are essential to a building and other artifacts, it is often difficult for us to abstract from them. From that perspective, it may be easier for a child, or someone who does not know much about houses and how we build and use them, to make a pure judgment of taste about them. But this makes Kant's concept of beauty in the arts problematic. After all, do we not need an understanding of musical composition, variation, counterpoint and the like, to appreciate the music of Bach? Do we not need to be educated and experienced in such matters to be able to appreciate this kind of music appropriately? That is, can we always, as Kant demands, abstract from concepts and still be left with the possibility of appreciating the object properly? With respect to mathematical objects, this problem becomes even more pressing, as we shall see later in the section "Can there be Beauty and Genius in Mathematics?" in chapter 7.

These matters are easier with regard to objects of nature: when contemplating them, we usually do not consider their functions or purposes. We do not construct and make flowers. They grow on their own, and hence we tend to know less about how the various parts of a flower function and what their purposes are. (In fact, it might be merely our projection when we say that certain parts of a flower have the "function" of reproduction or protection, say. After all, we do not know that those parts were intended for such purposes and thus really have those functions. What looks like a purpose or a function in nature may just be a coincidence. We might make a mistake. Not so with artifacts where we set the functions before we built the objects.)

If a botanist judges the beauty of a flower, he has to forget what he knows about flowers. At least his knowledge should not determine his judgment of taste. His judgment has to be free from conceptual considerations. Only if he does not presuppose a "concept of what the object ought to be" (section 16, 229) can his judgment of taste be pure. The object of such a judgment is then called a "free beauty." Kant gives various examples of such free beauties, such as flowers, birds (like the parrot, the humming bird, and the bird of paradise), "marine crustaceans," "designs à la grecque, foliage for borders or on wallpaper," and "music fantasias" (229). They all "signify nothing by themselves" (ibid.) and we are thus not easily led into consideration of them as beautiful because of what they signify. Again, the point here is that in the end it is not the object but our judging it that makes us call it a "free beauty." A free beauty is not beautiful in itself, due to some objective property. We simply know less about certain objects and are therefore more inclined to call them "free beauties" (if we find them beautiful); we are less distracted by our knowledge of them, their functions, and their purposes. In the end, whether something is a free beauty – or, rather, whether we call it so – depends mainly on us and how we look at the object. It is just that some objects are more suitable to being seen as free beauty.

Regarding "the beauty of a human being (and in this species that of a man, a woman, or a child), the beauty of a horse, of a building (such as a church, a palace, an arsenal, or a garden-house)" (section 16, 230), we know much about the functions and uses of these objects, and we have so many expectations regarding them that it is more difficult not to be distracted by considerations of perfection. It is therefore more difficult to make a free and pure judgment of taste about them.

Kant in this context distinguishes in section 16 between two kinds of beauty: free beauty (*pulchritudo vaga*) and dependent or adherent (*anhängende*) beauty (*pulchritudo adhaerens*). "The first presupposes no concept of what the object ought to be; the second does presuppose such a concept and the perfection of the object in accordance with it" (section 16, 229). After having argued against "philosophers of repute" (section 15, 227 – he has in mind Baumgarten and the Leibniz-Wolff tradition) and their idea that perfection can serve as a justifying ground of beauty, he now, after all, still has to make some room for accommodating their ideas: there is something such as a "dependent beauty." In sections 13 and 14, Kant argues against charm and emotion as playing a role in judgments of taste, and then in section 15 against concepts and perfection. Each of these makes the judgment of taste impure: "Just as the combination of the agreeable (of sensation) with beauty . . . hindered the purity of the judgment of taste, so the combination of the good (that is, the way in which the manifold is good for the thing itself, in accordance with its end) with beauty does damage to its purity" (section 16, 230). But regarding the latter, concepts and perfection, there still is a way of integrating them that does not make the judgment totally impure, but leaves room for something that Kant calls "dependent beauty," which is, after all, some kind of beauty.

The entrance of a gothic church, for example, its decorations and its shape, might be beautiful. But if it is essential that they belong to a church (or even more conceptually determined: a *gothic* church), their beauty is not free, that is, we are not free from conceptual considerations in our aesthetic contemplation of them. And this also has an effect on our aesthetic judgment of the church as a whole. On the other hand, Kant admits that "taste gains by this combination of aesthetic satisfaction with the intellectual in that it becomes fixed" (section 16, 230). Knowledge of gothic churches, of architecture, and of social history, forms a conceptual background against which taste becomes more "fixed" (preserved and stable over time) and, conversely, the church achieves its purposes, in part, also through beauty: Taste "becomes usable as an instrument of the intention with regard to" (section 16, 230) the church and the purposes of reason (devotion to God, for instance) that we connect with it.

We see that the borderline between free and dependent beauty is a fine one. Fluctuation is easily possible. The reason for this, the deeper reason within Kant's aesthetics, is that in the former we consider "the agreement of the manifold with a unity (leaving *undetermined* what it is supposed to be)" (section 15, 227), and that the satisfaction "is one that presupposes no concept, but is immediately [i.e. *not* mediated through a concept] combined with the representation" (section 16, 230); whereas in the latter, in the case of dependent beauty, we consider an agreement of the manifold with a unity that is given by concepts (the gothic church, the architecture and social history behind it), and taste is thus made dependent on these concepts and purposes. In both cases though, the "entire faculty of the powers of representation" is involved and "gains if both states of mind are in agreement," that is, if the free aesthetic state of mind is in harmony with the intellectual state of mind. The difference between free and dependent beauty is only that in the one case concepts matter more than in the other. In specific instances, when we are actually making a judgment of taste (and not just constructing a philosophical theory about it), it becomes difficult to determine whether there really are no concepts involved, i.e., that it really is a case of free and not of dependent beauty. In particular instances, it is hard to tell whether the satisfaction is really "immediately [without the mediation of concepts] combined with the representation." It is for these reasons that the borderline between free and dependent beauty is a fine one. But in theory, at least, the borderline is clear: "Strictly speaking . . . perfection does not gain by beauty, nor does beauty gain by perfection" (section 16, 231).

The distinction between free and dependent beauty becomes especially problematic when we consider works of art, because in that case considerations related to concepts, purposes, and perfection are more relevant than they are in the case of our contemplation of objects of nature or artifacts such as houses or computers; works of art are not only man-made, but are also created to be beautiful or at least to be aesthetically interesting. These issues will be discussed in the context of our discussion of art and genius in chapter 5.

Kant makes concessions regarding concepts and purposes but not regarding charm and emotion, not only because he wants to do justice to "philosophers of repute" and their attempts to reduce beauty to perfection, but also for deeper reasons. He wants to draw connections between beauty and morality, and because he sees elements of perfection but not of charm and emotion in morality, he allows for the former (perfection) and not the latter (charm and emotion) in matters of beauty as well. Of such connections there are at least two kinds in Kant's aesthetics. One is more sophisticated and is given in the form of an analogy of reflection. This is discussed in section 59 under the title "On beauty as a symbol of morality." We will devote a separate section to this in chapter 6. Another connection between beauty and morality is one that Kant brings up right after the distinction between free and dependent beauty. This happens in section 17 under the title "On the ideal of beauty." We will spend the rest of this section on this topic.

Kant's conception of an ideal of beauty, and in particular his claim that it is only the human figure that is capable of being an ideal of beauty, were probably influenced by Johann Joachim Winckelmann's book: *Thoughts about Imitation in Greek Sculpture and Painting*, which was popular and influential during his time. In this book, Winckelmann praised the Greek ideal of beauty that was to be found in the form and shape of the human body.

In section 17, Kant introduces three related notions, namely those of **idea**, ideal, and normal idea (*Normalidee*). "Idea signifies, strictly speaking, a concept of **reason**, and ideal the representation of an individual being [*eines einzelnen Wesens*] as adequate to an idea" (section 17, 232). An idea is a concept of reason, such as the idea of freedom or the idea of God, whereas an ideal is an empirical object (seen in a special light). A "normal idea" is also an empirical object, but as we shall see it is more abstract and in a certain sense less than an ideal.

Kant gives a "psychological explanation" of how we arrive at a normal idea, or, rather, he "attempts," as he says, to give such an explanation – "for who can entirely unlock its secret from nature?" (section 17, 233). If we recall in our imag-ination many examples of horses, say, and if we let them merge into one image that represents the average of all those examples, we then obtain a normal idea of a horse. We can do the same with any kind of objects, even with human beings. This is of course an empirical procedure, and the result depends on the examples chosen. Thus, it merely gives "the normal idea of the beautiful man in the country where this comparison is made; hence under these empirical condi-tions a Negro must necessarily have a different normal idea of the beauty of a figure than a white, a Chinese person a different idea from a European" (section 17, 234).

Once a normal idea has been established, the rules for judging a horse or a human being, say, can then be derived from this normal idea. The normal idea therefore precedes the rules and can be called "exemplary." It is the "image for the whole species" (234), and because of the way we have arrived at such a normal idea, it "cannot contain anything specifically characteristic" (235). It is merely "correct" and "does not please because of beauty, but merely because it does not contradict any condition under which alone a thing of this species can be beautiful" (235). (It would be interesting to compare this with what is called *"persona"* in Latin. *Persona* originally meant a mask that was used in Greek theater performances. Such a mask hid the individual features of the actor, who pre-sented a role and not an individual that would have personal characteristic features. Only later, under Christian influences, was the word "persona" used to express the individual and its uniqueness. The normal idea as well as the Greek mask express something more abstract, such as fate or the idea of a species. The personal and the beautiful on the other hand seem to be more on the side of the individual.)

In the general discussion of normal ideas, Kant even ventures as far as to say that nature itself uses such ideas as "the archetype underlying her productions in the same species" (234). However, such a normal idea is "merely academically correct" (235) and does not give the *ideal* of beauty. An ideal of beauty is more. It is not just "academically correct." Actually, it often breaks such rules of correctness. Previously, Kant asked: "How do we attain such an ideal of beauty? A priori or empirically? Likewise, what species of beauty admits of an ideal?" (232). The answer he gives is that we "attain" such an ideal of beauty by connecting the representation with *moral* ideas and the idea of humanity. This makes the ideal a priori but restricts it to the figure of a human being: "Only that which has the end of its existence in itself, the human being, who determines his *ends* himself through *reason*, or, where he must derive them from external perception can nevertheless compare them to essential and universal ends and in that case also aesthetically judge their agreement with them: this human being alone is capable of an ideal of beauty, just as the humanity in his person, as intelligence, is alone among all the objects in the world capable of the ideal of *perfection*" (233). This is a long sentence, and it is no easier in German. It is clear that Kant here wants to connect the ideal of beauty with the human being as the only being that is capable of considering its own ends (and thus capable of morality). But what allows him to claim such a connection?

What is missing from a normal idea when compared with an ideal of beauty is an *idea*, i.e. a concept given by reason (*eine Vernunftidee*). Now such a concept is of course not an empirical object. It cannot be perceived. It is in the mind. So an ideal of beauty must be an empirical object that is at least suitable to somehow *exhibit* such a concept, or idea. But what could that idea be? The third moment has taught us that beauty is grounded in purposiveness and reflective judgment. Kant here points out a parallel between aesthetic reflection and rational reflection (in this case a moral reflection about ends), and in this way singles out the human being. As in moral reflection we are at the same time the subject and the object of our thoughts, similarly, in aesthetic reflection, the object judged and the judging subject should also be the same. And since only human beings are capable of moral reflection, so only the human body will qualify as the object of an analogous aesthetic reflection.

We have to aesthetically judge a human body by identifying ourselves with it and at the same time by identifying ourselves with the idea of humanity that we see shining through this body. This is the only way something can be an ideal of beauty, because of the requirement Kant imposes on it in analogy to moral reflection about one's own ends. We must be able to see the idea of humanity in the other, and in his body "the effect of what is inward" (*Wirkung des Inneren*, 235), that is, of his character, his virtues, his "goodness of soul, or purity, or strength, or repose." In the human figure "the ideal consists in the expression of the moral" (235). It is this aspect of morality which adds something positive and universal to the normal idea that is otherwise merely empirical and "academically correct."

Thus, as Winckelmann wrote about Greek art and singled out the human body as an object of ideal beauty, so did Kant; but Kant was less interested in the human body and the Greek spirit of physical education in the *gymnasium* than he was in morality, and so he took over Winckelmann's praise for the human body by modifying it, establishing its ground not in beauty as such but in morality instead.

At this point something should be said about the particular position Kant chose for his discussion of free and dependent beauty in the third *Critique* and in his transcendental philosophy as a whole. In section 14 he talks about ornaments (*parerga*) and in section 16 about adherent beauty (*pulchritudo adhaerens*). All this serves to incorporate possible supplementary elements (*Beiwerke*) not only into objects of art but even into the judgment of taste in general. These elements can be *independent* (as are picture frames that can have their own existence and their own values), but they can also support and *serve* beauty. In fact, the more independent they are, the more effectively they can help and serve – Kant now incorporates these considerations of supplementary elements into his discussion of the third moment of taste. But why does he choose this moment and not another?

Here we should recall that the third moment is a central one. It establishes the a priori principle of subjective purposiveness, which in turn is a manifestation of an even more general principle: the a priori principle of purposiveness in general, be it subjective or objective. This general principle gives unity to the third *Critique* and it also unites the other two *Critiques*. It serves as a bridge between freedom and nature and practical and theoretical philosophy. (See the end of the section on the Dialectic and the supersensible below in chapter 6.) It is into this context, that Kant places his discussion of free and dependent beauty.

From this wider perspective, it is not too far-fetched to say that as *parerga* and *pulchritudo adhaerens* can serve beauty, so beauty in turn can serve morality (in everyday life) and the idea of a systematic unity between freedom and nature (in philosophy). And this is indeed what Kant is driving at toward the end of the discussion of the third moment, in section 17, when he singles out man as the only possible ideal of beauty, pointing out the human being and "humanity in his person" as "the ideal of perfection" (233). It is here that he allows for perfection again, but merely as an idea, and not in beauty of outer nature but in the realm of freedom and ends, uniting nature and freedom and outer and inner nature. The human figure can be the "visible expression of moral ideas" and help us in our pursuit of "goodness of soul, or purity, or strength, or repose," which otherwise requires "great force of imagination" (235). There is of course always the danger that the outward visual impressions (of a human body) might distract from the deeper "inward" values of morality; and similarly, there is the danger that *parerga* and *pulchritudo adhaerens* distract from the essential values of beauty. Nevertheless, they all can help us – *parerga* and *pulchritudo adhaerens* to develop our taste for beauty, and the beauty of our human body to strive for moral perfection.

Strictly speaking, the intellectual and the moral are fundamentally distinct from taste or beauty. They all have their own origins. Nevertheless, in reality they are not usually separate and pure but occur together and are in many ways intertwined. And there is nothing wrong with this. There is nothing wrong for instance when we judge "in accordance with an ideal of beauty." It is just that this then is "no mere judgment of taste" (236), and Kant certainly does not mean this negatively at his point. This is not a pure judgment of taste, but may nonetheless be an even more valuable one.

Further reading

Gammon, "*Parerga* and *Pulchritudo adhaerens*," draws on many sources such as the *Metaphysics of Morals*, the Reflections, the Lecture Notes, and also writings by contemporaries of Kant. He argues that "the Beautiful adheres to the Good." Rich in detail, well informed, and sensitive to the German.

Allison, *Kant's Theory of Taste*, pp. 290–8, asks whether Kant is committed to the claim that all artistic beauty is merely adherent.

Guyer, "Free and Adherent Beauty: A Modest Proposal," discusses three different interpretations of adherent beauty and possible relationships between form and function, showing that all three interpretations make sense and do not contradict each other. The treatment in his earlier *Kant and the Claims*, pp. 215–25, sees more problems and is less favorable.

Derrida, *The Truth in Painting*, is not only about Derrida but also contains a good deal about Kant, especially on adherent and dependent beauty, frames and *parerga* – often in Derrida's own terminology though, and possibly even on "his terms" (pp. 91–102 and at other places).

Kulenkampff, *Kants Logik des Ästhetischen Urteils*, has a section on adherent beauty, normal ideas, and ideal beauty, pp. 150–65 (1st edition: 140–55).

4

Necessity: Fourth Moment

Exemplary Necessity

Since Kant has been "guided by the logical functions for judging" (section 1, footnote), he accordingly ends his analysis of the judgment of taste by addressing himself to the last group of those "logical functions for judging": the functions of "modality." The first question one would naturally ask now is "what the modality of a judgment of taste is" (title of section 18). Because modality is concerned with possibility, actuality, and necessity, one might think that the question should be whether a judgment of taste is possible, actual, or necessary. But what could that possibly mean? It might make more sense to ask whether an object is possibly, actually, or necessarily connected with the pleasure we feel when we judge it to be beautiful. But Kant is too careful to phrase the question like this. Instead of addressing himself directly to the relationship between the object and our feeling, he asks what we commonly *say* or *think* of this relationship in the latter three respects (a twentieth-century analytic philosopher of language might appreciate this move). Kant then observes: first, that we can always "say" that an object, or a **representation** of it, is *possibly* related to pleasure; secondly, that we "say" of the agreeable that it *actually* produces pleasure; and thirdly, in the case of the beautiful, one commonly "thinks" that it "has a *necessary* relation to **satisfaction**" (section 18, 236). Kant thus simply pays attention to how we speak and think when we make aesthetic judgments. Only then does he go on to deeper philosophical reflections.

This simply paying attention to how we, as judging subjects, speak and think is in tune with Kant's general concept of modality, because the "modality of judgments is a quite special function": it "contributes nothing to the content of a **judgment** . . . but rather concerns only the value of the copula *in relation to thinking* in general" (*Critique of Pure Reason*, A 74/B99–100). It is in accord with this general remark from the first *Critique* that Kant, in section 18 of the third

Critique, does not address himself directly to the relation between an object and our feeling but merely observes our *attitude*, what we 'say' and how we 'think' regarding such a relation.

But what exactly does the necessity of a judgment of taste consist in? What do we think is the "necessary relation" (section 18, 236)? Is it a relation between the object and our feeling that is thought to be necessary? Or is it agreement of others with my judgment? In any case, the necessity of a judgment of taste cannot follow from the "logical functions for judging" or the a priori **categories** from the first *Critique* (these are primarily elements of cognition and are too fundamental to explain the specific nature of the judgment of taste's necessity). Nor can the necessity follow from empirical **concepts** (these would never do justice to the a priori nature of judgments of taste). Thus it is not an epistemic necessity. Nor is it based on free will and rational reflection about the categorical imperative, and it is therefore not a practical (moral) necessity either. Both are ruled out since there can never be any rules of taste. The "necessary relation" that we think of in a judgment of taste does not follow in a quasi-mechanical way from other elements or presuppositions, in the way the statement "Socrates is mortal" (necessarily) follows from the statements "all human beings are mortal" and "Socrates is a human being." We will see that the necessity is instead in some way *instantiated* by the judgment of taste itself.

We have already pointed out that what is special about the **universality** of a judgment of taste is the fact that someone actually has to make a judgment of taste before a claim to universality can be made. The subjective universality of a judgment of taste cannot be derived in a formal, logical way. Rather, one must first allow one's **faculties** of cognition to engage in free play of a certain kind before a claim to universality can be made at all. If we keep this in mind, we will not be surprised that Kant writes that the necessity that we think of in a judgment of taste is *"exemplary*, i.e., a necessity of the assent of all to a judgment that is regarded as an *example* of a universal rule that one cannot produce" (section 18, 237). Someone has to step forward, so to speak, and actually make a judgment of taste before anyone can be expected to agree to anything. The judgment itself is exemplary. It looks like an example of a rule, *as if* a general rule preceded it. But in fact there is no rule to start with, and it is the judgment of taste that comes first, that simply occurs, that stands on its own feet, so to speak, and is exemplary for other human beings to follow.

Here we can draw a useful parallel between the production of an aesthetic judgment and the production of beauty in fine art. A work of fine art brings something new into the world, and others often take it as a *model* that they imitate, as if they could read the rules of production from it. We take a work of art as an exemplar for imitation, and even the person who produced it cannot spell out the rules of production as far as beauty is concerned. There may be techniques that have to be learned, and the artist can possibly explain some of the ideas he or she had in mind while creating the object. But there are no rules for beauty, no rules for beautiful art, and also no rules for the production of beautiful art. We regard a work of art as an example of a rule that we cannot state. Kant himself later spells all this out in the sections on genius (from section 46 on). Similarly, we may – and in fact do – regard the judgment of taste itself "as an example of a universal rule that one cannot produce" (section 18, 237).

The judgment of taste thus is, I would suggest, like a work of art itself, insofar as it is something original that actually has to be brought into existence by someone and cannot be derived in a quasi-mechanical, formal logical way. ("Existence precedes essence," we might be tempted to say in an existentialist spirit with Sartre.) The features of originality and autonomy are of course more prominent in a genius, but they can also be found in judgments of taste, and the exemplary necessity of such judgments should be seen in the light of these features of originality and autonomy.

Formally, there are at least two different things that can possibly be thought to be necessary in a judgment of taste: the agreement of others to my judgment, and my own satisfaction with the object. In section 18, Kant talks of the "necessity of the *assent* of all to a judgment that is regarded as an example of a universal rule that one cannot produce," and in section 21 he argues much about conditions of universal *communicability*. Thus it seems Kant is focusing on the necessity of assent. But in fact, in the end, when he gives his "definition of the beautiful" after section 22, it is the *satisfaction* that he calls "necessary." To see what is actually going on, we must focus on what the necessity is based on, and then we will see that both, the agreement *and* the satisfaction, can be thought of as necessary.

The judgment of taste is based on the free play of our faculties of cognition and on the a priori principle of subjective purposiveness; and on these grounds, both features of a judgment of taste are felt to be necessary: the satisfaction I feel and the agreement I demand. One simply cannot do otherwise than to feel, demand, and assent – provided the correct justifying grounds are in place!

Having already answered in the first section on modality (section 18) the question of what the modality of a judgment of taste is, Kant spends the remaining four sections of the "Analytic of the Beautiful" discussing the role of the **sensus communis**. Although the *sensus communis* is the topic of our next section, let us say something here about how it is related to exemplary necessity.

Guided by the "logical functions for judging" from the first *Critique*, Kant looked for some kind of necessity in judgments of taste and found what he called exemplary necessity: "a necessity of the assent of all to a judgment that is regarded as an *example* of a universal rule that one cannot produce" (section 18, 237; actually, the German says: *was wie ein Beispiel . . . angesehen wird*, which could also be translated as: "that is regarded *as if* it were an example"). This exemplary necessity is not objective or practical. There is no rule from which it would follow. But because the justifying grounds are nevertheless (intersubjectively) universal (being basically the free play and the a priori principle of purposiveness), it seems to us *as if* there were such a rule. And at this point Kant introduces the *sensus communis* as an idea of a common feeling: a sense or feeling that we share, that decides about beauty and that therefore could take the place of such a rule. Now how does this relate to exemplary necessity?

There term *"sensus communis"* is a Latin expression, and there are several related terms in other languages: "common sense" in English, *"Gemeinsinn"* in German, and *"sens commun"* and *"bon sens"* in French. They all have their own histories and their own connotations. In particular, the English "common sense" should not be identified with the *"sensus communis."* We will see in the next section that Kant in fact wants to draw a line between these two. The reader at this point might want to have a look at the beginning of that section, where I give a brief historical account of the *"sensus communis"* that should be helpful for what follows.

The judgment of taste itself appears as an *example* of a rule that would guarantee the necessity we feel, and the *sensus communis* steps in, so to speak – or, rather, we *imagine* it to do so (after all, it is only an idea) – to fill in what the desired rule alone cannot provide. The rule cannot be sufficient, because we don't know how to "subsume" something under it, Kant says, and maybe such a rule in the strict sense of an objective rule is impossible anyway. (On the other hand, by subsuming "Socrates" under the concept "human," we can derive "Socrates is mortal" from the premise "Humans are mortal.") Now something has to take its place, and we are entitled to demand some kind of *sensus communis* to step in, because in a judgment of taste we feel the need for such a rule. In this way the judgment of taste appears as an "example" of the *sensus communis*, and accordingly, Kant suggests, the latter, the *sensus communis* (together with its history), should be understood in the light of the former (the judgment of taste). In fact, we will see in the next section that free play and the principle of subjective purposiveness are in the end, for Kant, the essential ingredients that make up (and allow us to explain) the *sensus communis* and whatever tradition has thought it to be.

For Kant, the traditional understanding of the *sensus communis* is merely an idea, an ideal norm, or an ideal feeling that would provide such a norm – maybe something to strive for (section 22). For him, the best we have achieved so far in our human history is the ability to make judgments of taste. These are real. These we can take as pointers toward such a norm. He calls them – and actually "offers" or at least "indicates" (*angeben*) them to his readers as – an "example" of such a norm: "The common sense [*Gemeinsinn*], of whose judgment I here

NECESSITY: FOURTH MOMENT   81

offer my judgment of taste as an *example* and on account of which I ascribe *exemplary* validity to it, is a merely ideal norm, under the presupposition of which one could rightfully make a judgment . . . into a rule for everyone" (section 22, 239). Thus the judgment of taste is an example of the *sensus communis*, and at the same time the judgment's validity, its grounds and its claim to universal and necessary intersubjective validity, are also examples of the validity of the *sensus communis*.

In short: the judgment of taste is, by the nature of its universal validity and exemplary necessity, an example of the *sensus communis*. The necessity "that is thought" (section 18, 237) in the judgment of taste, i.e., the necessity of the agreement of others as if the judgment were an example of a rule, is an example of the *sensus communis*. But this aspect is only an aspect on the surface. It merely reflects the functions (of necessity, agreement, and communicability). On a deeper level we can say that, for Kant, it is the grounds of the judgment of taste, the free play and the a priori principle of purposiveness, that are examples of the *sensus communis*.

Further reading

Gammon, "'Exemplary Originality': Kant on Genius and Imagination," focuses on the Kant before the third *Critique*. Gives useful separate sections on contemporaries of Kant who had an influence on his ideas: Hamann, Winckelmann, Tetens, and Feder. Such material is otherwise very difficult to get hold of. Goes into great detail with German words (sometimes almost too much). Discusses four kinds of exemplarity, *Nachfolge*, *Nachahmung*, *Nachmachung*, *Nachäffung*, and how Kant and others understood them. Also has a section on "moral exemplarity."

Kant's Interpretation of the *sensus communis*

Having introduced the notion of "exemplary necessity" at the beginning of the discussion of the fourth moment, in section 18, Kant makes much use of it in the course of integrating and redefining the traditional notion of the *sensus communis* within his third *Critique*, particularly in sections 19–22, but also later, in section 40.

Before going into any details in Kant, we should have a brief look at the general history of the *sensus communis*, the "common sense," and what Kant calls the "*Gemeinsinn*." This story is rich and complex, not only because it is long – it begins at least with Aristotle – but also because there are several strands in it that have developed and that have been interwoven at different times and different places with different emphases and interests. Aristotle argued that there must be a central cognitive faculty that combines our five senses. Cicero saw the *sensus communis* in the light of rhetoric and politics as something we should pay attention to in order to persuade others and act properly. We can thus distinguish roughly between two different strands: the idea of something that is common to, or unites, the different senses in *one* individual (the Greek origin), and the idea of something that is common to, and thus unites different individuals (the Stoic and Roman tradition). In short, there is an *intra-* and there is an *inter*-subjective aspect of the *sensus communis*. In both we find elements of **sensation** and **cognition,** something that will continue throughout the ensuing history. In Britain and especially in Scotland, we find at the end of the eighteenth century a widespread theory of so-called "common sense," which was theoretical as well as moral and familiar to Kant. This theory proposed intuitively known principles, including moral ones, and Kant was not very much in favor of this. So we find him arguing (if only indirectly) that the *sensus communis* should be a **feeling** rather than some kind of **understanding**: If we have to decide whether taste – which for Kant is fundamentally different from cognition – should be called *sensus communis* or some kind of "healthy" or "common" understanding, *gesunder* or *gemeiner Menschenverstand*, he votes for the former, thus drawing a line between *sensus communis* and understanding: "taste can be called *sensus communis* with greater justice than can the healthy understanding" (section 40, 295).

At first blush, the English term "common sense" might seem to be a good translation of *Gemeinsinn* and *sensus communis*, and the reader might wonder why I still drag along the old Latin term *sensus communis*. But there is a good reason for doing this. The English term "common sense" has its own history, mainly through Berkeley, Hume, and the Scottish school. It already has a specific meaning: a healthy understanding that is opposed to skepticism or nonsense. Now this is not at all what Kant has in mind when he speaks of the *Gemeinsinn* or the *sensus communis*. In fact, he wants to distance himself from such an understanding of the *sensus communis* (see quote above). Translating *Gemeinsinn* and *sensus communis* as "common sense" therefore in the end only creates confusion and is not a good idea. I thus prefer to use the Latin term.

After this short historical excursion, let us now return to the text. When introducing the *Gemeinsinn* and the *sensus communis*, Kant poses the same question he asked in his discussion of the second moment: what justifies my demand that everyone should agree to my judgment of taste? How can we communicate the feeling that we find in our satisfaction in the beautiful? On what grounds can such a communication possibly be based?

Traditionally, the *sensus communis*, some kind of common feeling or sense among human beings, has been invoked in this context. If there is such a common feeling, or sense, that we share and that also decides about beauty, then whoever has it will also agree to our judgment – supposing that we ourselves do have such a feeling or sense. Now for Kant the story is not that easy. He does not want to introduce just another sense. What would a merely postulated sense explain after all? It would be some kind of *deus ex machina*, it would not really explain anything, and it would, as we shall see, undermine Kant's vision of human autonomy in the spirit of the Enlightenment. Instead of an additional sense, he wants to explain our demand for agreement in matters of taste by what he has introduced already: the faculties of cognition and their free play. On the other hand, it is also important for Kant to suggest that if the *sensus communis* plays any role here, it should certainly not be some kind of understanding or reason (as in the English tradition of "common sense") but rather a feeling, a feeling of our own state of mind. (Kant values reason too highly to have it entangled with sense or feeling; and also he wants taste to stand on its own feet instead of being merely some kind of inferior cognition.)

Kant now refers back to his notion of free play of our cognitive faculties and the **a priori principle** of **purposiveness** as the proper ground for justifying our demand for agreement. These faculties have already been established in the first *Critique*, and it now suffices to explain the idea of a *sensus communis* in terms of these faculties. It is not necessary to introduce a new element in the form of a new sense called *"sensus communis."* Instead, introducing a new relationship between already established elements suffices. There really is no additional sense, and if we still wish to think of a sense here, a *sensus communis*, we should think of it as a *result* of the free play.

Kant begins to make room for his introduction of the *sensus communis* by noting in the title of section 19: "The subjective necessity that we ascribe to the judgment of taste is *conditioned* [maybe better: *conditional*]." That others should agree to our judgment of taste is a demand that is "pronounced only conditionally even given all the data that are required for the judging" (section 19, 237). Given my perception of the object and various kinds of background knowledge, I still have no way of convincing others of the beauty of the object by means of proof. The common ground that would justify my demand for necessary agreement seems to be missing. Such a common ground would be the 'condition' of the necessity of the agreement of others. It is at this point that Kant introduces the traditional notion of *Gemeinsinn*, or *sensus communis*: "The condition of the necessity that is alleged by a judgment of taste is the idea of a common sense [*die Idee eines Gemeinsinnes*]" (title of section 20). There must be a principle based on which I can be justified in my demand for assent. "Such a principle," Kant writes, *"could* only be regarded [*angesehen*] as a common sense [*Gemeinsinn*]" (section 20, 238). Kant here is going to phrase his *own* theory of taste in terms that have been utilized by many other philosophers writing about the *sensus communis*. In this way, he can, at least superficially, agree with other philosophers who think that some kind of *sensus communis* is what is required here. By saying that what is required *"could [könnte,* as others have claimed] only be regarded as a common sense *[Gemeinsinn],"* Kant presents a way of arguing that is not exactly his own, but to which he does subscribe, provided we understand the notion of a common sense properly, i.e. in *his* way. He is here saying to the reader: if you insist on using the notion of a *sensus communis* here, you have to understand it the way I do. Kant is now modifying the notion.

Indeed, only a few sentences later, Kant adjusts the above argument regarding the role of a *sensus communis.* It is indeed true that "only under the presupposition that there is a common sense . . . can the judgment of taste be made" (section 20, 238), but he adds in brackets that by such a common sense *"we* do not mean any external sense but rather the effect of the free play of our cognitive powers" (section 20, 238). "We," refers to Kant and his readers. After having followed Kant so far, "we" know how to understand the *sensus communis,* "we" know that it is "the *effect* of the free play." We know that we feel this free play within ourselves. If we wish to speak of a "sense" here, it is an inner sense rather than an outer sense. It is a sense by which we feel our own state of mind.

Something more should be said about sections 21 and 40. In section 21, Kant argues that we have "good reason to presuppose a common sense *[Gemeinsinn],"* and he does so in a very general way, arguing about universal communicability of our state of mind and the universal communicability of our feeling for this state of mind, and he does not restrict himself to a state of mind in aesthetic reflection but considers the state of mind in general and with respect to cognition in general. His way of arguing here is similar to what we have already seen in section 9, and so are the problems, for instance whether his arguments really work for judgments of taste or only for those of cognition, or whether his arguments tend to see judgments of taste too much like judgments of cognition. As we went into great detail with section 9, the reader should find his way in section 21 himself (see also the list of further reading).

In section 40, Kant returns once more to the topic of the *sensus communis,* right after the **deduction** (section 38) and a section on communicability (section 39), and just before discussing empirical and intellectual interests in the beautiful (sections 41 and 42). Here the scope of discussion is naturally much wider, and in particular the connections with autonomy and morality are more pronounced. Thus he connects taste with his "maxims of common human understanding." In aesthetic reflection we demand the agreement of others, thus we reach out to them, we think of them as being in our situation. To do so we have to abstract from what is private and particular to us, we have to abstract from charm and emotion in "seeking a judgment that is to serve as a **universal** rule" (section 40, 294), and our "faculty for judging" must take "account (a priori) of everyone else's way of representing in thought, in order as it were to hold its judgment up to human reason as a whole" (293). In particular it is thus the second maxim that is close to the power of judgment: "To think in the position of everyone else" (294). At the end of section 22, Kant alluded to moral ends; and he does this here again, at the end of section 40. Producing a *sensus communis* (Kant uses the word *Gemeinsinn*) might serve "higher ends" that are set by "higher principles of **reason**," that is moral reasons (section 22); and there might be a moral "interest" behind the "mere communicability" of a feeling, that would explain "how it is that the feeling in the judgment of taste is expected of everyone as if it were a duty." It might then be a duty to develop taste for beauty, because this would develop our *Gemeinsinn* and our ability to reflect about others as is required in moral actions. All this makes more sense after section 59: "On beauty as a symbol of morality," which we will discuss later in chapter 6 in the section with (almost exactly) that title.

There is one more question I would like to pose here. According to Kant, necessity and universality often go hand in hand (see section 19 of the *Prolegomena*). So one may wonder what, after all, the difference between the second and the fourth moment is, and why Kant did not introduce the *sensus communis* earlier, in the discussion of the second moment. Indeed, it may seem that Kant could easily have introduced the *sensus communis* in the context of the discussion of subjective universality. But he first had to develop his notion of free play, since he wanted to use it as a basis for deriving what others call the *sensus communis*; and in order to give the notion of the free play its a priori basis, he also had to introduce the a priori principle of purposiveness, which belongs to the third moment. Therefore, if Kant wants to derive the *sensus communis* from his notion of free play, he can do so only after the discussion of the third moment, and then a natural place for its inclusion would be in the discussion of the fourth moment.

If we think for a moment of the history of the *sensus communis* again, we see that Kant's account, going back to his notion of the free play of our cognitive faculties, is in a certain sense closer to Aristotle's and the older Greek notion of an inner sense or faculty that unites our five senses than it is to the Roman or British idea of an intuition or understanding that is shared by different human beings: the free play unites our senses. On the other hand, the connection to the Roman and British tradition is preserved in his linking aesthetic reflection with morality.

Here is an interesting side note. Looking for a moment at the twentieth and the twenty-first centuries, it seems to me that many of the currently discussed issues in the philosophy of mind are actually (at least systematically) very much related to what we have been discussing here. Unfortunately, those working nowadays in the philosophy of mind are usually not interested in Kant's aesthetics, nor are they familiar with the history of the *sensus communis* and its interpretations. Kant is much more up to date than many of them think.

Further reading

Gadamer, *Truth and Method*, pp. 19–30, gives a rich and fascinating account of the *sensus communis* from a historical perspective, especially with respect to Vico and in the general context of questions of truth, experience of art, culture (*Bildung*), and humanism. This leads Gadamer to a discussion of Kant's "subjectivization of aesthetics" (pp. 42–81).

Allison, *Kant's Theory*, pp. 144–59, offers a detailed discussion of the question whether Kant argues for a cognitive or an aesthetic conception of common sense. To do so, he reconstructs the dense argumentation of section 21, paying close attention to the argumentative roles of communicability, cognition in general, and skepticism (compare section 9 in Kant).

Lyotard, *Lessons*, has a good chapter on communication of taste (pp. 191–224) and gives a seven-step reconstruction of Kant's arguments in section twenty-one (pp. 200–2) and a discussion of section twenty-two. He also gives a creative discussion of how a mind can possibly feel itself (pp. 9–13).

Guyer, *Kant and the Claims*, pp. 248–73, sees Kant's chapter on modality as a first attempt to justify the judgment of taste and finds much fault with and confusion in Kant's arguments, especially those in section 21.

Saville, *Aesthetic Reconstructions*, pp. 142–61, reconstructs Kant's arguments about the (cognitive and aesthetic) *sensus communis* and the "aesthetic ought" (our duty to acquire taste). Analytic in style and relatively free of Kantian terminology.

Hampshire, "The Social Spirit of Mankind," does not explicitly discuss the *sensus communis* but focuses on the role of culture in Kant's third *Critique*, arguing that it is culture and especially the cultural aspects of our communication of feeling that actually bridge the gap between nature and freedom. This makes a nice complementary reading from a higher perspective.

Kaulbach, *Ästhetische Welterkenntnis bei Kant*, pp. 131–46, discusses the *sensus communis* as a feeling for being part of society and as a general point of view. Many examples, not technical, reconstructive.

Fricke, *Kants Theorie*, pp. 161–76, discusses aesthetic and objective "proportions" (*Proportion, Zusammenstimmung*) between imagination and understanding, the problem of communicability, and aesthetic and objective *sensus communis*. She sees "order" (*Ordnung*) in the manifold of intuition (*Anschauung*) as the common denominator (p. 175) between the aesthetic and the objective here.

Model, *Metaphysik und reflektierende Urteilskraft*, pp. 247–258, shows how Kant stresses sensibility against rationalism (Leibniz) and modifies the traditional conception of the *sensus communis*.

The Deduction

"Deduction" means justification, and what is in question is the judgment of taste's claim to **universal** intersubjective validity. This claim needs to be justified.

NECESSITY: FOURTH MOMENT 87

And because the claim is a universal one, one that does not allow for any exception, the justification has to be one in the sprit of **transcendental** philosophy – that is, non-empirical (a priori) **grounds** must be provided. Section 38 is entitled "Deduction of judgments of taste," and one thus expects it to be the culmination of the whole Deduction part, which comprises as many as 25 sections (sections 30–54), and one also expects it to give the deduction in a nutshell. But this section is surprisingly short, filling just about one page. Hence one should not expect to find all the necessary arguments given in full detail and starting from scratch. Nevertheless, the section is indeed a culmination point. Although it presupposes that the reader has gone through most of the previous sections and has grasped the main points given there, especially those of the second and the third moment, section 38 still tries to embrace the essence of many previous arguments and to unite them in a single thought – or at least in almost a single sentence.

Before going into the details of this section, let us briefly see how it is situated within the Deduction as a whole. Kant begins the Deduction with methodological considerations about the task and nature of the deduction, arguing that it has to deal only with beauty and not with the sublime (section 30) and explaining how one has to proceed in this deduction (section 31). Then he summarizes the problems of what he calls the first and second "peculiarity" of the judgment of taste: their being seemingly subjective and seemingly objective (32 and 33), discusses the possibility of subjective versus objective principles (34 and 35), reaches back to the first *Critique* by recalling overarching questions of transcendental philosophy about the **synthetic** a priori, and then jumps right into the deduction (section thirty-eight) to give the desired justification (of the claims to universality made in judgments of taste). The rest of the Deduction then offers various applications of previous results and discoveries, such as the applications to the *sensus communis*, art, and **genius**.

From the beginning, Kant takes it as a fact that in judgments of taste we reach out to others and make claims to universality (claims with which everyone should agree). The question then arises whether this is really possible, whether this reaching out to others is in vain or whether there are good reasons for it. Kant's analysis of such judgments then reveals the second and the third moments of the judgment of taste, which he briefly summarizes at the beginning of section 38: these are the nature of free play, in which satisfaction in the beautiful is (intrinsically) "combined," as Kant rather vaguely says, with the "mere judging" (*Beurteilung*) of the object's **form**; and "the subjective purposiveness of that form for the **power of judgment**," which we feel in that satisfaction. Kant thinks of this "power of judgment," and even more so of that "satisfaction," as subjective. Nevertheless, this power and the free play underlying the satisfaction are not "merely" subjective, because the elements involved (**understanding** and

imagination) are universal (the same for all of us) and they are involved in a way that relates them to cognition. Kant hinted at this, and makes room for it from the very beginning of the third *Critique*, for instance in section one, where he says in the very first sentence that we relate the representation "by means of the imagination (perhaps combined with the understanding) to the subject and its feeling." Not only is (the faculty of) understanding the same in all of us and the means for objectivity, but also imagination is a faculty that we share and that is needed in any empirical objective judgment. We need imagination to see a house or hear a melody. We are not just causally affected by what we see. Rather, in perception our minds are also active: we combine, memorize, and bring things to our attention, and imagination is an integral part of this synthesizing activity. "Synthesis," Kant wrote in the first *Critique* (A 78/B 103), "is . . . the mere effect of the imagination, of a blind though indispensable function of the soul, without which we would have no cognition at all." For Kant, imagination is not just fantasy.

In empirical cognitive judgments, a given **intuition** (of a house, say) is subsumed under a concept (the concept of a house). Here imagination (needed "for the intuition and the composition of the manifold of intuition," as Kant explains in section 35) is regulated (the concept of a house comes with rules for its application) and determined by understanding's "lawfulness." In judgments of taste, by contrast, imagination is free from such constraints and instead playfully interacts with understanding. In section 35, Kant recalls the results from section nine, for instance that "the judgment of taste must rest on a mere sensation of the reciprocally animating imagination in its freedom and the understanding with its lawfulness" (section 35, 287). This life-like animation (*Belebung* – perhaps a hint at **teleology** and the second part of the third *Critique*) takes place within the judging subject and is felt by that subject and not by others. It is thus subjective. But as far as the elements involved and especially their relation to "**cognition in general**" (no matter which object is perceived) are concerned, we can "presuppose," Kant says, that they are the same in all of us and that we are justified in "assum[ing]" (section 38, 290) that *if* we indeed make a pure judgment of taste, we make it with respect to these elements and that relation. Only then does the representation "correspond" with those "subjective conditions of the use of the power of judgment in general" as is "requisite for possible cognitions in general" (290). This "correspondence" is based on subjective purposiveness and must play the decisive role in our satisfaction in the beautiful. We feel this "correspondence" and through it the deduction becomes possible. (See Baudelaire's poem at the beginning of this book.)

At this point something should be added by way of comparison with the agreeable. After a long walk, we often think everyone (who walked with us) should find it agreeable to have a good rest, or that everyone should find it agreeable to have a good meal. But this does not mean that the satisfaction involved is a satisfaction in the beautiful. For this to be true our mind must be actively involved in a certain way. In Kant's terms, understanding as the faculty of concepts, of rules and objectivity, must be involved. Only when it is based on the free play of our cognitive faculties and when it is in "correspondence" with cognition in general, can the satisfaction be a satisfaction in the beautiful.

In section 38 Kant stresses a distinction between two levels, or perspectives, one of which is subject to doubt and the other is not. There is "no doubt," Kant says, that a judgment of taste's claim to universality is justified *if* it is indeed a judgment of taste, i.e. if the judgment is properly based on the free play and the a priori principle of subjective purposiveness. Nevertheless, Kant also says that there is always *room for doubt*, whether or not the actual judgment one makes is really a judgment of taste, i.e. whether or not it is really based on those grounds that make it a judgment of taste. Kant adds a "Remark" and a footnote in which he points out this double-sidedness, or two-step structure. First, the "subjective conditions" are (no doubt) the same for all of us as far as their "relation" to "cognition in general" is concerned. Second, the judgment of taste must take "into consideration" only those "conditions" (and not mere feeling or concepts), and we can always make an "error" with respect to the second part. But a wrong application, Kant stresses, does not touch on the authority of the first part, the principle that is applied.

That such an error in application is easily made can be explained within Kant's aesthetic theory as follows. The "subsumption" of imagination under understanding, of which Kant repeatedly speaks with respect to the judgment of taste, is actually a mere *quasi*-subsumption. Whereas in judgments of cognition an intuition (of a house) is subsumed under a concept (the concept of a house) such that the concept provides rules for the subsumption (by, for instance, guiding imagination in synthesizing the visual appearance), in judgments of taste it is the whole faculty of intuition, imagination, that is "subsumed," Kant says, under the understanding. But what exactly is this supposed to mean?

Kant also says that imagination is subsumed "under the *condition* that the understanding in general *advance* from intuitions to concepts" (section 35, 287). Here we are dealing with a "condition" of advancement, not a real advancement but a *possible* one. An actual "advance[ment] from intuition to concepts" takes place only in cognition (or in mental activities with the aim of cognition) but not in aesthetic reflection. In the process of cognition we either create a concept from intuitions (for instance, the concept of a house from seeing several houses) or we recall a concept if we already have it at our disposal (when we see parts of a house and then recognize it as a house). But in making a judgment of taste we merely subsume what we perceive (without having to recognize it as a such and such) under general conditions for something (the "advancement," an act of cognition) that does not actually take place within the judgment of taste itself. We subsume our perception, an empirical intuition, under the general conditions of possible cognition (not under any specific conditions for some specific cognition involving this or that concept). For this reason, I would suggest, Kant speaks of a subsumption of the whole faculty of intuition, imagination, under the faculty of concepts, the understanding. It is left open what concept might be applied. The faculty of imagination is not "regulated" by any concept, but free from any such specific regulation. Nevertheless imagination does not create chaos either. It creates something that suits some concept or another and in fact a whole range of possibilities of what the thing perceived might be. To do so it must at least create something that renders itself open to possible conceptualizations, and this means that imagination must pay respect to the conditions of conceptualization. In this sense imagination is "subsumed" under the understanding. (For those who are familiar with the first *Critique* we might say that imagination is "subsumed" under the requirements of the categories and schematization.)

A judgment of cognition might follow, or precede the judgment of taste, but for Kant the two judgments are always distinct. There are no **rules** for this kind of "subsumption," at least no rules like the ones we have with concepts. (With the concept of a house goes a rule for deciding what counts as a house). We merely feel the subsumption, but with a very special feeling, namely the satisfaction in the beautiful. That is why I call this subsumption of one faculty under another a "quasi"-subsumption.

Kant also says that in a judgment of taste we have to subsume what we perceive under the "subjective condition of the power of judgment" and under a "relation that is merely a matter of sensation." Part of what he means by this is that the subsumption and the relation are only felt but not cognized. Because feelings are not reliable, this quasi-subsumption "can easily be deceptive" and always leaves room for doubt. The "conditions," by contrast, under which we must subsume what we perceive if our judgment is to be a judgment of taste, are not just a matter of mere feeling but are related to the possibility of conceptualization and objectivity and are therefore universal and binding for all human beings.

At this point the reader might be disappointed. Is that the whole deduction? Is that all? But I think this is similar to the situation in mathematics, where it often takes a long time to find a proof for something one believes to be true (since Kant believes that there are a priori grounds for the judgment of taste). The first proof one comes up with is long, winding, and complicated. After some years the proof has not only been polished and streamlined, but often a whole theory has been developed around it, and within that new theory the desired theorem falls out easily (as the deduction seems to fall out easily in section 38). Nevertheless, if one wants to understand the theorem, one still has to familiarize oneself with the whole mathematical theory first, which takes many pages of hard work and much thought. Only then does the solution fall out so easily. Kant himself begins his "Remark" to section 38 by saying: "This deduction is so *easy* because . . . the judgment of taste . . . asserts only that we are justified in presupposing universally in every human being the same *subjective conditions* of the *power of judgment* that we find in ourselves" (290). But to get "a taste," so to speak, of what those "subjective conditions" involve and what exactly this "power of judgment" is, one has to go through many arguments and complex thoughts, which are provided in all those sections that lead up to section 38. So there really is no shortcut. There is no point in just reading section 38 and thinking one gets it all there.

There are still many questions leading back to difficult issues in the first *Critique*, questions about the nature of concepts and rules, judgment and imagination. These issues are still to a great extent open, not only in Kant, but also in arguably similar contemporary discussions in philosophy of mind and even in neuroscience. If we look at current discussions of "concepts," for instance, we will see that we have still not come up with a satisfying theory for them. There are so many different understandings of concepts – they are viewed as "stereotypes," "pictures," "intensions" – and they are viewed from many different standpoints – such as concept-possession, etc. – the merits of which continue to be debated. Because of this continued debate, it seems to me that many of Kant's thoughts on the interplay of imagination and understanding and their functions (in cognition as well as in aesthetic contemplation) are still "up to date."

Having said all this, there are still some points worth discussing: (1) Why is there no deduction for the sublime? (2) Does the overall structure of the deduction make sense when compared with the **Analytic** and the **Dialectic**? (3) Does the deduction imply that all objects are beautiful and thus in the end prove too much? (4) What exactly is the subject's autonomy in matter's of taste and is there room for erroneous judgments of taste?

1. At the beginning of the Deduction, in section 30, Kant claims that we do not need a deduction for the judgment about the sublime. Although this judgment is an a priori aesthetic judgment as well, its exposition already provides its deduction, so Kant says. He gives the following two reasons. First, in the case of the sublime, the object is "formless and shapeless," and in the end it is not the object but ourselves and our human nature that are sublime; the object merely triggers an activity in us, but it is we who create the feeling for the sublime. Second, in connection with this human nature in us, the feeling for the sublime is at least partially based on morality and our "faculty of ends (the will)" (section 30, 280), which already has an a priori basis of its own. In the case of beauty, although there is an intrinsic relation to cognition in general, Kant thinks we still need a new and separate kind of a priori principle. But in the case of the sublime,

where there is a relation to morality, he thinks this relation is sufficient to justify the judgment about the sublime as an a priori judgment. One wonders whether these two cases are really that different.

2. Where exactly does Kant give the main, essential, or sufficient arguments for the deduction? According to the section titles, they should be found in the part that is called "Deduction" and in particular in section 38 therein, which is entitled "Deduction of judgments of taste." But one can argue that the necessary arguments have already been provided in section 9, where the "key" solution to the critique of taste and the notion of free play of the faculties have been introduced. One can also argue that the deduction has been given in sections 20–22, where the *sensus communis* was introduced, especially in section 21, where Kant discusses the universal communicability of a feeling. Alternatively, one might say that neither what has been offered in section 9 nor what has been added (if anything at all) in section 38, nor for that matter in any of the sections from the entirety of the Analytic and the Deduction, is sufficient to justify the judgment of taste's claim to necessity and universality, and that this justification is completed only in the Dialectic, where the link to morality (beauty as the symbol of morality) is introduced. For these questions and the relevant secondary literature, I refer the reader to the relevant sections in this book: "How to read Section 9" in chapter 2, "Kant's Interpretation of the *sensus communis*" in chapter 4, and "The Analytic, the Dialectic, and the Supersensible" in chapter 6. For the most part, in each of them I defend Kant's overall argument and its structure.

3. The justification Kant gives for the judgment of taste's claim to universal validity makes much use of this judgment's affinity to judgments of cognition (the relation to "cognition in general"). Thus there is the danger that this affinity might be so close and the two judgments so similar that all objects of cognition turn out to be necessarily beautiful. To make sure that this does not happen, one must have the right kind of theory of "harmony" between imagination and understanding, a harmony that allows for enough freedom from the understanding and its concepts and rules (to make sure that judgments of taste are not judgments of cognition) but that is still close enough to the general function of understanding in relation to cognition in general to allow for the deduction. In addressing these questions, I refer the reader to the sections of this book on free play, purposiveness, perfection, and necessity.

4. There is at least one more problem worth discussing here, the problem of autonomy and error. In matters of taste one has to rely on one's own resources: one should not listen to others but should judge for oneself. (Kant says that the power of judgment "gives rules to itself" – as it were, we might want to add, because there are actually no rules allowed here, such as rules for what counts as a house. At best, we have guidelines such as disinterestedness and the

principle of subjective purposiveness.) In section 32 Kant gives the example of a young poet who "does not let himself be dissuaded from his conviction that his poem is beautiful" (282). The interesting point here is that Kant thinks the poet might actually be wrong, since he adds that later, when the poet is more experienced and his judgment is sharpened, he voluntarily changes his mind. Now, should we say that the poet's earlier judgment was not really a judgment of taste? Or should we rather say that it was one at the time when it was made, and that one is allowed to "change one's mind" in matters of taste? Or was it already a wrong judgment of taste then? There is much room for discussion here. In any case, autonomy seems not to be enough for making a judgment of taste. One might want to say that it must be "the right kind" of autonomy, one based on the right kind of factors (which are given in the four moments of taste). Kant's distinction between our certainty about the principle and our uncertainty about its proper application should be kept in mind here.

Further reading

Allison, *Kant's Theory of Taste*, has a section on the deduction (pp. 160–92), with separate subsections that deal with problems from sections 30 to 38 and with criticisms by Guyer and Savile, against which Allison argues in defense of Kant. Allison here gives a detailed account that is not too technical.

McCloskey, *Kant's Aesthetic*, pp. 80–93, discusses the relevance of finality, in particular of "forms final for perception," for the deduction.

Kemal, *Kant's Aesthetic Theory*, has a section on the deduction of judgments of taste (pp. 73–115) and a subsection discussing other writers on this issue.

Coleman, *The Harmony of Reason*, discusses the possibility of erroneous aesthetic judgments (pp. 79–84) and the role of autonomy (pp. 144–57).

Kulenkampff, *Kants Logik des ästhetischen Urteils* (pp. 97–111, especially 103–7, 1st edition) argues that the deduction merely repeats the analytic and that there is no way it could ever do more than just that.

Fricke, *Kants Theorie des reinen Geschmacksurteils*, offers, besides discussions of free play (pp. 38–71) and the *sensus communis* (pp. 161–76) a separate discussion of the deduction from section 38 (pp. 151–60).

5

Fine Art, Nature, and Genius

Fine Art and Why It Must Seem like Nature

Going to a museum is very different from taking a walk in a forest. Looking at a painting by Edvard Munch or a Chinese vase from the Ming Dynasty is very different from looking at a flower that happens to grow on the wayside, and listening to a fugue by Bach is different from listening to the singing of a bird. We know that these are works of art and that whoever created them had certain skills and a purpose in mind. They were intended to be works of art. The artist had a concept of what he or she was doing, and we who see or hear the result are aware of this. Now, this raises certain problems in Kant's account of beauty, because, according to Kant, no **concepts** should determine our judgment of taste. We are thus faced with a question: to what degree or in what way could concepts possibly be involved in beautiful art?

To appreciate a painting by Munch appropriately, we need to understand the symbols he employed. To know what is going on in a fugue, we need to know something about themes, variations, and counterpoint. Otherwise, how can we make sure that we appreciate the music appropriately, i.e. that our judgment of taste does not miss the point? Kant demands that a liking for the beautiful be without interest and that no perfection or any other kind of objective **purposiveness** play a decisive role in a judgment of taste. But in creating works of art, artists are usually pursuing certain interests by which they continually judge their progress during the process of creation, of bringing the work into existence. To this end, they have to learn and to develop certain techniques and skills, and they make plans, more or less detailed, before beginning to work, or while engaged in work. They try something out and see how it fits. They often modify their plans as they go along. And they also want their works to please or at least to be appreciated, be it by themselves or by others. All these activities on the part of the artist make use of aims and purposes, which, in one way or another, become part of the result, i.e. the piece of art.

Now, given the fact that the artist has certain **purposes** in mind, do we have to abstract from the artist's intentions and ideas so that our judgment of taste will be free from conceptual determinations? And, if so, do we then still judge the object *as art*?

It may well be that Kant was not a connoisseur of art. But he certainly was aware of the fact that there is a tension between rules and freedom when it comes to objects of art. To explain this phenomenon, the tension and the apparent contradiction, he notes that fine art looks like nature: "In a product of art one must be aware that it is art, and not nature; yet the purposiveness in its **form** must still seem to be as free from all constraint by arbitrary rules as if it were a mere product of nature" (section 45, 306). Even though we may know much about Munch and his symbolism, or about Bach and the structure of his fugues, and even though such knowledge may even be necessary to appreciate the works appropriately or correctly, there still must be room for some kind of purposiveness that is "free from all constraint by arbitrary rules as if it were a mere product of nature." Without this kind of freedom, there would be only rules and no room for beauty. Such purposiveness must be truly subjective and not a hidden objective purposiveness. Subjective purposiveness must be irreducible and real. It must not just appear to be subjective due to a lack of understanding on the part of the person making the judgment of taste. There must not be the possibility that a closer look and further analyses reveal that what seemed at first to be a "purposiveness without purpose" later reveals itself to be a "purposiveness with purpose" once we know the rules and purposes that guided the artist and have better scientific insights into the workings of the mind. Even though we are aware of certain rules and purposes involved in the production of works of art, such works must provide enough *room* for aesthetic contemplation *beyond* those conceptual constraints.

Although aesthetic contemplation must sometimes take certain concepts into account, it must *also*, I would suggest, in some essential respect *surpass* and *go beyond* them. Only then is it possible for our judgment of taste to be based on purposiveness without purpose, as we find it in the case of the beauty of nature, and still be about a work of art as such. We have to be aware of the relevant concepts (to know that it is an object of art), but we also have to go beyond these concepts and must not be bound by them (to experience the object as if it were given by nature): "Art can only be called beautiful if we are aware that it is art and yet it looks to us like nature" (section 45, 306).

The artist who creates an object of art *intends* it to be a work of art. This sounds innocent enough; however, understood within Kant's aesthetics this turns out to be a peculiar phenomenon. For the artist does not want to produce something that merely pleases the senses (that is, an object of a liking for the agreeable). Nor does the artist want to produce something that we like for its functionality or perfection (an object of a liking for the good). Rather, what the artist intends to create is something that we call beautiful, i.e. something that *"pleases in the mere judging"* (section 45, 306; Kant's emphasis). (Of course, there are problems with this: must art always be beautiful? Certainly not! But I do not want to get into a discussion of this here. I just would like to note that I think Kant's theory of free play and purposiveness can, with appropriate modifications, still be very useful to explain art that is *not* supposed to be beautiful. We will say a little more about this in the section "Can Kant's Aesthetics Account for the Ugly?" in chapter 7.) What Kant means by this can only be understood in the light of section 9, where he argued that a certain kind of "judging" precedes the liking for the beautiful. This judging is essentially the free play of the **faculties** in which we find the object suitable for this very play. The work of art must provide room for such play. It must be suitable for it by providing a good basis for discovering various kinds of purposiveness without a purpose. Beyond all the rules that went into its production, there must be possibilities for different perspectives from which to view the object and different possible combinations of such perspectives, which we enjoy playing with and which we find purposive beyond the determination of the rules that went into the production of the work of art. We may even play with those rules themselves. A work of art must create exactly such possibilities. The structures of the mind (the free play and its various internal and enlivening ways of purposiveness) that underlie a judgment of taste, explain the fact that art looks like nature: "The purposiveness in the product of beautiful art, although it is certainly intentional, must nevertheless not seem intentional; i.e., beautiful art must be regarded as nature, although of course one is aware of it as art" (section 45, 306–7).

The artist's intention to create a piece of art is, in a certain sense, a peculiar phenomenon. It is peculiar because the artist has to produce a work that provides substance and space beyond any rules and academic forms, an open space that we enjoy filling, so to speak, with the free play of our faculties. But how can an artist produce such a space? There cannot be any rules that determine the procedure for creating such free space. Hence the artist creates something that in a certain sense goes beyond his or her own skills and understanding, i.e. beyond those skills that consist in following certain rules and that can be taught and learned. It is at this very point that Kant has to introduce his notion of "genius."

Further reading

Zammito, *The Genesis of Kant's "Critique of Judgment,"* pp. 124–47, discusses Kant's philosophy of art in 1788, emphasizing its development and the historical background. Good introduction.

Allison, *Kant's Theory of Taste*, pp. 271–301, discusses the compatibility of art and genius with Kant's main theory of taste.

Crawford, *Kant's Aesthetic Theory*, devotes the last chapter to appreciation, creativity, and art criticism.

Guyer has a chapter, entitled "Nature, Art, and Autonomy" in his book *Kant and the Experience*, pp. 229–74, in which he demonstrates the "underlying modernity of Kant's apparently old-fashioned preference for nature over art." Also contains a discussion of the views of several contemporaries of Kant.

Kemal, *Kant and Fine Art*, arrives at the contrary conclusion: fine art is to be preferred over nature, because the link to morality is intrinsic to art whereas it is merely extrinsic in the case of nature. Guyer has criticized this conclusion in a postscript to the above-mentioned chapter, pp. 271–4. Kemal also has some sections on art in his book *Kant's Aesthetic Theory*, pp. 135–51, stressing the relevance of culture and social community.

Gaiger, "Constraints and Conventions: Kant and Greenberg on Aesthetic Judgment," discusses the writings and seminars of twentieth-century art critique Greenberg, who often referred to Kant. Topics include the form- and content-based approaches to art, the relevance of reflective self-criticism, and the relevance of knowledge of media and conventions in art (where the empirical and the transcendental part company).

McCloskey, *Kant's Aesthetic*, pp. 105–47, offers an introductory reading of passages on fine art with an emphasis on aesthetic **ideas**, dependent beauty, and universal communicability; she discusses examples from Pushkin and Shakespeare, and (which is maybe the most interesting part) confronts Kant's philosophy of art with the expressionist theory of Collingwood, pointing out the superiority of Kant's theory over the latter.

Kivy, "Kant and the *Affektenlehre*," discusses Kant's treatment of music, asking whether Kant said something original about its emotive character. He argues that Kant missed the opportunity to apply his theory of aesthetic ideas to music, and that this was probably due to the fact that he was ignorant of music as art.

Weatherston, "Kant's Assessment of Music," discusses composition, free and adherent beauty, and aesthetic ideas with respect to music. He shows that it was Kant's lack of appreciation and lack of understanding, especially regarding composition, pitch, and timbre, that led to his low estimation of music.

Menzer, *Kants Ästhetik in ihrer Entwicklung*, draws from many otherwise hard-to-find sources, such as lecture notes of Kant's students and notes by Kant himself, to give insight into the development of Kant's aesthetics. Here we find a detailed picture of the young Kant's knowledge and opinions regarding literature and poetry (pp. 1–23), Kant's classification of fine arts (pp. 169–74), the beauty of art and nature (pp. 174–80), and his ideas of aesthetic education (pp. 187–96).

Kuypers, *Kants Kunsttheorie und die Einheit der Kritik der Urteilskraft*, is a full-length study on Kant's theory of art, offering several sections on the third *Critique* as a whole and as a bridge between the first and the second *Critiques*.

Basch, *Essai critique sur l'esthetétique de Kant*, has a chapter, pp. 401–99, on art, the artist, and the arts. Many examples, detailed, critical, and original.

Kaulbach, *Ästhetische Welterkenntnis bei Kant*, has a section on art, pp. 232–62, discussing the production of works of art, genius, rules in the arts and the sciences. Many examples, reconstructive, not technical.

Genius and Taste

Viewed within Kant's aesthetics, the phenomenon of the beauty of art makes us aware of a certain problem. Simply put, the beauty of art must be at the same time with and without rules. We will see that a more finely tuned picture based on Kant's notion of genius provides the solution to this apparent contradiction.

On the one hand, a work of art is not an object of nature but a man-made thing, something that was produced under the influence of certain rules, the rules that lie at the basis of skills, purposes, intentions, deliberations, and whole traditions of artistic practice. On the other hand, a work of art is something that we find beautiful – at least usually, and this judging it to be beautiful must, according to Kant's theory, be independent of rules. Hence the rules that went into the production of the work of art must somehow disappear, so to speak, in the free play that underlies the liking for the beautiful. These rules should not play a decisive role in this free play. At least the rules should not hinder it. The problem now is that, on the one hand, we are aware of the rules when we contemplate and understand a work of art as a work of art, and, on the other hand, we like the work of art in a way that is free from any constraints of those rules. Whoever has produced a work of art, therefore, must have produced something that goes beyond his or her understanding and makes room for free play and contemplation. It is at this point that Kant introduces his notion of genius.

According to Kant, "Genius is the inborn predisposition of the mind (*ingenium*) through which nature gives the rule to art" (section 46, 307). This says at least three things. First, genius is an "inborn mental predisposition," a gift, something that cannot be learned. Second, genius is something "through" which nature gives rules. Somehow, nature makes use of genius, and the genius, i.e. someone who has genius, does not fully understand what was going on when the work of art was produced. A genius cannot fully explain how the work was produced, where the ideas came from, and why it was that those ideas and not others occurred to him or her and went into the work of art. Other ideas might have occurred to the artist, and the result would then have been different. Kant simply says that it is "nature" that works through the artist. Third, rules are somehow *given* to art: Nature, "through" genius, "gives the rule to art." All this sounds rather metaphorical, poetic, or abstract, and we have to see what exactly Kant wants to say here.

There are no rules and proofs to decide what is beautiful and what is not. Works of art are, insofar as we find them beautiful, subject to this condition as well. Nor, therefore, can there be rules of *production* of beautiful art, because such rules would turn into criteria for judging what is beautiful and what is not. This explains why a genius cannot fully explain and comprehend what he or she has produced. But this does not explain why we think certain people have genius and others do not. Nor does it explain how a genius goes about his or her work, or how nature works through genius.

If we find beauty in a work of art, we often wonder how the artist did it, how the artist was able to bring the object into existence. We do not believe that this was mere chance, and nor do we think that it is all only a question of having the right skills, skills that anyone can acquire through learning, skills that can be learned according to rules. Furthermore, we take certain pieces of art as models for imitation and inspiration. Such pieces of art have not been created by means of merely following rules. It is, rather, the other way around: the individual work of art seems to create, or instantiate, a new rule, or at least something that seems to be a new rule. Other artists try to learn from masterpieces as if they could read the rules of creation from them; however, Kant thinks that a piece of art is an *exemplar* and not just an example. It is an exemplar, because it seems to live on its own and to speak to us. It opens new horizons and does not follow from rules. A world of art comes into existence first. It is only later that it sometimes seems to us as if it were produced according to a rule.

Still, we wonder how the artist did it, and Kant still needs to explain what he means by saying that "nature gives the rule to art" and that nature does so "through" a genius. What kind of source of inspiration is "nature" here? And what is the "rule" that flows from it?

Before we look into what Kant has to offer by way of an explanation here, we should ask ourselves what kind of answer to the above questions we can reasonably expect to receive. Whatever the source of inspiration turns out to be, we should not expect it to be something predictable. In other words, given a description of it, we should not be able to predict what will flow from this source. We should not expect something as explicit as a mathematical function $f(x)$ that allows us to compute the value y for any argument x. Otherwise, we would be looking for rules of genius and rules of beauty. Nevertheless, we are entitled to expect something more than a dark metaphysical entity, something better than some *deus ex machina* that solves all problems at the last minute.

At this point, we can return to the question of what is meant by "nature" when Kant says that nature gives the rule to art. Is it the nature we find surrounding us, which is studied by physics, or is it something in us, something human? For Kant it is the latter: The "nature in the subject (and by means of the disposition [attunement, *Stimmung*] of its faculties) must give the rule to art" (section 46, 307). As it was a harmonious relationship between **imagination** and **understanding** in free play that gave substance to the concept of taste, so it is the "disposition of its [the judging subject's] faculties" that makes genius possible. That is, both taste and genius are explained in terms of imagination and understanding, their functions, and the harmonious relationships they engage in.

A natural question to ask with respect to taste and genius is which one comes first and is the fundamental one? There are two facts one should be aware of here. First, in the third *Critique*, Kant begins with an analysis of taste and only much later introduces the notions of fine art and genius. Secondly, the notion of genius is introduced to explain fine art and not taste. So it may seem that the notion of genius is only an appendix to taste and fine art. But reading through sections 46–50, the notion of genius comes to play a larger and larger role, and one becomes more and more aware of the importance of the notion of genius for Kant's aesthetics. A closer look at the phenomenon of artistic creation shows us that genius and taste are interwoven. A genius certainly has taste. A genius pays attention to what he or she is doing. The artist almost continuously evaluates his or her work during the process of creation by making judgments of taste, although these judgments do not have to be consciously or even explicitly made. The artist engages in a free play of his faculties while creating the work of art, stops or makes changes when finding the play to be disharmonious, and otherwise goes on, more or less encouraged by those continuous aesthetic evaluations on the way. This is a pre-cognitive state, and when the artist makes, explicit or not, judgments of taste in the process of creation, the satisfaction he or she feels in making these judgments is disinterested.

Similarly, when we make a judgment of taste, be it about an object of nature or an object of art, we play with various features of the object, rearranging and recreating them. We ourselves play the role of an artist, and possibly even that of a genius. We see that taste and genius go back to the same source. Hence Kant is not at all ill-guided when he tries to base both taste and genius on the same grounds, namely a certain relationship between our faculties of **cognition**. But to give more substance to this relationship in the case of the genius – after all, not every person who has taste and is an artist is a genius – Kant introduces the notion of aesthetic **ideas**. Only the genius, Kant explains, is able to bring something into the work of art that gives us much to think about and enlarges our minds.

Kant gave substance to the notion of a free play of our faculties underlying a judgment of taste by introducing the principle of purposiveness. Similarly, the relationship of the faculties, as we find it in the mind of a genius creating a work of fine art, is made more explicit by introducing the notion of aesthetic ideas. This then is what Kant does at this point in the development of the third *Critique*.

Further reading

Schlapp, *Kants Lehre vom Genie und die Entstehung der Kritik der Urteilskraft*, is still the richest source of material on the development of Kant's theory of genius.

Tonelli, "Kant's Early Theory of Genius," is a sequence of two papers focusing on the early Kant between 1770 and 1779. Tonelli reconstructs the development of Kant's ideas on genius and traces their sources in Kant's cultural background. He draws from many sources and discusses expressions such as "spirit" (*Geist*), "mind" (*Gemüt*), "talent," "rule," "intelligence" (*Kopf*), "vivification" (*Belebung*), "wit" (*Witz*), and others, and how they were used at the time. At the end he discusses a "four-step process of genial invention." A rich historical account.

Bäumler, *Das Irrationalitätsproblem*, offers a great variety of material and ideas on taste, feeling and genius in eighteenth-century Europe. It has a section on imagination, wit, and genius and the distinction between *ingenium* and *acumen* (pp. 141–66); another section on the logic of invention (pp. 170–87); and one on the *analogon rationis* (pp. 188–97).

Menzer, *Kants Ästhetik in ihrer Entwicklung*, gives an account of the development of Kant's ideas about genius before the first *Critique* (pp. 83–9) and a critical assessment of Kant's theory of genius (pp. 163–9). See also the entry on this book by Menzer in the further reading section on p. 97.

Gould, "The Audience of Originality: Kant and Wordsworth on the Reception of Genius," draws parallels between these two quite different and not in any obvious way connected writers, an undertaking that is already interesting because of its idiosyncratic nature.

Genius and Aesthetic Ideas

A genius must have taste, but that alone is not enough. A genius must also have "spirit" (*Geist*). What he creates is not only beautiful; it also animates our faculties, enlarges our minds, and gives us much to think about. It is in his discussion of genius that Kant introduces the notion of "aesthetic ideas" (section 49) to give more substance to his notion of genius and also to suggest connections between beauty and morality that go beyond what mere analysis can reveal, touching as they do on the realm of the **supersensible**.

An aesthetic idea is a "**representation** of the imagination that occasions much thinking though without it being possible for any determinate thought, i.e., concept, to be adequate to it, which, consequently, no language fully attains or can make *intelligible*" (section 49, 314). A work of art is a representation of the imagination, it is given in **intuition**, and it is something we can perceive and contemplate for a long time. There seems to be an infinite richness of material that escapes any attempt of expression in a conceptual and exhaustive way. Even a poem, although written in words and thus being a product of language, seems to go beyond language – that is, ordinary, conceptually determinate, and (in that sense) "intelligible" language (see quote above).

Kant gives the example of a poet, who "ventures to make sensible rational ideas of invisible beings, the kingdom of the blessed, the kingdom of hell, eternity, creation, etc., as well as to make that of which there are examples in experience, e.g., death, envy, and all sorts of vices, as well as love, fame, etc., sensible beyond the limits of experience, with a completeness that goes beyond anything of which there is an example in nature" (section 49, 314). An aesthetic idea works, so to speak, by means of "supplementary representations" (*Nebenvorstellungen*) and "aesthetic attributes" (section 49, 315). An empirical object is presented to our senses so that it may evoke certain rational ideas in us which the artist is aiming at. The object, or parts or aspects of it, can help to make the idea more vivid in our mind. They give additional support to the otherwise abstract idea and serve as "aesthetic attributes." Kant gives the following example: "Jupiter's eagle, with the lightning in its claws, is an attribute of the powerful king of heaven" (section 49, 315). The eagle with the lightning in its claw is an object of the senses, and it can serve as a "supplementary representation" and an "aesthetic attribute" of an abstract idea, namely the rational idea of the powerful king of heaven, i.e. God. The sharp eye of the eagle, the fact that he can overlook his territory from above and that he can strike at any moment, all these are images and characteristics that we usually associate with an eagle and that we carry over, so to speak, to our concept of the "powerful king of heaven." We make use of such images, because they give the imagination cause "to spread itself over a multitude of related representations [*verwandte Vorstellungen*], which let one think more than one can express in a concept determined by words" (section 49, 315). This "multitude of related representations" cannot be fully grasped or even surveyed. It is not fixed or determined. Instead, the representations spread – to borrow a Wittgensteinian expression – like "family resemblances" that do not follow rules but create new ones. That is, such representations make us recall or create other representations, one after another, whole chains of images and concepts, so that one is linked to the next, but without an overall rule that would determine the next step or link.

The more remote a concept from reality, the more difficult it becomes to give an example of it. I can *show* you a tree and a table. The anatomist "*demonstrates* the human eye when he makes the concept that he has previously expounded discursively intuitable by means of the dissection of this organ" (section 57, remark I, 343). Similarly, we can demonstrate the Pythagorean theorem geometrically on a piece of paper; however, this becomes more difficult in algebra and higher mathematics, where we increasingly rely on symbols and abstract concepts. Furthermore, I have to explain even more to show what "death, envy, and all sorts of vices," or the "kingdom of hell, eternity, creation, etc." are (section 49, 314). Finally, regarding God, free will, and morality, it may seem utterly impossible to find an appropriate visualization, such that one may not even want to try to find a corresponding image or any other way of representing and exhibiting such an idea in intuition (*Anschauung*). The genius can help with this by offering aesthetic ideas in works of art. Such ideas are intuitions for which no adequate concept can be found, but that make us reflect and search for one. We thus have an intuition which we can "hold on to" as we go through the process of aesthetic reflection. The image of the eagle, for example, provides such an intuition. And this intuition helps us discover more and ever more thoughts in relation to the abstract concept the artist wants to show and communicate to us, such as that of God, immortality, or virtue.

By introducing aesthetic ideas, Kant puts beauty and genius into a wider context that goes beyond mere aesthetics. He writes: "One readily sees that it [an aesthetic idea] is the counterpart (pendant) of an idea of reason, which is, conversely, a concept to which no intuition (representation of the imagination) can be adequate" (section 49, 314). This connects aesthetics to the first and the second *Critiques*, since typical ideas of reason are the ideas of God, freedom, immortality, and morality, which are presupposed by metaphysics and moral science. A genius transcends the physical and creates, "as it were, another nature" (ibid.). What Kant has in mind here is humanity and our moral nature. Accordingly, he later on relates aesthetic ideas, genius, and beauty to morality. He does so in the **Dialectic**, in the remarks to section 57, and in section 59. His discussion of the relations between beauty, genius, aesthetic ideas, and ideas of reason, are speculative in character. These relations are not constitutive parts of the moments of a judgment of taste. They do not belong to the elements of a judgment of taste. Instead, they belong to a wider and more speculative field and are dealt with in the Dialectic, where they become the central topic. Although Kant is very much interested in issues of morality and possible connections between beauty and morality, he nevertheless keeps these issues out of the Analytic, and he does so for a good reason. In the Analytic, he wants to explain the phenomenon of beauty, which should be independent of morality. Only after having shown that beauty can stand on its own feet, so to speak, does he draw connections between morality and beauty. Only in this way is it possible to see how beauty can give support to morality.

Aesthetic ideas are counterparts of the ideas of reason. Both lack what the other abounds in. Both are incomplete and make us strive for completeness. Both make us touch on the "supersensible." The supersensible (*das Übersinnliche*) transcends our capacities of perception as well as of cognition. We can think it, but we cannot fully grasp and comprehend it. There is no (theoretical) cognition of it. The first *Critique* showed us the "supersensible substratum of (all) appearances" (section 57, 341; and remark I, 343), the second the "supersensible substratum of humanity" (section 57, 340), the "indeterminate idea of the super-sensible in us" (section 57, 341), and the "idea of transcendental freedom" (section 57, remark I, 343). Now, in the third *Critique*, we see that a genius creates a work of art that goes beyond mere physical nature and that can makes us realize the supersensible in us. The aesthetic idea in the work of art can function as a counterpart to ideas of reason and hence assist us in entertaining such ideas of reason. A piece of music or a painting can show us something that makes us realize certain features of our human and moral nature.

But already mere beauty, be it beauty of nature or beauty of art, has a rela-tionship to morality, because the free play of our faculties, and the subjective pur-posiveness that we find in ourselves in relation to nature around us, together tell us that we fit into nature in a way that goes beyond the physical. We find that we can be autonomous. In a judgment of taste, "the power of judgment . . . gives the law to itself, just as reason does with regard to the faculty of desire" (section 59, 353; "reason" here means "practical reason", reason in the context of moral-ity). Beauty and morality thus find a common ground "in which the theoretical faculty [for cognition] is combined with the practical [in matters of morality]" (ibid.). There are certain features of our faculty of judgment (in its reflective function) that are common to the judgment of taste and moral judgments, such as reflection about others and how they might feel in our position. And it is for this reason that we find similar and even isomorphic structures in beauty and morality. Such a structural isomorphism is a case of what Kant calls "symbol-ism." He now can speak of "beauty as a symbol of morality" (*Von der Schönheit als Symbol der Sittlichkeit*, title of section 59). In fact, Kant even claims that "the beautiful is *the* symbol of the morally good" (later, in the middle of section 59, 353), thereby giving taste and the judgment of taste a role that cannot be taken by anything else. More will be said about this in our section "Beauty as the Symbol of Morality" in chapter 6.

Further reading

Basch, *Essai critique sur l'esthétique de Kant*, has a section (pp. 519–52) on aesthetic ideas and genius, drawing connections between aesthetic ideas and the thing in itself.

Gibbons, *Kant's Theory of Imagination*, has a chapter on "imagination and reflective judg-ment" (pp. 79–124), with subsections on the ideals, ideas, genius, fine art, rules and exemplarity, focusing on the role of imagination and drawing connections with the first *Critique*.

Lüthe, "Kants Lehre von den Ästhetischen Ideen," investigates Kant's theory of aesthetic ideas, which he thinks has been too much overlooked. He argues that they are essen-tial not only in contemplation of art (*Rezeptionsästhetik*) but also in production of works of art (*Produktionsästhetik*); that they not only provide an intuition for rational ideas (as is usually said) but also enrich the empirical realm as such (*assoziative Erweiterung der sinnlichen Fülle der Erfahrung*); that they help us (our *Geist*) not only to extend but also to focus, limit, and "shape" our associations (leading to *gestaltete Erlebnisfülle*).

Nuyen, "The Kantian Theory of Metaphor," discusses the symbolic process from section 59 and shows how it creates metaphorical meaning and aesthetic ideas (in contrast with Davidson's view that there is no metaphorical meaning in addition to literal meaning).

Verhaegh, "The Truth of the Beautiful in the *Critique of Judgment*," questions the separation of aesthetics and truth. Making use of Davidson's theory of metaphor to point out certain enhancements in aesthetic judgments, he argues that natural beauty is an expression of aesthetic ideas.

Savile, *Aesthetic Reconstructions*, pp. 168–85, discusses Kant's notion of aesthetic ideas, especially with respect to the "aesthetic ought," our duty to acquire taste. Savile's argumentation is reconstructive and analytic in style, relatively free of Kantian terminology.

Kivy, "Kant and the *Affektenlehre*": see the further reading at the end of the first section of this chapter on p. 97.

6

Beyond Beauty

The Sublime

The sublime is more complex than the beautiful in at least two ways. First, the **judgment** about the sublime involves a two-step structure (involving a negation) that is foreign to the beautiful. Furthermore, there is a distinction between what Kant calls the "mathematical" sublime, which has an analogue in his conception of the beautiful, and the "dynamical" sublime, which has no such analogue. But in spite of this structural complexity and its novelty, and also in spite of the general interest in the sublime during Kant's time, he nevertheless calls "the theory of the sublime" a "mere appendix to the aesthetic judging of the **purposiveness** of nature" (section 23, 246). Why there is such a distinction into mathematical and dynamical sublime and why the theory of the sublime is a mere appendix to Kant's aesthetic theory are questions that have no obvious answers in the text and that we shall try to answer here. But first we have to introduce Kant's theory of the sublime.

As typical examples of what we call sublime, Kant gives the following: "the wide ocean, enraged by storms" (245), the pyramids in Egypt and "St Peter's in Rome" (252), "shapeless mountain masses towering above one another in wild disorder with their pyramids of ice" and "the dark and raging sea" (256), "bold, overhanging, as it were threatening cliffs, thunder clouds towering up into the heavens, bringing with them flashes of lightning and crashes of thunder, volcanoes with their all-destroying violence, hurricanes with the devastation they leave behind, the boundless ocean set into rage, a lofty waterfall on a mighty river" (261), "mountain ranges towering to the heavens, deep ravines and the raging torrents in them, deeply shadowed wastelands" (269), and, finally, "the starry heavens" above us (270). Except for the pyramids and St Peter's dome, all of these are phenomena of nature. All are large, mighty, and overwhelming. They exceed our power of **imagination** by their sheer size and force. They are almost frightening, and they make us aware of our physical limitations in comparison with them.

That we call such objects "sublime" is due to their size and force, and to the fact that they appear "to be contrapurposive for our **power of judgment**, unsuitable for our **faculty** of presentation, and as it were doing violence to our imagination" (245). We have problems apprehending and comprehending such objects in one **intuition** and we feel "pushed almost to the point of the inadequacy of our faculty of imagination" (253), which "demonstrates its limits and inadequacy" (257). What is required (to make judgments about the sublime) in addition to these merely "negative abilities" of imagination and **sensibility** are certain positive aspects of **reason** connected with a demand for totality. I will now give a long list, but this will provide a good picture of what Kant has in mind regarding the sublime:

- a "voice of reason, which requires *totality*" (254);
- the ability "to think" of something "as a whole" which "indicates a faculty of the mind which *surpasses* every standard of sense" (254);
- a "vocation for adequately realizing" the "idea of the comprehension of every appearance that may be given to us into the intuition of a *whole*," a vocation for realizing "the presentation of the *idea of reason*" (257);
- an "enlargement of the mind which feels itself empowered to *overstep* the limits of sensibility from another (practical) point of view" (255);
- the "*idea of humanity* in our subject" and the "*substitution* of a respect for the object instead of" the respect for that idea (257);
- our "capacity for *judging ourselves as independent*" of outward nature and to "regard those things . . . (goods, health and life) as trivial" (261); and, finally,
- the ability of our mind to "make palpable to itself the sublimity of its own *vocation* even over nature" (262).

We can see that for Kant the sublime – or rather a judgment about it – has a twofold structure, which includes a negative and a positive aspect. The first aspect is unpleasant and contrapurposive (too big, too forceful) for the operation of the imagination, whereas the second aspect (the discovery of the sublime in us) is pleasant and purposive for reason and our moral vocation as a human being.

From a higher perspective we can say that "**ideas** of reason . . . [are] provoked and called to mind precisely by this inadequacy" of what is given to our senses (245), and that "the mind is incited to abandon sensibility and to occupy itself with ideas that contain a higher purposiveness" (246). On a more basic level, we can say that, as a phenomenon, the sublime makes itself known through a "feeling of a momentary inhibition of the vital powers and the immediately following and all the more powerful outpouring of them" (245).

Having now introduced his notion of the sublime, we are in a better position to ask what Kant understands by the "*mathematical*" and the "*dynamical*" sublime and why he makes such a distinction in the first place. This is not going to be an easy matter. In the first *Critique*, Kant introduces two distinctions, one between mathematical and dynamical syntheses (A 160/B 199), the other between mathematical and dynamical **principles** (A 162/B 201). In a footnote to his discussion of the latter distinction, added in the B-edition of 1787, Kant explains that "all combination" (*conjunctio*) is either "composition" (*Zusammensetzung, compositio*) of homogeneous parts that do not necessarily belong together, or it is "connection" (*Verknüpfung, nexus*) of heterogeneous parts that necessarily belong to one another (B 201). So there are two kinds of combination: composition and connection; and there are two criteria to distinguish between the two: homogeneity and necessity. A composition is homogeneous and not necessary, whereas a connection is just the opposite: not homogeneous but necessary.

An example of the former kind is the composition of "the two triangles into which a square is divided by its diagonal" (B 201, footnote). These two triangles make up a square and they are homogeneous parts in space and can therefore be treated mathematically (making use of Cartesian coordinates). Furthermore, they just happen to be side by side (forming a square). They could be anywhere (within a Cartesian coordinate system; there are linear transformations that are isomorphisms and that could move either of the two triangles around in space without changing its inner structure). Therefore they do not necessarily belong together.

Examples of connections are the connection between cause and effect and the connection between substance and accident. Here the two parts are heterogeneous (a cause is essentially different from its effect, and so is a substance from its accidents). But at the same time they are necessarily connected with each other (every cause has its effect and every substance its accidents).

We should keep all this in mind (from the first *Critique*) – the two kinds of combination, the two criteria (homogeneity and necessity), and the examples (triangle, cause and effect, substance and accident) – when we now turn back to Kant's treatment of the sublime, especially to his distinction between the mathematical and the dynamical sublime (in the third *Critique*).

Let us look at the mathematical aspect first. In a judgment about the sublime, the imagination tries to apprehend and comprehend an intuitively given object as a whole. Imagination has to "compose" the parts into a whole. These parts are given in time and space and therefore inherit certain mathematical properties from time and space, such as divisibility, dimensionality, and homogeneity. In mathematics, one says that a manifold is "homogeneous" if it "looks locally the same" everywhere, that is, if for any two points of the manifold, there is a (local) neighborhood for one point, and another neighborhood for the other point, such that these two neighborhoods are "isomorphic" (i.e., have the same properties in the mathematical theory one is presupposing, and are thus mathematically indistinguishable).

Now time and space are homogeneous in that sense. There is also no logical or causal connection between any parts in them, such as ground and consequence or cause and effect, that would establish any necessary connections between any of its parts. Also things *in* time and space can therefore be regarded as "homogeneous" and as "not necessarily" belonging together. They inherit these properties (from time and space). Now Kant wants to say that there is going to be a problem with the composition of such parts (those things in time and space), or rather of our *perceptual* composition of them. This is going to be not a logical but an "intuitive" problem: a problem of intuition (*Anschauung*).

If we regard the composition as logical (*comprehensio logica*), there is no problem, since "the logical estimation of magnitude proceeds unhindered to infinity" (section 26, 254). We can use a basic unit (the height of a tree, of a mountain, or the diameter of the earth) and then apply numbers to express the given magnitude. In this way we are not overwhelmed by the size of the objects. We use numbers to express the size and there is no problem in coming up with big numbers. On the other hand, the basic measure used in such a mathematical and logical composition is something we must "immediately grasp . . . in an intuition" (the height of a tree, for example), and therefore "in the end all estimation of the magnitude of objects of nature is aesthetic" (251) – 'aesthetic' in the old (Greek) sense of being related to perception (*aesthesis*).

Now, so Kant argues, there is a limit to how large such a basic measure can be and still be an aesthetic one, i.e. grasped in a single intuition. As apprehension advances, the ability of our imagination to hold the parts of what we imagine (the parts of the tree) together "soon reaches its maximum" (252). Thus, "for the aesthetic estimation of magnitude there certainly is a greatest" unit of measure (which "brings with it the idea of the sublime," 251). And in any case, being face to face with the object, being exposed to it in an immediate way, it is our senses that are overwhelmed, and against this it does not help to try to do mathematics (adding up pieces and parcels of perception).

We thus find the mathematically sublime in the mere size of objects and in the aesthetic composition of their parts that are regarded as homogeneous and not necessarily connected. Like the two triangles in a square, the lengths of the parts of the tree, the first meter of the trunk, the second meter, etc., are homogeneous but not necessarily connected. This aesthetic composition through mere imagination, without the concept of a number, comes, Kant argues, to its limits and thus "demonstrates a faculty of the mind that surpasses every measure of the senses" (250). This faculty is reason (not practical, but theoretical reason), because it has the ability to demand "absolute totality" (250) and to think "the given infinite" (254). Although what we take in through the senses can surpass our ability to imagine it in all detail and in its full size, reason tells us that it is all out there.

This leads us to the dynamically sublime. Keeping in mind what we have quoted above from the first *Critique*, we may see that the dynamically sublime depends on a synthesis of *heterogeneous* parts that *necessarily* belong to one another. At the beginning of his discussion of the dynamically sublime, Kant gives the following definition: "Nature considered in aesthetic judgment as a power that has no dominion over us is dynamically sublime" (section 28, 260). Nature's power and the momentary fear it arouses in us make us look for something that we can hold against this power. As we are physically no match for the forces of nature, we shift the perspective and find a very different and "heterogeneous" element in our inner human nature, an element that we think of as greater and more powerful than nature around us. This element is the idea of humanity and morality, which we discover in ourselves as persons. In this respect we are, so to speak, untouchable. The forces of outer nature (objects in time and space) do not reach into our inner nature (the idea of humanity and morality in us, something not in time and space). Thus we connect two "heterogeneous" elements in a judgment about the sublime: the size and power of outer nature on the one hand, and the idea of (theoretical) absolute totality and (practical) humanity and morality in us on the other. The experience of our physical limitations triggers – we may even say *causes* – the experience of the sublime in us, and, in that sense, the two experiences are "necessarily" connected to each other. Our experience of the limitation causes our experience of the sublime, and the latter thus necessarily follows upon the former. From the above, we see that the twofold structure of the sublime fits, at least to some degree, the distinction between the mathematical and the dynamical as introduced in the first *Critique*. Thus, we can assert that Kant's twofold structure of the sublime in the third *Critique* is an extension of the two-part structure of syntheses and principles from the first *Critique*. This answers the first of our questions.

This still leaves us with the second question: Why did Kant think of the "theory of the sublime" as "a mere appendix to the aesthetic judging of the purposiveness of nature" (section 23, 246)? At least two explanations can be given here.

First, as was the case with the ugly, the sublime is more complex than the beautiful. It involves a negation. Therefore, it should be dealt with only after having completed the analysis of the (less complex) beautiful. This answers why the beautiful should be treated first and the sublime second, but not why the latter is a "mere appendix" to the former. But once this path has been taken and

the beautiful has been analyzed, the subjective principle of purposiveness will
have been successfully introduced and established, so that the analysis of the
sublime (and the ugly) will not be necessary any more – at least not with respect
to the establishment of this a priori principle of purposiveness, which, after all,
is Kant's main concern in his aesthetics, if not in the third *Critique* as a whole.

Second, the beautiful shows us that we *fit* into nature. When we find something beautiful, we discover that nature suits our capacity for a free play of imagination and **understanding**, that we can "feel at home" in nature. Beauty is a gift,
and the man of taste is a happy man, a *felix aestheticus*. Additionally, **teleology**
also shows us that nature suits our mind in its structure and its demand to find
order in nature. Thus, subjective (aesthetic) as well as objective (teleological) purposiveness reveal to us that we are part of nature. The sublime, by contrast,
pushes us out of (outer, physical) nature and instead forces us to look into ourselves and our inner nature. The purposiveness that we find in the sublime is
merely an indirect one, one based on a negative purposiveness. The outer object
is counterpurposive for our power of imagination, but this proves, in a second
step, to be purposive for our inner powers: practical reason, our capacity to
engage in moral reasoning.

Both the judgment about the ugly, which we will examine later in a separate
section, and the judgment about the sublime involve negation. But only the
latter involves reason, too. We already find the negative purposiveness of the
ugly within the domain of imagination and understanding, but the negative
purposiveness of the sublime leads us out of that domain and into the realm of
reason.

We have seen that the so-called "sublime objects" are contrapurposive for our
power of imagination, but that this in turn is purposive for reason. This distances
and even separates us from outer nature, and for that reason there is in the
sublime "so little that leads to particular objective principles and forms of nature
corresponding to these" (246), and the sublime "indicates nothing purposive in
nature itself, but only in the possible use of its intuitions to make palpable in ourselves a purposiveness that is entirely independent of nature" (ibid.). This latter
purposiveness we thus find, and create, within ourselves. It addresses the idea of
humanity in us and is "entirely independent of [outer, physical] nature." Thus,
if we think of the sublime as merely *indicating* something in us (our moral nature)
and as something to the discovery of which the outer, physical nature merely
serves as a trigger, and if we think that on the other hand the beautiful *establishes*
something *positive* in our relationship to outer nature, then the claim that Kant's
theory of the sublime is "merely an appendix to the aesthetic judging of the purposiveness of [this outer] nature" does make sense.

It is very likely that Kant wrote the section on the sublime rather late, when
most of the other parts of the third *Critique* were already finished. But pointing

this out certainly is not a good explanation for why he calls his discussion of the sublime a mere appendix.

Further reading

Crawford, "The Place of the Sublime in Kant's Aesthetic Theory," gives in the second part of his paper a nice introduction to the historical background, showing what the general mood and opinions were at that time and what Kant might have known from Longinus, Burnet, Addison, Burke, Hogarth, and many others. He also shows that most of the components of Kant's account of the sublime were already well known before him.

Zammito, *The Genesis of Kant's "Critique of Judgment,"* pp. 275–83, asks why Kant included his analysis of the sublime so late, when most of the third *Critique* was already written, and sees this in the light of a "cognitive" and an "ethical turn" that must have happened toward the end of composing the third *Critique*. Good introductory reading.

Coleman, *The Harmony of Reasons: A Study of Kant's Aesthetics*, presents the "ancestors" of the Kantian sublime (pp. 120–7), its "presuppositions" (pp. 85–108), and its "defects" (pp. 108–20). This is an exposition that draws from many sources, from Kant as well as others, philosophical and literary. Beautifully written, with many illustrations, and not at all technical.

Crowther, *The Kantian Sublime: From Morality to Art*, offers brief insights into the backgrounds from Addison and Burke, discussions of the connections to morality, reconstructions of Kantian ideas in general aesthetic terms, and applications to works of art.

Budd, "Delight . . . Part III: The Sublime in Nature," discusses the mathematically and the dynamically sublime, the feeling of the sublime, and the purity of the judgment about the sublime. Introductory, not technical.

Burnham, *An Introduction to Kant's "Critique of Judgment,"* has an introductory section on the sublime, pp. 88–105, offering detailed discussions of examples.

Allison, *Kant's Theory of Taste*, pp. 302–44, offers a thorough and detailed analysis of the sublime, focusing on the tension between the sublime as a mere "appendix" on the one hand and its being highly relevant for morality on the other.

Gibbons, *Kant's Theory of Imagination*, comments on the sublime against the background of Kant's epistemology and his notion of imagination (pp. 124–51).

Guyer, "Kant's Distinction between the Beautiful and the Sublime," offers detailed discussions of logical, linguistic, and epistemological aspects as compared with phenomenological and psychological ones, showing how Kant exploits these aspects instead of conflating them.

Lyotard, *Lessons on the Analytic of the Sublime*, is, as Lyotard modestly says, "a collection of lessons" and "a file of notes in preparation for the oral explication of the Analytic of the Sublime." But it certainly is much more than that. Not only does he make many new and stimulating connections with the other two *Critiques*, Lyotard is too much an original thinker himself to restrict his "lessons" to a close reading and allows himself to do creative and speculative philosophizing, which fortunately never loses sight of the text (even often being very sensitive to the German) and is helpful and thought provoking.

Kaulbach, *Ästhetische Welterkenntnis bei Kant*, has a section on the sublime, pp. 161–206, with many examples, much about Schiller and Goethe, subsections on the mathematically and the dynamically sublime. Expository, reconstructive, not technical.

Myskja, *The Sublime in Kant and Beckett*, applies Kant's theory of the sublime to works of literary art, such as Beckett's novel *Molloy*.

Beauty as the Symbol of Morality

There are two German words that are both translated by the English word "morality": *Sittlichkeit* and *Moralität*. But there is a difference between the two. *Moralität* goes "deeper": it is related to our free will, motivation, and moral laws. *Sittlichkeit*, on the other hand, is more on the surface. It is more about empirical and social phenomena of behavior, manner, politeness, and customs. It is more visible (not as visible as a house or a tree though; it requires some insight into culture to know what proper behavior is and to recognize it as such). We will see that we should keep these two apart, *Sittlichkeit* and *Moralität*, if we want to understand what Kant says about the relation between beauty and "morality." But already at this point we can guess that what we find beautiful is an object of the *senses* and therefore closer to *Sittlichkeit*, whereas the **grounds** for our judging it to be beautiful, grounds that go deeper, that are on the level of purposiveness and **reflection**, are closer to *Moralität*.

Kant relates beauty to morality in several places in the third *Critique*. One is at the end of section 17, when he connects the *ideal* of beauty with morality (*Ausdruck des Sittlichen*). We have already commented on this at the end of our section on free and dependent beauty in chapter 3. Another place is in section 42, entitled "On the intellectual interest in the beautiful." A third is in the Dialectic, where Kant devotes an entire section to the relation of beauty and morality: section 59. The title of this section already announces the kind of connection Kant has in mind: "On beauty as a symbol of morality [*Sittlichkeit*]."

In general, we can say that Kant wants beauty and morality (*Moralität*) to be understood as being "basically" independent of each other. Not only should each be dealt with separately, at least in a first attempt (in two separate *Critiques*, the second and the third), they should also be understood as being themselves independent of each other, i.e. as each having its *own* justifying grounds. The analogy works only on parts of these grounds. Kant argues that it is merely through an *analogy of reflection* that there is a connection between the two. This analogy is to be found mainly between certain ways of reflection that underlie our aesthetic and moral judgments. This is a fundamental but non-**determining** level – the

level of judgment in its general reflective function – and it is basically due to a
similarity on this level that there is an affinity between beauty and morality. But
this connection is not strong enough to guarantee a necessary implication in one
way or the other; i.e. a person of taste need not be morally good (*moralisch gut*),
or vice versa (first paragraph of section 42).

Some people, Kant observes, tend to think that it is "a sign of a good moral
character [*guter moralischer Charakter*] to take an interest in the beautiful in
general," be it beauty of nature or beauty of art, whereas others contradict them,
pointing out virtuosi of taste who are "usually vain, obstinate, and given to cor-
rupting passions" (section 42, 298). Both sides offer good grounds that speak in
favor of their opinions, but, strictly speaking, Kant argues, neither side is correct.
It is only 17 sections later, in section 59, that he gives an explanation for our inclination to draw such parallels between beauty and morality. He also explains there
why these can be parallels but nothing more that that. At this point, however, in
section 42, Kant takes the opportunity to point out a feature that is peculiar to
the beauty of nature and cannot be found in the beauty of art:

> I do assert that to take an immediate interest in the beauty of *nature* (not merely
> to have taste in order to judge it) is always a mark of a good soul, and that if this
> interest is habitual, it at least indicates a disposition of the mind that is favorable
> to the moral **feeling** [*moralisches Gefühl*], if it is gladly combined with the *viewing
> of nature*. (Section 42, 298–9; Kant's emphasis)

It is not mere taste as such, that is a "mark of a good soul," because we find taste
also in matters of fine art and Kant here stresses beauty of nature and not beauty
of art. This of course raises the question how art and morality might be related.
But the answer to this question has to be postponed, because at this point Kant
focuses on nature. He explains that we must have something else in addition to
good taste, namely a taste for the beauty of *nature* together with a readiness to
"view" (see above) nature as such, that is, to *respect* nature and to take a certain
interest in it: "Someone who . . . considers the beautiful shape of a wildflower, a
bird, an insect, etc., in order to marvel at it, to love it, and to be unwilling for it
to be entirely absent from nature, even though some harm might come to him
from it rather than there being any prospect of advantage to him from it, takes
an immediate and certainly intellectual interest in the beauty of nature" (section
42, 299). What is required is an awareness of the fact that the object we are contemplating is an object of nature: "the thought that nature has produced that
beauty must accompany the **intuition** and reflection" (299). We enjoy the song
of a nightingale and feel elevated by it. The song seems to "contain a language
that nature brings to us and that seems to have a higher meaning" (302). But all
this is destroyed if we find out that we have been deceived by "a mischievous lad
who knew how to imitate this song" (302).

The fact that nature has produced a vast multitude of objects that we find beautiful, as if they were made for us, makes us think that we somehow *fit* into nature. It seems to us as if this were a *gift* or blessing given to us by nature or by God. From the perspective of human autonomy, we might also say that it is not that nature does us a favor, but the other way around: we do nature a favor by finding it beautiful. But in any case, Kant suggests that this makes us think that ideas and higher purposes of our inner nature, like freedom and morality, may be realized in outer nature and society where human beings live together (*sittlich*) under moral laws (*moralisch*). Reason thus takes an interest in any sign or trace in nature that might indicate a bridge between freedom and nature.

> Since it . . . interests reason that the ideas (for which it produces an immediate interest in the moral feeling [*moralisches Gefühl*]) also have objective reality, i.e., that nature should at least show some trace or give a sign that it contains in itself some sort of ground for assuming a lawful correspondence of its products with our satisfaction that is independent of all interest . . . reason must take an interest in every manifestation in nature of a correspondence similar to this; consequently the mind cannot reflect on the beauty of *nature* without finding itself at the same time to be interested in it. Because of this affinity, however, this interest is moral [*moralisch*], and he who takes such an interest in the beautiful in nature can do so only insofar as he has already firmly established his interest in the morally good [*am Sittlich-Guten*]. We thus have cause at least to suspect a predisposition to a good moral disposition [*moralische Gesinnung*] in one who is immediately interested in the beauty of nature. (Section 42, 300–1; Kant's emphasis)

Kant suggests that we must already have been exposed to what is morally good (*sittlich gut*) in society in order to be able to see the deeper moral significance (*Moralität*) in the beauty of nature. When we encounter something in society as *sittlich gut*, we can take it as a manifestation of something deeper: *Moralität*; and when we find something beautiful in nature, we can take it as a sign of something deeper as well: that we fit into nature and that nature appears as if it were made for us.

There is a deeper ground based on which beauty and morality can strengthen and serve each other and together promote our development as human beings. If finding something beautiful automatically gave rise to moral interest, adding the latter would not add anything new, and vice versa. What they share can only be part of their grounds. What they share might be fundamental, and in fact is, but it is still non-determining in each case. Both judgments of taste and moral judgments presuppose a "broad-minded way of thinking" (section 40, 295) and strengthen our ability to "think in the position of everyone else," which is one of the "maxims of the common human understanding" central to enlightenment

(294). What is common to judgments of taste and morality is my ability to reflect, to reflect about the other person's position as compared with mine, and to reflect about various forms of purposiveness (implicit or explicit, subjective and objective, aesthetic or teleological). Kant refers to this common ground when he wants to give meaning to "the cipher by means of which nature figuratively speaks to us in its beautiful forms" (section 42, 301). It is in section 59 that Kant will be more explicit about this common ground. There, in the Dialectic, he can make use of aesthetic ideas and rational ideas in the context of **antinomies** of reason. There he refers to the **supersensible**, develops a theory of symbolization, and reflects on broader and methodological issues regarding the position of **transcendental** idealism versus empiricism and rationalism.

To be able to follow Kant in section 59, we have to step back a little. According to Kant, if we want to represent a **concept** in intuition (*Anschauung*), we do so either in a schematic or in a symbolic way. The schematic way of **representation** has been laid out in the first *Critique* and applies to concepts of the understanding: By means of the **categories** we associate a representation in intuition with a concept. It is by associating the concept of a tree, for instance, with an intuitive representation of it (a mental picture), that we see a tree *as* a tree. There are rules for such associations, and there are rules that say what it means for an intuition to be adequate to a concept. There are ways of finding a concept for a given intuition and there are, the other way around, ways for finding an intuition for a concept. The concept might be empirical, like that of a tree; and it might be non-empirical, like that of a triangle (for the concept of a triangle we can create an intuition through geometrical construction). This is all about concepts of the understanding. On the other hand, given a concept of *reason* – just think of our concepts of justice, morality, or God – there is no adequate intuition, and a symbolic way of associating it (more freely) with some intuition is needed: "To a concept which only reason can think, and to which no sensible intuition can be adequate, an intuition is attributed with which the power of judgment proceeds in a way merely *analogous* to that which it observes in schematization, i.e., it is merely the rule of this *procedure*, not of the intuition itself, and thus merely the form of the *reflection*, not the content, which corresponds to the concept" (section 59, 351).

Symbolic representation is merely an *indirect* representation of a concept. There is more freedom in this kind of representation, it is less determined by the concept, and there are no fixed **rules**. The intuition we use does not directly correspond to the concept, but merely serves to provide us with an object of the senses about which we reflect in a way that captures what is essential in the concept we started out with. A body with a soul, Kant suggests, can be used to symbolically represent (in intuition) a monarchical state that is ruled in accordance with laws internal to the people (a concept of reason). The relation between the monarch and the people can be thought of in a way analogous to the relation between the parts of the body and its soul. (Here the body together with its soul should be understood as an object of intuition, an object of the senses.) Kant gives another example: a machine, for instance, a hand-mill, can be used to represent (in intuition) a monarchy that is ruled despotically by a single absolute will (a concept of reason) and not according to the laws internal to the people. Both the body and the hand-mill are symbolic representations, because neither corresponds directly to a monarchy, and in both cases it is merely our way of *reflecting* about the empirical object, the body and the hand-mill, that brings out what is essential to the concept of the monarchy we have in mind. There is a visible effect that the monarchy (good or bad) and the empirical object (body or hand-mill) share. In one example (the body) it is the harmony in the state and the harmony of the body and its soul; in the other the oppressed people and the ground coffee-beans, which share a common fate, so to speak.

Kant observes that our language is full of such indirect representations. We often even use the *same word* for two different things merely because there is an analogy between the ways we *reflect* about them. The word "ground," for instance, can be used to refer to the ground of an argument as well as to the foundation of a house. Both kinds of ground give some kind of support to something else, that is, either an argument or a house; and accordingly, there is a formal analogy between our reflecting about the ground of an argument and our reflecting about the ground of a house. The analogy manifests itself on the level of reflection: The two reflections are structurally isomorphic. Making use of such analogies can be useful in cases when we know how to reflect about something abstract, like a monarchy, justice, morality, or God, without being able to find an appropriate sensible representation for it, that is, when reflection seems to be floating or suspended in the air, so to speak, and when we wish to represent it, or at least in some way to fix and give support to it in intuition. Human history is full of symbols for concepts like God, honesty, or justice.

Now what is particular in our reflection in matters of beauty and morality? We have already seen that the aspect of abstracting from private interests and reflecting instead about other human beings is something that can be found in moral judgments as well as in judgments of taste (think of the first and the second moment of the judgment of taste). Objects of judgments of taste, which are objects of intuition, can thus serve as symbols of morality. In order to find them beautiful, we must reflect about them in ways that are similar, analogous, or isomorphic to the way we reflect on matters of morality. Here it is useful again to distinguish between *Moralität* and *Sittlichkeit*. The former is more abstract, involving deeper acts of reflection, whereas the latter is more of an empirical and social phenomenon. Similarly, the justifying grounds of a judgment of taste go deep, whereas the object we find beautiful is an empirical object that we perceive through our senses. The symbolic relation between beauty and morality lies essentially on the level of reflection, but it also depends on the empirical world, the objects we find beautiful and the human beings that live in harmony under moral laws.

Beauty is thus a symbol of morality. In fact, Kant writes that it is *"the* symbol" of morality (section 59, 353). Thus it is *only* in making judgments of taste that we engage in an activity that is analogous to moral reflection. Only aesthetic reflection about the beautiful (or the ugly) is formally analogous to moral reflection. Beauty and the judgment of taste thus play a role that cannot be taken over by anything else. There is no substitute for them in this respect.

We should also notice that beauty is the symbol of morality regardless of whether what we find beautiful is an object of nature or an object of art. This is different from the previous connection between beauty and morality that Kant drew earlier on, in section 42, regarding a certain "intellectual interest in the beautiful." There, beauty of nature was favored over beauty of art because this specific connection was shown to exist between morality and beauty of nature, not between morality and beauty of art.

To see the reason for this change, or this extension, we have to pay attention to a further aspect of the relationship between beauty and morality, which complicates matters in fascinating ways. Aesthetic ideas, as we have seen, are a suitable counterpart to rational ideas, because they provide much to think about. They not only support but also enrich rational reflection. Artists, therefore, often make use of symbolic presentations in their works. They can intentionally inject aesthetic ideas into their works, which nature cannot (unless you adopt a point of view, such as pantheism, according to which nature has intentions, or if you allow God to play a role). In this respect, the beauty of art offers more than mere beauty of nature does. But, on the other hand, if the object represented by the work of art is an object of nature (like a landscape in a painting), the power of aesthetic ideas might rely not only on the general features of reflection outlined in section 59, but also on those that are specific to objects of nature, namely the accompanying intellectual interests which Kant discussed in section 42. In this way, the features that are particular to beauty of nature, and that allow us to draw connections to morality, are inherited, so to speak, by objects of art. Art thus reaches out into nature.

But in any case, whether we focus on the general features of reflection or on the more specific intellectual interests, the fact that, in matters of taste, nature has to look like art *and* art like nature (section 45), allows us to admit *both* possibilities, the possibility that judgments of taste depend on intellectual interests when their objects are regarded as products of nature (section 42), and the possibility that they depend on general features of reflection when their objects are regarded as products of art (section 59).

Further reading

Allison, *Kant's Theory of Taste*, pp. 195–267, discusses the transition from nature to freedom – the relation between beauty, duty, and interest – and, finally, beauty as a symbol of morality. In general, Allison is good in giving support to various Kantian claims. His discussion is competent, detailed, and sophisticated. Especially helpful for the advanced reader. Not an introduction – at least, not an easy one.

Budd, "Delight . . . Part II: Natural Beauty and Morality," discusses three connections Kant draws between morality and immediate interest in natural beauty (the possibility, inevitability, and significance of this interest), concluding that Kant's arguments are not compelling. Introductory, not technical.

Munzel, "The Beautiful is the Symbol of the Morally Good," gives a helpful discussion of the distinction between *Sittlichkeit* and *Moralität* and the kind of "proof" the analogy can provide. Particularly sensitive to the German and providing helpful insights from this.

Guyer, *Kant and the Claims*, has a chapter on aesthetics and morality (pp. 312–50) with a special section on beauty as the symbol of morality (pp. 331–45). He suggests, following Crawford who had already argued this in *Kant's Aesthetic Theory* (pp. 143–56) that Kant tried to use connections between beauty and morality in order to complete his otherwise incomplete justification of the judgment of taste's claim to universality. Allison takes the opposite view, as I do. Guyer later wrote two longer essays on duty, nature, and beauty, *Kant and the Experience*, pp. 304–93. These essays approach aesthetics from the side of ethics and investigate the development of Kant's views before and after the third *Critique*.

Cohen, "Why Beauty is the Symbol of Morality," is unusual in that it gives a reconstructive interpretation and concentrates not on section 59 but on just one passage from section 8, which has otherwise received little attention in connection with the problem of beauty as the symbol of morality. In particular, Cohen discusses issues of certainty, the other, and purposiveness without purpose, as they can be found in both beauty and good will.

Kinnaman, "Symbolism and Cognition in General in Kant's *Critique of Judgment*," uses the theory of beauty as the symbol of morality to cast some light on Kant's philosophical system as a whole and his concept of cognition in general (*Erkenntnis überhaupt*).

Zammito, *The Genesis of Kant's "Critique of Judgment,"* pp. 306–26, gives a nice discussion of Kant's ideas of man as end-in-himself and the unity of mankind, which Zammito argues are among the most central ideas of the whole third *Critique*.

Henrich, *Aesthetic Judgment and the Moral Image of the World*, contains four highly original essays of wide scope that connect the judgment of taste with morality, human rights, and the French Revolution. Kulenkampff, *Kants Logik*, pp. 188–96 (only in the 2nd edition), gives a critical account of Henrich's book.

The Analytic, the Dialectic, and the Supersensible

In this section, we will discuss the Dialectic and the supersensible. The Dialectic is the last part of Kant's aesthetics, where he tries to make various overarching connections within his system of transcendental philosophy as a whole. In the following, we will first briefly say what a "dialectic" is for Kant, in general and not only in the third *Critique*. Second, we will discuss the "dialectic of taste" and its solution and compare this with the Analytic. Third, we will see how Kant introduces the supersensible as an "indeterminate concept." Finally, we will discuss the question of whether the Analytic is complete in itself or whether it is completed only in the Dialectic.

1 What is a "dialectic"?

Each of Kant's three *Critiques* has two parts: an Analytic and a Dialectic. The Analytic establishes the basic elements and is usually more constructive in nature and positive in its results. Roughly put, it is more "down to earth." The Dialectic then forms the second part, following the Analytic, and its task is basically a negative one, namely to dispel what seem to be contradictory statements at the level of reason. It is our human nature to ask for unconditional final answers, and we are thus often led into contradiction when speculating about ideas and principles, for instance about immortality, freedom, the highest good, or God. Kant makes use of the results of his Analytic to translate such traditional problems into his own system of transcendental philosophy, and he then discusses and resolves them there, on his own grounds. The Dialectic is thus also a place to test the results of the Analytic, a place where Kant can show that his system is the best and only possible one: the only one that can solve those traditional problems. The Dialectic hence also becomes a place of defense of Kant's philosophy of transcendental idealism in general, a philosophy in which we fundamentally distinguish between things as they appear and things as they are in themselves.

For Kant, a "dialectic" arises when we begin to "reason," or "rationalize" (*vernünfteln*: section 55, 337) beyond our capacity, that is, when we make claims to universality on *a priori* grounds in such a way that we are led to seemingly contradictory statements: a "thesis" and an "antithesis." Kant must make sure that the a priori grounds which his Analytic has established do not really lead to a contradiction.

2 What is the "dialectic of taste" and what is its solution?

In section 56, Kant "introduces" or "presents" (*Vorstellung*, as the title says) the "antinomy of taste." He does so by first presenting two widespread opinions, two "commonplaces" about taste, and then by transforming them into a "thesis" and an "antithesis":

A1   "The judgment of taste is not based on concepts"
A2   "The judgment of taste is based on concepts"

There are no proofs in matters of taste, so A1 must be true. But there must be some kind of concept on which a judgment of taste is based, because otherwise people would be content to leave each other alone with their personal opinions (which is not the case). Thus A2 must be true as well.

There is an apparent similarity, as Kant himself points out at the beginning of section 57, with the two "peculiarities" (*Eigentümlichkeiten*) of taste that were discussed earlier in the Analytic, in sections 32 and 33:

E1   The judgment of taste claims universality, "as if it were objective" (281).
E2   "The judgment of taste is not determinable by grounds of proof at all, just as if it were merely subjective" (284).

E1 is similar to A2, and E2 is similar to A1. But because these peculiarities, E1 and E2, have been dealt with already in the Analytic, there must be a fundamental difference between them and the thesis and antithesis, A1 and A2, from the Dialectic. Otherwise, why should Kant have to write such a Dialectic? Kant already asserted at the end of the previous section 55, that a "dialectic of the aesthetic power of judgment" can only arise if there is "an antinomy of the *principles* of this faculty, which makes its lawfulness and hence also its inner possibility doubtful" (337), and he makes similar comments at the beginning of section 57. The difference must thus be in the antinomy's reference to principles.

I suggest that the thesis and antithesis, which create the antinomy (in the Dialectic), should be understood as generalizations, or inflations, of the two earlier peculiarities. The thesis and antithesis are talking *about* the judgment of taste and about its *general* nature and principle. The contradiction of the antinomy should be seen as one of those principles and justifying grounds, those "concepts" that are mentioned in the thesis and antithesis. On the other hand, the contradiction that one finds in the judgment of taste and its peculiarities (in the Analytic) should be seen more on the level of the judgment of taste itself, for instance in the case where my judgment about this rose goes against yours, where I find the rose beautiful whereas you do not (and where I demand that you and everyone else should agree to my judgment). That is, I suggest, the antinomy takes place on a different level (the level of principles).

How the thesis and antithesis should be understood becomes more apparent when we look at Kant's solution to the contradiction between them. Both the thesis and the antithesis mention a "concept," but, as Kant explains, they do not mean the same *kind* of concept. The thesis talks about *concepts of the understanding*, where proof and scientific investigation are possible. The antithesis talks about *concepts of reason*: concepts that are undetermined and even undeterminable, that is, that can never be exhibited in sensible intuition, such as the ideas of God and freedom. (If they could be exhibited, scientific investigation would become possible and the quarrel in matters of taste would disappear.) So the solution to the antinomy of taste is given by a *disambiguation* of the term "concept."

Let us briefly compare this with the Analytic. There, after the analysis of the judgment of taste (sections 1–22) has been completed, Kant introduces (*vorstellig machen*) the two peculiarities (sections 32 and 33), which are commonplaces, too, and which he uses as *starting points* for his deduction. He then explains these commonplaces and peculiarities within his own system by making use of the results from his analysis (the free play and the principle of subjective purposiveness). Similarly here, in the Dialectic, Kant "introduces" the antinomy (*Vorstellung der Antinomie*) by using "commonplaces" (*Gemeinörter*) as starting points. He transforms them into thesis and antithesis and then resolves what seems to be a contradiction between them (the antinomy) by distinguishing between two kinds of concept, that of the understanding and that of reason. The "concept of reason" in question here will be interpreted by Kant as the "supersensible," or various forms of it, as we shall see shortly. It is only here in the Dialectic that Kant can avail himself of such concepts of reason.

On the one hand, the Dialectic does not need to offer a priori grounds for the judgment of taste. That has been done already in the Analytic. On the other hand, the Dialectic is not restricted to the level of *understanding* and imagination (where concepts can always be exhibited in intuition), but it can make use of ideas and concepts of reason, concepts that can never be exhibited in intuition. Such indeterminable concepts are admissible in the Dialectic and sufficient to resolve the antinomy. The mere *possibility* of such an indeterminable concept being referred to in the antithesis suffices to avoid the contradiction. The task of the Dialectic is thus a merely negative one: It must show that no contradiction arises from the a priori grounds, which the Analytic has provided, and that reason together with the power of judgment, as the seat of such a priori grounds, does not run into contradictions within itself and through its own principles.

3 What is the "supersensible"?

The indeterminable concept to which the antithesis refers cannot be exhibited in sensible intuition and is an idea of the "supersensible." However, it cannot be just any idea. It must be an idea that somehow corresponds to the problem of taste and its a priori ground, the principle of subjective purposiveness. This principle must allow for some kind of connection to something supersensible at the level of ideas: It must be *"the correct* concept of taste" (*der richtige Begriff des Geschmacks:* section 57, 341). It must be "correct" in two senses: (1) It must establish the judgment of taste as an a priori judgment, so that an antinomy of principles (not just an empirical contradiction between particular judgments of taste) can arise; and (2) it must allow for a solution to this antinomy. This solution then helps to "make reason self-consistent" (*die Vernunft mit sich selbst einstimmig zu machen:* section 57, 341), i.e. to show that reason is without contradiction, or, rather, that our philosophical concept of it is without contradiction.

The principle of subjective purposiveness does indeed satisfy these two requirements. It gives an a priori basis and allows for the antinomy; and it is indeterminable and thus allows for the solution. But there is more. This principle of subjective purposiveness gives an explanation to our aesthetic feeling that we *fit* into nature, and it creates a link between *us* and *outer nature* by showing how nature is *purposive* for our aesthetic contemplation of it. Correspondingly, the idea of the supersensible will show features of our *inner* nature as well as features of *outer* nature: on the one hand the "supersensible substratum of humanity" (section 57, 340) and the principle of the ends of freedom (346), and on the other the "the substratum of nature" and "the principle of subjective purposiveness of nature for our faculty." Kant mentions such concepts of reason and the "supersensible" in eight different places in section 57 and the two short appendices which follow it. Kant here connects outer, physical nature (first *Critique*) with inner, moral nature (second *Critique*), thereby uniting his three *Critiques*.

At this point one should have a look at sections 76 and 77. They do not belong to Kant's aesthetics but to the second part of the third *Critique*, Kant's teleology. Nevertheless, they say much about the supersensible, and Kant here writes much more freely about his general ideas of transcendental philosophy. In the following, I will say a few words about these two important later sections. They are profound and speculative in character, and they give an idea of the place of Kant's

aesthetics in his overall system and of its significance even beyond the third
Critique.

Kant is famous for drawing distinctions, and in the first two *Critiques* he took
great care to distinguish between nature and freedom, the general and the particular, the possible and the actual, understanding and sensible intuition, and,
most fundamentally, appearance and the thing in itself. But here in the third
Critique, and even more so in his later writings, we see that his wish to bridge
these gulfs is becoming increasingly pronounced. He wants to see his own distinctions overcome, of course not on the level where they were drawn – there
they shall remain as they are – but from a higher point of view. It is also at this
point more than at any other that we may say philosophers such as Hegel were
greatly inspired by Kant and took over.

This higher point of view is that of an almost God-like non-human understanding: an "intuitive understanding." For human beings, sensibility and understanding are two *separate* sources of knowledge that always need to cooperate.
Intuitions without concepts are blind, and concepts without intuition empty.
Intuition and understanding are separate and we do not have an "intuitive
understanding." We cannot intuitively understand nature at a single glance.
Instead, we have to investigate it, empirically and step by step, if we want to learn
about particular empirical objects and about particular laws of the natural sciences, such as physics, chemistry, and biology. For us there is always an element
of contingency in nature, because neither the individual (for instance a tree) is
fully understandable and fully describable through general concepts and scientific laws (our concept of a tree or our scientific knowledge about trees), nor is
the web of such scientific laws (especially in biology) given a priori. For Kant,
although some very basic laws of the natural sciences are given a priori, many
particular laws are not. Nevertheless we have the ability to discover such laws,
and we may thus say our mental faculties happen to fit a world that affects our
outer senses.

In aesthetic contemplation we can at least feel this kind of fitting, and as
philosophers we can point out the principles of purposiveness to explain this phenomenon: subjective purposiveness (as studied in aesthetics) and objective purposiveness (the subject of teleology). An intuitive understanding, on the other
hand, would not have any of this; it would not need it.

We can try to imagine a being with such a higher point of view, equipped
with an understanding different from ours, as underlying ourselves, outer nature,
and the subject–object distinction. Such a being could understand nature at a
single glance. We can even try to imagine a creative understanding for which the
merely imagined and possible are already what is real. There would then be
no distinction (and also no conflict) between freedom and nature for a being
with such an understanding. Many gaps would be bridged if there were such a

supersensible being, or if we had at least a better understanding of such an idea. But we cannot comprehend it, although we feel compelled to do so. Kant later in his life turned to the concepts of space, matter, and ether, hoping they might allow him to make these unifying thoughts more clear.

What is important for us to see here, or at least to get a glimpse of, is the role of subjective purposiveness and thus aesthetics in the larger picture of Kant's plan and his hope for a unified transcendental philosophy. After this brief but sweeping excursion, let us return to the Dialectic.

4 Is the Dialectic the completion of the Analytic?

Certain passages in the Dialectic easily give one the impression that the Analytic is not complete and that it is only here, in the Dialectic, that the justification of the judgment of taste, which should have been given already in the Analytic (in the deduction), is finally provided: "A concept of this kind . . . is the mere pure rational concept of the supersensible . . . For if one did not assume such a point of view, then the claim of the judgment of taste to universal validity could not be saved" (section 57, 340). Kant is here referring to the "point of view" of transcendental philosophy, where one distinguishes between appearance and the thing in itself. He is referring to the fundamental and systematic layout from the first *Critique*. It is only from this point of view that the right concept of our power of judgment and the "correct concept of taste" (see above) could be developed. The supersensible then is a possible ground for all this, and pointing it out is sufficient for the purposes of the Dialectic.

Both the Analytic and the Dialectic have distinct "tasks" (*Aufgaben*), make use of their own "keys" (*Schlüssel*), and present their own "solutions" (*Auflösungen*). Kant uses all of these three expressions in both parts, the Analytic and the Dialectic. But they have different meanings in these two contexts. The task in the Analytic is different from the task in the Dialectic, and so are the keys and the solutions. Let us look at this more closely. We saw a "key" already in the Analytic, namely "the *key* to the critique of taste" (section 9, 216). This key was explicitly called the "solution" (*Auflösung*) to a "problem" (*Aufgabe*). That problem was given in the title of section 9: "Investigation of the question: whether in the judgment of taste the feeling of pleasure precedes the judging of the object or the latter precedes the former." The solution there was given on the level of the faculties of cognition, imagination and understanding, namely by establishing the concept of free play of these faculties and by discovering the principle of subjective purposiveness. This was a solution in a somewhat *constructive* way, comparable to the way a solution to a geometrical problem is carried out by means of compass and ruler. There, too, we are given a "problem" (*Aufgabe*) and asked to find a "solution" (*Auflösung*).

The situation in the Dialectic is different from the very start. It is not required that we establish any kind of foundation. It suffices to show that there is no contradiction of principles. For this it is enough merely to "indicate" how the contradiction can be avoided, and to do so we can even avail ourselves of ideas, such as the idea of the supersensible: "The subjective principle, namely the indeterminate idea of the *supersensible* in us, can only be *indicated* as the sole *key* to demystifying this faculty which is hidden to us even in its sources" (section 57, 341). Pointing out the possibility of such an idea (which has become a real possibility through the Analytic) suffices to solve the antinomy. The "correct concept of taste," built on Kant's concept of the power of aesthetic judgment, has created the right kind of *open space* for such an idea.

Further reading

Allison, *Theory of Taste*, pp. 236–54, gives a detailed and close reading of the antinomy of taste.

Posy, "Imagination and Judgment in the Critical Philosophy," compares the role of imagination from the first *Critique* with that, or rather the lack thereof, in the supersensible realm of morality and the sublime. From the empirical, to the beautiful, the sublime, and the moral, we increasingly go beyond the limits of perception and imagination and enter the realm of ideas, where we find completeness and totality. Posy briefly discusses examples from poetry, music, and algebra.

Pippin, "The Significance of Taste," discusses the question of whether the teleological, moral, and sociocultural aspects Kant offers are mere addenda to judgments of taste or actually necessary to establish them and their subjective universality. Nicely sketches a "continuum" ranging from narrower to wider perspectives.

Lyotard, *Lessons*, pp. 207–18, has sections on the antinomy, "limit ideas," and how the supersensible "signals itself" in the three "facultary orders."

Brandt, "Analytic/Dialectic," gives an account of the concepts of Analytic and Dialectic in all three *Critiques*, and he then argues that the deduction in the "Critique of Aesthetic Judgment" is actually incomplete and completed only in the Dialectic.

Allison, "Is the *Critique of Judgment* 'Post-Critical'?" argues against Tuschling (see the German article below) that Kant did not try to "found" purposivness on some kind of non-human, intuitive understanding. This article presupposes much knowledge of the first *Critique*.

Brandt, "Die Schönheit der Kristalle und das Spiel der Erkenntniskräfte," focuses on Kant's detailed discussion of crystallization from section 58, pointing out an analogy between the free play of our faculties and the free formation of crystals that should be seen in the context of the purposiveness of nature from an idealist perspective.

Dumouchel, "Genèse de la *Troisième Critique*: le rôle de l'esthétique dans l'achèvement du système critique," does not focus on the Dialectic but gives a good account of the function of Kant's aesthetics within the third *Critique* and in Kant's critical system as a whole.

Bartuschat, *Zum systematischen Ort von Kants Kritik der Urteilskraft*, discusses the third *Critique* as a whole and also as an integral part of Kant's system. At the end he focuses on the supersensible and the question of its relevance (pp. 246–66).

Baum, "Kants Prinzip der Zweckmässigkeit und Hegels Realisierung des Begriffs," discusses Hegel's reading of Kant's third *Critique*, especially of sections 76 and 77, asking whether purposiveness can be construed as realization of ideas.

Förster, "Die Bedeutung von §§76 und 77," discusses the influence Kant's idea of an intuitive understanding had on Goethe, and through Goethe and his botany on Hegel. Förster argues that there is a distinction between two kinds of intuitive understanding in Kant, which has been overlooked by many but nevertheless played a decisive role in Hegel's development.

Tuschling, "The System of Transcendental Idealism: Questions Raised and Left Open in the *Kritik der Urteilskraft*," asks what exactly Kant thought the unity of his transcendental idealism was. He shows how Kant was searching for a higher unifying principle that could bridge the gaps between "nature" and "freedom" and between "apriority" and "absolute aposteriority." He argues that such a higher principle must be seen as based on a non-human, intuitive understanding, and that this was indeed already Kant's opinion and not just how Hegel later read Kant. Considering the difficulty of the topic, this article is relatively easy reading. Unfortunately, it often quotes from the German without giving translations.

Mertens, *Kommentar zur Ersten Einleitung*, gives an introduction and commentary to Kant's "First Introduction" to the third *Critique*. This introduction by Kant is quite long and was never published in his lifetime. In it he laid out his overall plans from a higher perspective.

7

Two Challenges

The discussions in the following two sections, about the ugly and the beautiful in mathematics, could perhaps have been inserted elsewhere, dotted about in the other sections. I chose not to do so for several reasons. Kant has no separate sections on these issues; he brings them up as side issues or in a few words without further justification at different places in the third *Critique*. His arguments never focus on these issues. Especially regarding the ugly, it is apparent that all his arguments are directed at **judgments** about the beautiful, so one naturally wonders whether they would work for the judgment about the ugly as well. But it is also natural first to go along with Kant as he establishes his theory of judgment about the beautiful and only then to see whether his arguments also work for the ugly. Similarly, Kant does not focus on issues regarding beauty and genius in mathematics, and one wonders what he would say about such issues. Again, one should tackle this problem only after the judgment of taste has been properly understood. One can then use these issues and problems to challenge Kant's theory and to see whether it is good enough to deal with them successfully. The questions about the ugly and beauty in mathematics are not just academic, but also very natural questions to ask; and it can be fun to see how Kant's theory deals with them.

Can Kant's Aesthetics Account for the Ugly?

In his aesthetics, Kant is mainly concerned with judgments about the beautiful, and he says almost nothing about the ugly. Kant calls judgments that claim that an object is ugly *"negative* judgments of taste." Similarly, the displeasure we feel when we see something that appears ugly to us is called "negative pleasure." His discussion of the four **moments** of taste is directed mainly at positive judgments of taste, judgments about the beautiful, and not, at least not directly, at negative judgments of taste, i.e., judgments about the ugly. So it is only natural to ask if his arguments would work, possibly with minor modifications, when applied to negative judgments of taste. Furthermore, we might ask whether Kant intended his analysis of judgments of taste to apply to judgments about the ugly. This question, in turn, raises a number of other questions. Are such negative judgments of taste disinterested? Is there some kind of free play of the **faculties** of **cognition** underlying such judgments? Do they have an a priori **principle**? And what, exactly, would that principle be?

One might easily believe that Kant's theory cannot account for judgments about the ugly, because one might think that when we find something ugly there is neither a free harmonious play of the faculties nor a subjective **purposiveness** underlying such a **feeling** and such a judgment. Nevertheless, as we will see, such a belief is premature and wrong.

We shall see that there are good reasons to believe that Kant's *Critique of Aesthetic Judgment* is intended also to cover judgments about the ugly, in fact, to treat them on equal grounds with those about the beautiful. Judgments about the ugly are in a certain sense (as we will explain) just as "positive" as are judgments about the beautiful (which are the so-called "positive judgments of taste"). Furthermore, we will suggest minor modifications to those arguments that Kant made specifically for the beautiful, so that they also work for the ugly.

At different periods of Kant's development, before and after the composition of the third *Critique*, we find in his writings and lectures a strong conviction that ugliness and beauty, as well as pleasure and displeasure, hate and love, blame and praise, positive and negative natural numbers should all be understood as having their own positive **grounds**. In the essay "Attempt to Introduce the Concept of Negative Magnitudes into Philosophy" (1763, *The Cambridge Edition of the Works of Immanuel Kant, Theoretical Philosophy 1755–1770*), Kant writes that "the sign '−,' as it occurs in the example '−9 − 4 = −13,' does not signify a subtraction but an addition, in exactly the same way as the sign '+,' as it occurs in the example '+9 + 4 = +13', signifies addition" (ibid., p. 173). This is also in accord with the way in which addition and subtraction are introduced in higher mathematics courses at universities today. Kant gives further examples of the need for positive grounds for what we often think of in negative terms. Thus, "impenetrability just as much presupposes a true force in the parts of a body, in virtue of which they collectively occupy a space, as does the force in virtue of which another body strives to enter this space" (179); displeasure must have positive grounds just as pleasure does (181); "aversion can be called a negative desire, hate a negative love, ugliness a negative beauty, blame a negative praise" (182). Kant kept this basic conviction throughout his life. In 1772 he wrote: "Ugliness is something positive, not merely lack of beauty, but the existence of something opposite to beauty" (*Logik Philippi, Akademie Ausgabe* XXIV, 364), and as late as 1792:

"Ugliness is something positive, as well as is beauty" (*Logik Dohna-Wundlaken*, XXIV, 708).

These passages show that we should expect Kant to have believed that there were a priori grounds for negative judgments of taste. But there are also systematic reasons for asserting this. If a judgment about the ugly had no a priori grounds, then it would have no basis for a claim to subjective **universality**, and the possibly infinite dispute in matters of taste, which Kant takes as a given fact from the very start, could not even arise. Furthermore, without the possibility of conflicting a priori grounds, there would be no grounds for *reason* possibly contradicting itself, and thus no **antinomy** and no **dialectics**. Based on these historical and systematic considerations, we should expect Kant's aesthetic theory to be applicable, with appropriate modifications, to negative judgments of taste as well as to positive judgments. If this is so, then why did Kant not explicitly account for the ugly in his third *Critique*? In defense of Kant, we can say that he concentrated on the analysis of judgments about the beautiful simply because this analysis suffices to discover the notion of a free play of the faculties and the a priori principle of subjective purposiveness, the establishment of which is his main interest in the third *Critique*. Kant may have taken for granted that a similar analysis applies to negative judgments of taste.

At the end of each of the four analyses of the judgment of taste, according to the four moments, Kant gives a definition of the beautiful. This definition can easily be modified to fit the ugly. However, the arguments involving free harmonious play and the principle of subjective purposiveness are problematic in the case of the ugly. If we find something to be ugly, there should be some kind of free *disharmonious* play of our faculties underlying our dissatisfaction. The play would still be free, insofar as intuition is free from conceptual determination; and it would be play, because the ugly can be fascinating and it can occupy our minds as much as does something that is beautiful. The play would not be harmonious, but disharmonious. It would be a quarrel. But Kant's argumentation, especially in the key section 9, relies on communicability and subjective universal validity, and we therefore have to ask whether a disharmonious relationship between **imagination** and **understanding** is as communicable as is the harmonious relationship. Crucial to Kant's argumentation is the following claim: "Nothing . . . can be universally communicated except cognition and **representation** so far as it belongs to cognition" (section 9, 217), i.e. insofar as it can serve in cognition. Kant argued that in free harmonious play the representation "belongs to cognition." If we accept this, we should, I suggest, also accept that the representation in free *disharmonious* play "belongs to cognition." The point is that in both cases the faculties of cognition are engaged in some kind of interaction, be it a harmonious or a disharmonious play, and that this interaction strengthens the faculties and is related to **cognition in general** without having to lead to a

determinate cognition (the aesthetic interaction might, in a specific case, happen to lead to a determinate cognition, but that would not be necessary, and it would be external to the aesthetic judgment as such). Harmonious and disharmonious play are two kinds of aesthetic reflection. Both require "more" and "less" than epistemic **reflection** that serves in cognizing the object. Aesthetic reflection requires more because it involves the feeling of pleasure or displeasure, which is not the case in epistemic reflection, and it requires less because it does not aim at cognition, as is the case in epistemic reflection.

The state of mind which underlies a judgment of taste, and which Kant analyses in section 9, can be that of a harmonious as well as that of a disharmonious play. Crucial for Kant's arguments is that this state of mind be universally communicable. He carefully writes: "it can be nothing other than the state of mind that is encountered in the relation of the powers of representation to each other insofar as they relate a given representation to cognition in general" (section 9, 217). These relations, we may add, must obtain in a harmonious as well as in a disharmonious play. Thinking of poems by Charles Baudelaire or paintings by Hieronymus Bosch, we can see how fascinating the ugly can be and how much beauty and ugliness can be interwoven. There is indeed a free play of our faculties possible also in the case of the ugly. And our judgment can be as disinterested as in the case of the beautiful.

Finally, we return to the principle of subjective purposivness. In addressing this topic, we have to introduce the notion of *negative* purposiveness. In chapter 3 we introduced a diagram indicating the threefold structure of subjective purposiveness. This will be useful here.

$$\text{understanding}$$

$$\text{object} \quad \xrightarrow{\quad P_1 \quad} \quad \updownarrow \; P_2 \quad \xrightarrow{\quad P_3 \quad} \quad \text{cognition in general}$$

$$\text{imagination}$$

The object of a positive judgment of taste is suitable (purposive) for free play, in which the two faculties, imagination and understanding, strengthen and enliven each other and thus are purposive for each other. All this in turn is suitable for cognition in general. So far this applies to the judgment about the beautiful. There are now at least two ways of introducing an element of negation into this threefold structure of subjective purposiveness. First, if we find something ugly, we find it *negatively* purposive (-P1) for a harmonious free play (P2), that is, the object resists our attempt to engender such a play among the faculties. Or, second, we may say that the object is indeed purposive (P1), but purposive not for a harmonious but for a *dis*harmonious (−P2) free play.

The ugly can be fascinating and hold our attention for a long time. We can even be obsessed by something ugly. No matter whether we introduce negation in P1 or in P2, the state of mind in aesthetic contemplation of the ugly can be seen as being purposive (P3) for cognition in general, because the cognitive powers are actively involved and strengthen each other in the attempt to find harmony. The fascination with the ugly can be a challenge to change perspective so that the disharmony disappears.

In beauty we often find an element of local disharmony that nevertheless creates harmony in a wider context. Just think of the element of negation in Japanese aesthetics: the "kire" in Zen, an element of sudden cutting and unexpected turning in Nô plays, in stone gardens, or in haiku poetry. Or think of music, when a chord that sounds unpleasant by itself becomes harmonious when placed in a wider musical passage. Here the disharmony is part of a harmony in a wider context. It enhances the experience and strengthens our faculties. But these are cases of *local* disharmony. In the case of the ugly there is no wider context available in which the disharmony would turn into harmony. Sometimes though, things that appear ugly at first become beautiful when taste is more "educated" and when we have learned how to take new perspectives. A more sophisticated play between imagination and understanding may produce harmony where earlier perception has produced only disharmony.

We have now given two kinds of reason, historical and systematic, for a judgment about the ugly to be a judgment of taste equal in status with the judgment about the beautiful. This can be established by introducing the notion of free and disharmonious play of the faculties of cognition and by introducing a negative version of the principle of subjective purposiveness. In this way we see that Kant's aesthetics can indeed account for the ugly.

Further reading

The articles on the ugly in Kant can roughly be divided into two groups: those that argue against the possibility of negative judgments of taste, and those that argue in favor of it. In the first group (contra) are Brandt, "Zur Logik des Ästhetischen Urteils," and Shier, "Why Kant Finds Nothing Ugly." On the other side (pro) we find Strub, "Das Hässliche und die 'Kritik der Urteilskraft'" (he does not believe in the possibility of a free disharmonious play between the faculties, though, but offers instead the idea of the faculties playing independently of each other); Hudson, "The Significance of an Analytic of the Ugly in Kant's Deduction of Pure Judgments of Taste"; Lohmar, "Das Geschmacksurteil über das faszinierend Hässliche;" and Wenzel, "Kant Finds Nothing Ugly?" (this argues explicitly against Shier, contains criticisms of Hudson and Strub, and gives a positive account).

Can there be Beauty and Genius in Mathematics?

Most of us would probably say that mathematics can be beautiful (at least those who have not been driven away from mathematics by impatient teachers and insensitive educational systems). Mathematical objects, proofs, and even whole theories can be elegant and beautiful – at least we often say so. But this creates a problem for Kant, because it is an essential ingredient in his theory that **concepts** should play no role in matters of taste. One therefore wonders if it is possible to find beauty in mathematics without any of the concepts that define mathematical objects playing any role in our aesthetic contemplation. Mathematics seems to be purely conceptual. Thus, nothing would be left if we had to abstract from the very concepts that are so essential to mathematics. Maybe we can find a rose beautiful without paying any attention to the concept of a rose, but is it possible to find beauty in a proof of the Pythagorean theorem without paying close attention to all the definitions, rules, and concepts involved in this proof?

We can see a sunset without having a concept of a sunset, but can we see a square – and see it as a *mathematical* object – without knowing something about lengths, sides, and right angles? Of course we can see a square drawn in the sand without such knowledge, as a small child or an animal might do, but do we then see it as a mathematical object? If we talk about mathematics being beautiful, we are not talking about the color and shade of the sand but about the mathematical structure of the square.

In sections 15 and 16, Kant argues against rationalist conceptions of beauty and stresses that beauty has to be kept separate from perfection: "Perfection does not gain by beauty, nor does beauty gain by perfection" (section 16, 231). But is it not perfection that we often find essential to what we think is beautiful and elegant in mathematics? If this is the case, then Kant might say that this is not pure beauty in his sense of the word. Indeed, he tends to reserve beauty for art and nature and to refrain from using it in the context of mathematics and the sciences: "There is neither a science of the beautiful, only a critique, nor beautiful science, only beautiful art" (section 44, 304). But we have to see whether Kant is right in this.

The problem becomes more complex if we also ask the question whether there can be any **genius** in mathematics and the sciences. To our surprise, we find that Kant has a tendency to deny this: "Newton was a man of great talent but not a man of genius, as he himself said. His book *Principia philosophiae naturalis* is the result of twenty years of diligence" (*Anthropology Lecture Notes Mrongovius* 1784/85, XXV 1311); or: "genius . . . is a talent for art, not for science" (section 49, 317). We will see that for Kant the question whether or not there can be genius in mathematics and the sciences is connected with the questions of what the nature of imitation and learning is, what can and what cannot be learned, what kind of ability can be acquired by everyone, and what abilities or talents count as gifts of nature. We will also see that all this raises the question of what mathematical concepts and rules are and what role they play in the process of learning and doing mathematics. It is in regard to these connections that the question of whether there can be beauty and genius in mathematics becomes complex. The problems involved here lead us into philosophy of mathematics and Wittgenstein's rule-following problem, and this brings us into deep water. Although I will refrain from going into the discussions around Wittgenstein and stay within Kant's aesthetics, certain similarities should become apparent to anyone familiar with those discussions.

The following quote makes it apparent how intricately interwoven the issues of beauty, genius, rules, imitation, learning, invention, and discovery are in the context of Kant's aesthetics. The italicized passages are problematic and will be examined more closely in this section.

> Everyone agrees that genius is entirely opposed to the spirit of imitation. Now since *learning is nothing but imitation*, even the greatest aptitude for learning . . . still does not count as genius. But even if one thinks or writes for himself, and does not merely take up what others have thought, indeed even if he invents a great deal for art and science, this is still not a proper reason for calling such a great mind . . . a genius, since just *this sort of thing* could also have been learned, and thus still lies on *the natural path* of enquiry and reflection *in accordance with* rules, and is not specifically distinct from that which can be acquired with effort by means of imitation. Thus everything that Newton *expounded* in his immortal work on the principles of natural philosophy, no matter how great a mind it took to discover it, can still be learned; but one cannot learn *to write* inspired poetry, however exhaustive all the rules for the art of poetry and however excellent the models for it may be. The reason is that Newton could make *all the steps that he had to take,* from the first elements of geometry to his great and profound discoveries, *entirely intuitive* not only to himself but also to everyone else, and thus set them out for posterity quite determinately; but no Homer or Wieland [a well-known German novelist of the time of Goethe] can indicate how his *ideas,* which are fantastic and yet at the same time rich in thought, arise and come together in his head, because he himself does not know it and thus cannot teach it to anyone else either. In the scientific sphere, therefore, the greatest discoverer differs only in degree from the most hard-working imitator and apprentice, whereas he differs in kind from someone who is gifted by nature for beautiful art. (Section 47, 308–9)

Now, what are mathematics and poetry? There is a difference between mathematics and doing mathematics and also a distinction between reading poetry and writing it. But these distinctions are not very strict, and yet much of the problem regarding the possibility of beauty and genius in mathematics and poetry depends on these distinctions. We can say that mathematics is distinct from doing mathematics if we adopt a Platonic point of view, that is, if we believe that mathematics exists already independently of us, and that we merely discover and do not create it. But, on the other hand, how do we know that the poetry we believe ourselves to create is not written down already in some Platonic realm as well?

Kant apparently thought that "mathematics by itself is nothing but rules" (*Reflection* 922, XV 410, *c*. 1776–8). But is this true? And what exactly are rules, and how do we apply them? Let us look at an example. If we read a mathematical proof of a theorem, say in analysis, we often find the following kind of lines: "Take f(x) = 17x + 5; let x = 0; apply the formula (23) from the previous paragraph," etc. If we study such a proof (a proof Newton might have "expounded" – see quote above), if we follow it and think it through until we get the ideas and can reproduce it, what exactly is it that we are learning? There is no rule that forces us either to "take" this formula and not another, or to "let" x = 0 and not x = 1, or to "apply" formula (23) at this point of the proof. In fact, there is no rule that tells us to take, let, or apply anything at all. There is no rule for applying rules. In any proof that is more than one page long, there are dozens of such instances where the author simply makes a choice without saying why one step is chosen and not another. The beginner often wonders why one has to do this first and that next; however, there is no complete justification for taking these steps and making these choices. Only if we go through the proof (and many others of its kind) several times do we realize, in hindsight, how the steps of the proof fit together if we do it this way. Once we have taken the time to study it in detail after it has already been laid down, it seems to us as if all the steps of the proof were necessary, as if these were the only steps that could have led to a proof of the theorem. But this is wrong. There are always many proofs of a theorem, and during the course of history the proofs change. Originally they tend to be very long and later, when new proofs are found, they become shorter and shorter. Thus there is no unique series of steps that constitutes "*the* path of enquiry and investigation," as Kant writes. It is not true that mathematics is "nothing but rules," because there are no rules that always tell us what to do.

One might argue that such considerations apply only to proofs and our doing mathematics, but not to mathematics "itself." But looking at higher mathematics, we easily see that the methods of today become the object of study tomorrow. Hence the methods turn out to be part of mathematics itself. Just think of conic sections, the complex numbers, differentiable manifolds, algebraic varieties, string theory, etc. If one insists that not only all theorems but also all possible methods and proofs are part of some kind of Platonic realm of mathematics, one has to wonder whether one might not equally well say that all poetry is written down already somewhere in a Platonic realm of poetry.

There is, then, no unique way to solve problems in mathematics that could count as "*the* natural path of enquiry and reflection in accordance with rules." Similarly, the expression "in accordance with rules" (*nach Regeln*) is problematic. It is rather vague and can be misleading. Rules do not prescribe how they have to be used. (The German word "*nach*" suggests an even stronger connection between reflection and rules than does the English expression "in accordance with.") There is always much freedom in how and where to make use of them, when and what to take, let, and apply to what. Rules even change. After all, there is a history of mathematics. The old rules usually do not turn out to be false. They simply apply to an older part of mathematics that is not being considered any more, that has been modified, or that has been integrated into another area of mathematics.

It is for these reasons that Newton cannot, contrary to what Kant wrote, make "entirely intuitive" all "the steps that he had to take" (see quote above), simply because he did not really have to take them and because other steps were possible, too. Just think of Leibniz's infinitesimal calculus as an alternative to Newton's. The steps are "intuitive" in the sense that we can reproduce them, that they do not violate other mathematical rules, that they make sense, and that they are part of a theory that works as far as we can see at the time and within a certain framework. The steps are intuitive in this sense, but not in an absolute sense, as if no other steps were possible. Moreover, a new theory often makes us look further and enlarge that framework, as was the case with relativity theory, for instance. The concept of what is "entirely intuitive" changes if we adopt a Kuhnian or Wittgensteinian perspective, making us more aware of historical, social, and cultural aspects.

Of course, in many respects mathematics is not like poetry. There are strict rules in mathematics that should never be violated, such as the rule of non-contradiction. So there is more freedom in poetry. And mathematics is more abstract than poetry, because you can sometimes change a line here and there and still say that it is the same proof, which is hardly so in poetry. There we would tend to say that changing a line is making another poem. But nevertheless, there are creative elements in mathematics that Kant might have underestimated. We will come back to this.

From the mid-1780s on we find several passages that relate rules to learnability and taste and at the same time separate all these aspects from genius and the arts:

> If I derive rules from other rules that are already known, this is a case of talent but not of genius. (*Anthropology Lecture Notes Mrongovius*, 1784/85, XXV 1310)

But we have already shown that a mathematical proof is not a simple matter of "deriving rules from other rules" – there are too many choices that have to be made on the way.

> Matters of genius are those that cannot be acquired according to rules. Mathematics and philosophy are not matters of genius. Mathematics can be learned. (*Anthropology Lecture Notes Mrongovius*, 1784/85, XXV 1311)

But we have seen that mathematics is not something that can be "acquired according to rules" – there are no rules telling you how to acquire rules and when and where and how to use them.

> [Genius] is a talent for art, not for science, in which rules that are distinctly cognized must come first and *determine* the procedure in it. (Section 49, 318).

But it is not true that the rules "determine the procedure." A mathematical proof is not an algorithm. To see this, no knowledge of non-Euclidean geometry or relativity theory is necessary. Contrary to what Kant claims, there is room for beauty and genius in mathematics and the sciences because, as in the case of the production of beautiful objects, there is some kind of freedom in these areas too. Ironically, Kant's theory of free play and subjective **purposiveness** turns out to be very suitable for explaining the role of beauty and genius in mathematics.

When we do mathematics we play with certain possibilities. This becomes apparent when we examine what a researcher or a child does. A researcher trying to answer a certain question initially moves within theories that are already known and well established. But then he goes further, loosening some aspects, dropping certain rules, concentrating on examples, considering borderline cases, trying something out, imagining possible situations (maybe even counterfactual ones), making hypothetical assumptions, seeing what the desired result implies, etc. Now a child learning how to add natural numbers and trying to grasp the rules underlying addition does something very similar, even though he is less aware of what he is doing. This certainly is a very creative process. Here we play with possible ways of making sense out of what we know so far. We often quite freely imagine different possibilities in order to see what fits, and forget about rules. It is often even necessary to forget about rules, because otherwise we cannot create a necessary dynamical process in our mind, and a child or a researcher can teach us that there is indeed much movement going on that is not rule-governed at all. It is only by means of playing with possible rules, associations, and combinations that we can choose well, that we know how to take, let, and apply, as I have indicated above, without any of these moves being necessary ones. It is in such playful processes between **imagination** and **understanding** that mathematical structures suddenly appear to fit, and that we then make a suitable choice. Kant might object here that this is a case of objective purposiveness, where objective elements fit together objectively, and not a case of what he calls subjective purposiveness, where something is suitable for our pleasurable free play of imagination and understanding without objective purposiveness being the ground for this. And this is a crucial claim in Kant's aesthetics as a whole, i.e. that subjective purposiveness cannot be reduced to objective purposiveness, and that beauty cannot be reduced to perfection. But how do we see what turns out to be the right thing, or at least one possible right thing, to do in mathematics? There are uncountably many choices possible in every step we take in a proof, and the structures are far too complex for us to comprehend them completely. We therefore have to rely on our feeling, not only for symmetry but also for *harmony* and *rhythm*. There is indeed much music in mathematics, in its formal and abstract nature, its mix of rules and freedom, and in its creation and composition. The harmony we feel in the free play of our imagination and understanding is indicative of what to try next, and it is here that we find the freedom and open space required for invention and discovery. Furthermore, because the choices we make and the methods we develop are the objects of tomorrow's inquiry, the aesthetic playfulness underlying our choices leaves its *trace* in the mathematics that we have now.

After having discussed the deep systematic problems involved in applying Kant's aesthetics to beauty in mathematics, let us now take a more historical perspective on the same topic. There was a time when Kant thought of beauty and genius as being compatible with mathematics and when he did not separate subjective and objective purposiveness. As a matter of fact, this distinction is new in the third *Critique*. In the following lecture note dating from 1772/73 I will indicate in square brackets what would count as objective [o.p.] or subjective [s.p.] purposiveness. In so doing, I will look back at this quote from the standpoint of Kant's critical philosophy using the conceptual vocabulary that he developed more than 25 years later:

> Demonstrations in geometry can be beautiful due to their shortness [o.p.], their completeness [o.p.], their natural light [?] [*wegen des natürlichen Lichts*], and their suitability for an easier understanding [o.p. and s.p.] [*leichter Fasslichkeit*]. It is the pleasure we take in the ease of proofs, which makes them appear beautiful [s.p.] to us. Here we find an agreement [*Übereinstimmung*] with the subjective laws of the understanding. (*Anthropology Lecture Notes Collins*, 1772/73, XXV 183)

It is clear from this passage, and others, that the pre-critical Kant had not yet introduced the distinction between subjective and objective purposiveness, and that he had not yet separated beauty and genius from mathematics and the sciences. Here is another passage:

> Objects that ease our perception of them [s.p. and o.p] give us pleasure and are beautiful. They accord with the subjective rules of **sensibility** [*den subjectiven Gesetzen der Sinnlichkeit gemäss*], they are suitable to strengthen our inner lives by bringing our powers of imagination and understanding into motion and action [s.p. – this is a forerunner of the notion of free play of the faculties] . . . Symmetry [o.p.] eases our understanding and is the proportion of sensibility [s.p. and o.p.]. Looking at a disproportional house [o.p.], I find it difficult to conceive it as a whole . . . Uniformity [o.p] of the parts helps my **representation**, increases my inner life [s.p.], and I therefore must find it beautiful [s.p.]. (*Anthropology Lecture Notes*, 1772/73, XXV 181)

In this passage, objective purposiveness, the fitting together of the parts, mutually and with respect to the object as a whole, is still thought of as a justifying ground for our finding beauty in the object and thus for what Kant later called subjective purposiveness. But the critical Kant no longer allowed for such a reduction (see *Critique of the Power of Judgment*, section 15). He made this kind of distinction not only with respect to the notion of beauty but also regarding that of genius. As we have seen, in 1790 Kant wrote that Newton should not be called a genius. It is only in his earlier period that we find him thinking that "in mathematics genius can be seen in the discovery of new methods" (*Reflection* 812, XV 362, c. 1776–8), and that "the talent of opening a new way in art or science is a case of genius" (*Reflection* 1510, XV 827, c. 1780–4). The arts and the sciences are being treated equally here. It is in the mid-1780s that a change took place in Kant's thinking. It is at that time that Kant began to develop the distinction between subjective and objective purposiveness, reserving beauty, genius, and the arts for the former only. When it comes to mathematics and the sciences, instead of speaking of genius, he now begins to speak of talent. In those areas, he thought, one can teach and learn all that there is to learn simply by being diligent. To some extent he also wanted to protect mathematics and the sciences from the far too many so-called geniuses of his time: "Now one calls, by way of misuse, every talent a genius" (*Anthropology Lecture Note Mrongovius*, 1784/85, XXV 1311), and "a science which, as such, is supposed to be beautiful, is absurd. For if in it, as a science, one were to ask for grounds and proofs, one would be sent packing with tasteful expressions (*bon mots*)" (section 44, 305).

Whatever caused the change in Kant's views during the 1780s, that change was radical, and even today it remains an open question what exactly the nature of rules and learning is, and whether a feeling, like the feeling for the beautiful (subjective purposiveness), can in the twenty-first century be explained by reference to physical phenomena (objective purposiveness), or whether it can even be reduced to them in a materialist or physicalist way. In any case, Kant argues in the third *Critique* against the possibility of such a reduction. Perhaps further philosophical reflection in the philosophy of mind, neuroscience, and the brain sciences will cast more light on these issues.

Further Reading

Zammito, *The Genesis of Kant's "Critique of Judgment,"* has a subsection on art and artifice (pp. 129–36), and one on art, science, and genius (pp. 137–42). He argues that Kant separates science and genius out of hostility against Herder and the *Sturm und Drang*, which he finds all too passionate.

Giordanetti, "Das Verhältnis von Genie, Künstler und Wissenschaftler in der Kantischen Philosophie," gives a rich account, mainly historical, of the development of Kant's conceptions of genius, artist, and scientist and their interrelations.

Wenzel, "Beauty, Genius, and Mathematics: Why did Kant change his Mind?," also discusses the development, especially the changes, of Kant's ideas during the 1770s and '80s, based on the recently published *Anthropologie Nachschriften (Lecture Notes)*. This article focuses more on systematic than historical questions.

Winterbourne, "Art and Mathematics in Kant's Critical Philosophy," draws parallels between schematism in mathematics and symbolism in art, arguing that imagination and construction function comparably in both disciplines.

Marc-Wogau, *Vier Studien*, has a section (pp. 186–93) on purposiveness and mathematics in the third *Critique*, discussing the example of the circle and the many rules and applications it embraces and unifies, and arguing that here we can see Kant moving from outer to inner purposiveness.

Model, *Metaphysik und reflektierende Urteilskraft bei Kant*, pp. 277–90, discusses the role of genius and purposiveness in the arts versus the sciences and mathematics. Much on Leibniz.

Summary and Overview

This section has three parts. The first, "Before Kant," offers a brief sketch of the historical background of Kant's aesthetics, indicating what the situation was in Germany before 1790. The second, "Kant's Aesthestics," outlines the main points of Kant's aesthetics. And the third, "After Kant," is historical again, offering brief accounts of the influence Kant's aesthetics had on later philosophers after 1790.

Before Kant

The *Critique of the Power of Judgment* appeared in 1790. It has two parts, the "Critique of the *Aesthetic* Power of Judgment" and the "Critique of the *Teleological* Power of Judgment." It was written in the spirit of the Enlightenment, especially the German Enlightenment (*Aufklärung*), which was supported by Frederick II, who became King of Prussia in 1740 and founded the Berlin Academy. There, French thought and British ideas were introduced and discussed, bringing an air of cosmopolitism into Germany. These new thoughts and ideas met in Germany with two traditions that stood strongly opposed to each other: German rationalism, whose main figures were Leibniz (1646–1716) and Wolff (1679–1754), and Christian pietism, led by Crusius (1715–75). Baumgarten (1714–62) revised Wolff's philosophy, and Mendelssohn (1729–86) helped introduce British and French ideas about beauty, art, and genius from the work of such figures as Shaftesbury, Addison, Hutcheson, Hume, Burke, Lord Kames, and Batteux. Kant tried to steer a middle course between rationalism and empiricism, and in matters of aesthetics it was Baumgarten on the one side and Burke on the other who had the greatest influence on him.

As the Enlightenment developed in Germany, Lessing (1729–81), Mendelssohn, and Kant defended more rationalistic views, whereas Hamann

(1730–88), Herder (1744–1803), the young Goethe (1749–1832), and Jacobi (1743–1819) initiated a more emotional, holistic, and sometimes (especially in Kant's view) irrational movement: the *Sturm und Drang*. Jacobi proved to be the sharpest and most enduring critic of Kant and the intellectualist German Enlightenment. It was in this cultural and political situation that Kant wrote his three *Critiques* (1781, 1788, and 1790). After the death of Lessing in 1781 and Mendelssohn in 1786, Kant became the leading figure of the German Enlightenment.

Kant's Aesthetics

The judgment of taste is a judgment of the form "This X is beautiful," where X is an object that we perceive. Although it is not a judgment of cognition, we nevertheless claim *universal* validity. That is, in making a judgment of taste we claim that everyone should agree. If we take this claim (to subjective universality) seriously, then there must be a priori grounds for it and the judgment of taste must be analyzable with respect to the categories (more precisely, with respect to the logical functions of judging) from the first *Critique*. This analysis reveals the following four "moments," the third of which gives the desired a priori ground of the judgment of taste.

First moment

Disinterestedness   "Taste is the faculty for judging an object or a kind of representation through a satisfaction or dissatisfaction without any interest. The object of such a satisfaction is called beautiful."

Three kinds of satisfaction   To clarify the notion of disinterestedness, Kant distinguishes between three kinds of satisfaction, or pleasure (*Wohlgefallen*): the satisfactions in the agreeable, the beautiful, and the good. The first is a merely subjective feeling and there is no claim to universality involved (it does not demand that others should agree), the second is subjective but nevertheless makes such a claim, and the third has an objective ground (it is based on concepts and rules). Only the satisfaction in the beautiful is free and disinterested.

Second moment

Universality   "That is beautiful which pleases universally without a concept." When we find an object beautiful, we ask that everyone who perceives it should find it beautiful too. But there is nothing in the object that we could point out and that would justify our claim. Instead, there are grounds in us and in our relation to the object that justify that claim. Such grounds must be universal – that is, valid for everybody.

Judging To establish the justifying grounds for the judgment of taste's claim to universality, Kant introduces a distinction between judging (*Beurteilung*) and judgment (*Urteil*) in matters of taste. The first justifies the latter and logically precedes it. The judging is a reflection about the universality of the grounds (the cognitive faculties that we share) that are involved in making a judgment of taste.

Free play With the help of the notion of a "judging" that precedes the judgment of taste, Kant develops the concept of a "free play" of our faculties of cognition. This is a play with our representation of the object and with respect to cognition in general. It is harmonious and pleasurable. This concept of a free play of imagination and understanding becomes fully understandable only with the result of the third moment, the a priori principle of subjective purposiveness.

Third moment

Purposiveness "Beauty is the form of the purposiveness of an object, insofar as it is perceived in it without representation of an end." An object that we find beautiful seems to be made for us and for our aesthetic contemplation of it. It fits our powers of cognition, imagination and understanding, without there being any determinate concept or rule for this. We merely play with the representation of the object through our powers of cognition. This play is suitable for cognition in general (*Erkenntnis überhaupt*), but it is not determined through any concepts. The purposiveness is "without purpose." This establishes the a priori principle of our power of judgment, the principle of subjective purposiveness, or purposiveness without purpose. This principle creates fundamental links between us, the free play, and nature around us. In the Dialectic we see that it also allows for a link with our inner nature: the idea of humanity in us.

Beauty versus perfection and charm Beauty should not be confused with perfection or charm. It should be understood as based on the *a priori* principle of purposiveness. This principle involves rationality and emotion but cannot be reduced to them. It is mistaken to think that charm may add to beauty, and it is also wrong to suppose that the satisfaction in beauty is merely a less-developed or lower form of cognition.

The ideal of beauty The idea of a supreme model of beauty is merely an idea, but we wish to represent it as an object of the senses. Such an object should have, and ideally even create, purposiveness within itself. But only man can give a purpose to himself. Thus only the human body can be an ideal of beauty. Kant here makes a first, tentative connection with morality and the idea of humanity in us. Later he will develop a stronger link by showing how beauty is the symbol of morality.

Fourth moment

Necessity "That is beautiful which is cognized without a concept as the object of a necessary satisfaction." If the first three moments are in place, then we cannot but judge the object to be beautiful. Kant uses this opportunity to introduce, and reinterpret, the traditional idea of the *sensus communis*. This is the idea of a sense that we share and that should explain this kind of necessity. But instead of introducing such an additional sense, Kant thinks it is better simply to explain this idea through his already established concept of the free play (second moment) and his a priori principle of purposiveness (third moment).

* * *

The sublime Besides beauty, there is the sublime. The feeling for the sublime is based on a two-step process. First, we perceive the object and find it overwhelming: too huge (mathematically sublime) or too powerful (dynamically sublime) for our perceptual capacities. But then, in a second step, we discover something within ourselves that is even greater (although of a totally different kind): the idea of humanity.

The two peculiarities The judgment of taste "determines the object with regard to satisfaction (as beauty) with a claim to the assent of everyone, *as if* it were objective," and "is not determinable by grounds of proof at all, just *as if* it were merely subjective." Kant explains this double "as if" by making use of the results from his discussion of the four moments of taste. Later, in the Dialectic, the two peculiarities appear again, but in a different form, namely as the "antinomy of taste."

Genius Genius is a talent, an "inborn disposition of the mind (*ingenium*) through which nature gives the rule to art." There are no rules of taste, so there should also be no rules of production of works of art (which are objects of taste). The artist, who has genius, produces works of art without fully understanding the process him- or herself. Rules come later, when a work of art has been produced and when other artists have come to recognize it as an exemplar and use it as a model for their own inspiration. The exemplar then takes the place of a rule.

Aesthetic ideas   There are concepts of reason, such as our ideas of morality, God or freedom, for which we can never find corresponding objects of the senses that would be adequate to them. Similarly, but the other way around, there are objects of the senses or representations of imagination, aesthetic ideas, that inspire us and that give us much to think about, but for which we never find an adequate concept. Symbols are often of this kind, and artists make use of such symbols and aesthetic ideas to express concepts of reason and to make them communicable. Kant explains the structure and the functioning of symbols and aesthetic ideas in connection with his theory of genius and against the background of his theory of the aesthetic power of judgment in general, involving the free play, subjective purposiveness without purpose, and cognition in general.

Nature and art   Beautiful art is man-made but it must look natural and not constructed. It thus must be the product of genius. On the other hand, beautiful nature looks like art. Kant explains this interconnectedness of beautiful art and beautiful nature through his theory of genius and aesthetic ideas and within his general theory of aesthetic power of judgment, involving the free play, the a priori principle of subjective purposiveness, and the possibility of the supersensible.

The Dialectic and the antinomy of taste   Since there is an *a priori* basis for the judgment of taste, we must make sure that there will not be a contradiction on another, higher level, namely within reason itself. There the two peculiarities give rise to an "antinomy of taste": The judgment of taste seems to be both based and not based on concepts. The contradiction can be resolved by distinguishing between two kinds of concept: of the understanding and of reason. The judgment of taste might be based on a concept of reason, an indeterminable concept, an idea of the supersensible. The grounds that Kant has discovered in the Analytic, the free play and the a priori principle of purposiveness must allow for such an interpretation and this solution of the antinomy in the Dialectic. They must give the "correct concept of taste."

The supersensible   This is the idea, or concept of reason, that possibly underlies the judgment of taste in a way that fundamentally connects us with outer nature. It is the idea of humanity in us and of a substratum of nature outside of us. Later, in the Dialectic of teleology, Kant introduces the idea of an intuitive, almost God-like understanding and there speculates about further connections between us and outer nature. These speculations in sections 76 and 77 go beyond the framework of the third *Critique* and had great influence on Hegel and other idealist philosophers after Kant.

Beauty as the symbol of morality Based on his distinctions between sensibility, understanding, and reason, and based on his theory of our power of judgment (especially in its reflective and aesthetic functions), Kant develops general theories of schemata, signs, symbolism, and aesthetic ideas. He then makes use of these theories and the idea of the supersensible to show how beauty and morality are connected.

After Kant

The German poet, playwright, and philosopher Friedrich Schiller (1759–1805) was very much taken by Kant's aesthetics, but he was also a friend of Goethe and the *Sturm und Drang*. He tried to combine their ideas. He was the first to develop further Kantian aesthetics (in particular the notion of free play) by applying it to specific problems of education (*Bildung*), culture, and history. Schiller developed Kant's formal aesthetics into a material aesthetics, focusing on practical aspects of our daily lives (education *through* art). He tried to develop Kant's theory of beauty as the symbol of morality in order to cast light on the historical and social impacts and *tasks* of the fine arts. Starting out from within Kant's systematic framework, but trying to transcend it (the endeavor of many philosophers after Kant), Schiller strived to reconcile the sensuous and the rational side of human nature. To do so, he developed, still relying on Kant, the concept of a "play drive" (*Spieltrieb*) and the concept of a "beautiful soul" (*schöne Seele*). His "Kallias Letters" (1793), "On Grace and Dignity" (1793), and especially his "Letters on the Aesthetic Education of Man" (1794/95) were influential at the time and had an impact on the literary genre of the *Bildungsroman* as well as on German aesthetic idealism (Fichte, Schelling, Hegel) and Marxist aesthetic theories.

Of the three *Critiques*, it was the third that impressed Goethe (1749–1832) the most. He was fascinated by questions about purposiveness in nature and the evolution of organisms. One can see clear traces of this in his novels such as *Elective Affinities* (*Wahlverwandtschaften*) (1809), but also in his studies of botany, which in turn influenced Schiller and Hegel, with whom he shared his ideas in private conversations.

Already a few years earlier, three young geniuses had become close friends around 1790 in the theological seminary at Tübingen, where they shared their ideas in long discussions and for some time even lived together: the romantic poet Hölderlin (1770–1843), the young Hegel (1770–1831), and the even younger Schelling (1775–1854). This was the time when Kant's third *Critique* appeared (1790). These three friends enthusiastically discussed not only the French Revolution (1789) and questions of theology, but also Kantian philosophy.

Schelling soon met Schiller and Goethe, and art, organicism, and vitalism came to play a central role in his philosophy. In 1798, at the age of only 23, Schelling became professor in Jena and a close friend and colleague of Fichte (1762–1814), and with Hegel he edited an influential philosophical journal during 1802–3. Both Schelling and Hegel were strongly influenced by the works of Kant, including his third *Critique*. Both referred to its sections 76 and 77 and pointed out the fundamental importance of the general ideas they contained. Schelling took from Kant the idea that both organisms and works of art must be understood teleologically, and in his own philosophy aesthetic insights were superior to theoretical and practical ones.

Hegel, whose philosophy developed much slower than that of his young friend Schelling, published his *Phenomenology of Spirit* in 1807. There he tried to overcome several strict distinctions that Kant had introduced and that he thought were artificial and "merely abstract." In his eyes, several fundamental Kantian notions had to be made fluid and enlivened. They had to be made "concrete" (from Latin *concrescere*: to grow together – see vitalism and organicism above), which could be done only through a dialectical thought-process and with an awareness of the role of history. Kant would probably not have agreed to such developments, but he himself planted the seeds of it in his third *Critique* by suggesting many overarching connections, especially in the Dialectic. Essential for the development of Hegel's dialectical method were ideas about organisms conveyed to him by Goethe (who in turn was inspired by Kant's third *Critique*).

The period after Kant's third *Critique* was no longer (just) one of struggle between Enlightenment and *Sturm und Drang*. It was also the time of rising early German Romanticism and German Idealism. With the decline of the Enlightenment movement, Romanticism grew. But in some respects, Romanticism was also a continuation of the Enlightenment (insisting on change, for instance).

The leader of the early German Romantic movement was Friedrich Schlegel (1772–1829). Kant's third *Critique* made a lasting impression on him, but he was more impressed by Schelling's theory of aesthetic consciousness and pure creativity. Like Fichte, Schelling, and Hegel, he found Kant's systematic philosophy too rigid and inflexible. Together with his brother August Wilhelm Schlegel (1767–1845), he edited the leading journal for early German Romanticism, *Athenäum*, in which literature, historical linguistics, and philosophy met. Not only the two Schlegel brothers but also Schleiermacher and Novalis contributed to this journal and they were all influenced by Kant's ideas and actively exchanged ideas with the German Idealists of the time. Goethe's *Faust* was considered a good example of Romanticism.

Schopenhauer (1788–1860), in his main work, *The World as Will and Representation* (1818), combines ideas from Kant, Plato, and Indian Philosophy (Buddhism

and Hinduism) in new and interesting ways. Schopenhauer was mainly influenced by the first *Critique*, less so by the third. His views on art, which occupy a
high position in his philosophy and about which he had much to say, rely more
on Plato and other sources. However, traces of Kant's notion of purposiveness
are clearly visible in his metaphysical philosophy of will, and he was impressed
by Kant's account of the sublime and followed Kant's distinction between the
mathematical and the dynamical sublime. Schopenhauer's work in turn had an
impact on Nietzsche and Wittgenstein, as well as on writers such as Tolstoy,
Conrad, Proust, and Thomas Mann.

The period surrounding Kant's lifetime was rich and complex. There was
much change taking place, politically, socially, culturally, and philosophically, and
Kant's ideas and thoughts were often present, if not directly then indirectly. To
see the historical influence of his aesthetics, one must allow for a wider context.
One must look at its place in his philosophical system as a whole and then trace
the influences of this system.

Let us briefly look at one example from the twentieth century. Jean-François
Lyotard (1924–98), a leading postmodernist philosopher, made a close study of
Kant's aesthetics (*Lessons on the Analytic of the Sublime*, 1991). He focused on the
sublime and on art (whereas Kant favored the beautiful and nature). Lyotard did
not try to unify opposing elements, as the German idealists had done. Instead,
he thought that differences must be left standing as they are, and that one must
be content with critical reflection – a critical attitude that he had already seen in
Kant.

Glossary

a priori Said of that which is (logically, not temporally) *prior* to experience, independent of experience, and usually the *condition of the possibility* of something that is in question. Universality and necessity are features of the a priori. Not only judgments can be a priori, but so can principles, rules, and various elements of cognition, such as intuition and concepts (in particular the categories).

aesthetic (*ästhetisch*) In Kant's third *Critique*, refers to the judgment of taste and the analysis and "critique" of this judgment. The aesthetic here must be distinguished from the Transcendental Aesthetic, the study of time and space from the first *Critique*.

analytic (*analytisch*) Said of a judgment, proposition, principle, or method; opposite to "synthetic." If one assumes something to be given and looks for its conditions, one uses an analytic method of investigation. Kant's aesthetics proceeds by analyzing the judgment of taste and is therefore analytic in method. A judgment is analytic if what is thought under the predicate is already thought under the subject, as in "bachelors (subject) are unmarried (predicate)." Analytic judgments do not increase our knowledge, which is different from synthetic judgments. Each of Kant's three *Critiques* consists of two parts, an Analytic and a Dialectic. See "Dialectic."

antinomy A contradiction between two statements that both seem to be true. The contradiction is not merely a conflict of empirical claims but seems to lie in the nature of reason itself. Antinomies make us realize that objects of appearance are not things in themselves. They force us to look beyond the world of mere appearance and to bring human reason in accord with itself on a higher level, the realm of the supersensible. Kant discusses antinomies in the Dialectic. See "Dialectic" and "reason."

apperception Self-consciousness, consciousness of oneself as a thinking subject, underlies and holds together our perceptions and our thoughts.

categories   Basic concepts of the understanding by means of which experience and cognition become possible. They are a priori because they are prior to experience, and they are pure because nothing empirical is mixed into them. Their origin is in us and thus *subjective*. But they are in *all* of us, and they are also *objective* because for us experience is possible only through them. Kant distinguishes twelve categories (in four groups) and studies them with respect to twelve forms of judgment, consciousness (apperception) and perception in his first *Critique*, in the notoriously difficult and famous "transcendental deduction [justification] of the categories."

causa efficiens   The moving cause, for instance the builder of a house or the hammering in of a nail; that through which something happens or comes to be. Sunshine is the cause of a rise in temperature.

causa finalis   Purpose, end, or aim (Greek: *telos*), that for the sake of which something exists or happens; for instance, the shelter (purpose) a house provides, or the attaching (aim of hammering) of a wooden board onto another. *Causa efficiens* and *causa finalis* both play a role in explaining what a thing is and how it comes into existence.

cognition (*Erkenntnis*)   A process or the result of such a process by means of which we obtain knowledge of objects. We usually have cognition through experience, but there are always a priori elements involved and the whole cognition can even be a priori (that is, we can realize that the judgment is *valid* a priori). Intuition (*Anschauung*) and concepts are the elements of cognition. Kant thought and wrote much in Latin, and the corresponding Latin term for German *Erkenntnis* is *cognitio*. Thus English "cognition" is a suitable translation. Kant studies cognition in his first *Critique*.

cognition in general (*Erkenntnis überhaupt*)   Cognition universally conceived, cognition as such, the very idea of cognition. This is not supposed to be a mere generalization of individual cognitions. It does not just have comparative generality. It is not based on induction and no exception is conceivable. It is a normative concept, not a descriptive one.

cognitive judgment or **judgment of cognition** (*Erkenntnisurteil*)   A judgment that is based on cognition and that gives us knowledge. See "cognition."

common sense   See *sensus communis*.

concept (*Begriff*)   That which can serve as predicate in judgments, as for instance in "This is a *house*," or "This house is *red*." It is by means of the concept *house* that I understand what makes a house a house, that I have a grasp of its characteristic features, and that I can recognize something as a house. A concept always comes with rules by means of which I know how to apply it. By using concepts we combine and order our representations (and thus bring them into one consciousness). Concepts and intuition are the elements of cognition and depend on each other. There are also a priori concepts, such as the categories. Kant has a sophisticated theory of concepts in his first *Critique*, involving the categories, perception, and consciousness. In German, *Begriff* comes with a verb, *begreifen*, which means "to grasp" and indicates an act of the mind. See "intuition."

deduction (*Deduktion*)   A legal term, meaning *justification* (of a claim). All three *Critiques* of Kant contain a "Deduction," a part that tries to justify a priori foundations for certain fundamental claims. In Kant's aesthetics, we are dealing with the judgment of taste's claim to universal intersubjective validity.

determining (*bestimmend*)   A function, use, or application of the power of judgment through which we determine that a given particular X is a case of Y, as in "This (X) is a house (Y)," or "This house (X) is red (Y)." Here the concept Y is given. If no Y is given, the power of judgment has to look for one. In that case it has to "reflect." See "reflecting," "power of judgment," and "subsumption."

Dialectic   The second part in each of the three *Critiques*, following the Analytic; deals with antinomies, dialectical transcendental illusions, and apparent contradictions of human reason with itself. See "analytic" and "antinomy."

disinterestedness (*Uninteressiertheit*)   Without interest, or devoid of interest, a characteristic feature of our satisfaction in the beautiful. See "satisfaction." Our satisfaction is disinterested if it is free of concerns about the real *existence* of the object that gives rise to it. In pure contemplation we are free of such concerns.

experience (*Erfahrung*)   Perception, or what we make out of perception, and what leads us to cognition. Experience always involves a priori elements of the mind (mainly the categories) that give it its unity and objectivity.

faculty (*Vermögen*)   An ability or power of the mind to cognize, feel, or desire; in particular, the faculties of cognition (understanding, power of judgment, and reason), and even more specifically the faculties of cognition (*Erkenntnisvermögen*) in the narrow sense, which are imagination and understanding. See "imagination" and "understanding."

feeling (*Gefühl*)   See "sensation."

form   Always comes together with matter. The distinction between form and matter goes back to Aristotle (*eidos* and *morphe* versus *hyle*). A stone, for instance (matter), is given a certain shape (its form). In biology an individual creature belongs to a certain species by virtue of the "form" which determines its development and essence. Kant uses the term "form" to describe our ways of perceiving and thinking (in general our ways of ordering what is given) in contrast to that which is perceived and thought (matter). The distinction between form and matter becomes problematic when applied to sensations. See "sensation."

Gemeinsinn   See *sensus communis*.

genius (Lat. *genius*; Germ. *Genie*)   A talent for producing great works of art, or the person who has such talent. Genius, as a talent, is innate and a gift of nature. An artist can have genius and produce something new, a new style in art. Through a genius, new rules are given by nature to art, and even the artist him- or herself cannot fully explain how this happens.

ground (*Grund*)   A foundation, justification, or reason. For Kant it is usually a justifying basis; less an argument than the deeper layers on which the argument is built.

idea (*Idee*)   In the first *Critique*, a concept of reason that aims at an object that we can think of but never experience, such as God or freedom, an object that is unconditioned and that answers our demand for ultimate explanations. Such ideas can nevertheless be useful in guiding our investigations (which is what is meant by a regulative idea). In the third *Critique*, Kant also discusses *aesthetic ideas*, which belong to imagination and make us think, although (and because) we cannot find a single concept that would be adequate to them. Aesthetic ideas are important for Kant's discussion of genius.

imagination (*Einbildungskraft*)   One of the two faculties of cognition. The other is the understanding. For Kant, imagination plays an essential part in cognition and is not just fantasy. By means of imagination we take up, recollect, and creatively combine what is given to us through the senses. In this, imagination is guided by concepts of the understanding, empirical and (more fundamentally) a priori ones. Imagination mediates between sensibility and understanding. See "sensibility" and "understanding."

intuition (*Anschauung*)   What is immediately given to us through the senses or, in the case of pure intuition, what is given by the forms of intuition, time, and space. Intuitions are part of what gives concepts their content, and, through concepts, intuitions mean something to us. Intuitions without concepts are "blind," and concepts without intuition are "empty." See "concept."

judgment (*Urteil*)   The act by which we combine, in our conscious mind, representations (concepts and intuitions) into an objective unity. This combination is guided by the categories, which give it its objectivity. See "power of judgment," "determining," and "reflecting."

judgment of cognition (*Erkenntnisurteil*)   See "cognitive judgment."

manifold (*Mannigfaltigkeit*)   A manifold of sensations is given to us through the senses and in intuition. It is then an empirical manifold of intuition. A manifold of intuition can also be pure, as is the case in geometry, when we create it by drawing a line or by constructing a triangle. In this case we give the manifold to ourselves.

matter (*Materie*)   The counterpart to form. See "form."

moment (*das Moment*, neuter) A term originally used in physics to mean a moving force or its effect (acceleration). Without making the connection with this original meaning sufficiently clear, but having it in mind, Kant distinguishes four "moments" of the judgment of taste. "Moment" here should not be confused with a moment of time (*der Moment*, masc.), although deep down they might be related. See the section "The Moments of a Judgment of Taste" in my Introduction.

power of judgment (*Urteilskraft*) A faculty of the mind, more specifically a faculty of cognition, by means of which we subsume the particular (an intuition or concept) under the general (a concept, rule, or law). The power of judgment can be determining or reflecting. See "subsumption," "determining," and "reflecting."

principle (*Prinzip*) A basic proposition or law of reason, from which, or according to which, specific kinds of particular knowledge can be derived. The principle of the purposiveness of nature, for instance, says that the various particular laws of nature that we discover should fit each other and form a system. This is a regulative principle helping us in our scientific investigation of nature.

pure (*rein*) Free or independent of (not made impure by) what is given through the senses (the empirical). In special situations it can also mean free of influences that are pure in their own right.

purpose (*Zweck*) Primarily a concept of practical reason. When we set ourselves a purpose or aim, we direct our will toward it and act accordingly. In our study of nature, especially in biology and evolution theory, we often discover what seem to us to be purposes set by nature itself or by God.

purposiveness (*Zweckmässigkeit*) That which fits as if it were arranged according to some plan, intention, or purpose. In an organism for instance, the parts fit and cooperate harmoniously with each other as if they were designed that way.

reason (*Vernunft*) In a wider sense, the higher faculty of cognition taken as a whole, including theoretical and practical (i.e., moral) reason. In a more narrow sense, the higher cognitive faculty that exists outside and above the understanding and which supervises it.

reflecting, reflective (*reflektierend*) A function of the power of judgment, through which we try to find a suitable concept for a given particular, when, for instance, we see something and wonder what it might be. It is the task of the third *Critique* to find an a priori principle for the power of judgment in its reflective function. This principle will turn out to be the principle of purposiveness. See "power of judgment" and "determining."

representation (Lat. *representatio*; Germ. *Vorstellung*) In general, what is in front of the mind's eye, so to speak. Of course we do not literally see representations. We have them. We have representations of an object. For Kant, a representation might be an intuition, a perception, or a concept. They are combined through the understanding to form a cognition, and the categories play the fundamental role in these acts of combination.

rule (*Regel*) A regulation that relates a concept to whatever falls under it, that is, to which it can be applied. By means of the concept of a house and its rules of application, for instance, I recognize something as a house and I can think about houses as such. As the understanding is the faculty of concepts, so it is also the faculty of rules. It is only through rules that combinations (acts of synthesis) of intuitions and concepts are *objective*, that is, that they give us objective knowledge of objects.

satisfaction (*Wohlgefallen*) A feeling, of which Kant distinguishes three different kinds: the satisfaction in the agreeable, the satisfaction in the beautiful, and the satisfaction in the good. Only the satisfaction in the beautiful is "disinterested." "Satisfaction" might not seem a happy translation, and *Wohlgefallen* has also been translated as "pleasure," "delight," or "liking." But these translations have their own problems.

sensation (*Empfindung*) What we feel or obtain through the senses. There is a subtle ambiguity here (in English as well as in German) and Kant points it out in section 3. Sensation can be inner sensation, as of pleasure or agreeableness; he calls this sensation "feeling" (*Gefühl*). But sensation can also be outer sensation, sensation through our five senses, which gives us a representation of an object, such as a house that we see. Agreeableness, for instance, is subjective sensation, and the perception of the green color of a meadow an objective sensation. In general, we can distinguish between the two by deciding whether or not the sensation in question can serve (the person who has it) for a cognition (of an object). If it can, it is referred to an object; if it cannot, it is referred to the subject and called a feeing. This distinction is crucial, because taste seems to straddle the two. To avoid confusion, Kant wants to reserve the word "sensation" for objective sensation and "feeling" for subjective sensation.

sensibility (*Sinnlichkeit*) The receptivity of the mind. Sensibility makes it possible for us to be affected by objects of the senses (perception). It gives us intuitions (*Anschauungen*) (whose forms are time and space), which in turn require concepts so that these intuitions, perceptions, and objects of the senses can be thought. Sensibility and understanding are thus the two sources of human cognition, sensibility being the faculty of intuitions, understanding the faculty of concepts. See "intuition" and "concept."

sensus communis (Latin); ***Gemeinsinn*** (German) Some kind of common sense, or rather a variation of it. The idea of a common sense goes back at least to Aristotle and has gone through various modifications in meaning. The English term "common sense" usually means a healthy understanding that is opposed to skepticism or nonsense. This must be distinguished from what *sensus communis* or *Gemeinsinn* means for Kant: the ground for our ability to take into account (or reflect about) other people's ways of looking at things and the ability to take their points of view into account. The *sensus communis* allows one to avoid taking one's personal opinion for the general and objective one. For more details and a brief historical account, see the beginning of the section "Kant's Interpretation of the *sensus communis*" in chapter 4. See also in that chapter the second half of the section "Exemplary Necessity."

subsumption   A particular is said to be "subsumed" under the general. The particular might be an intuition or a concept. For instance, when I say "This is a villa," I subsume my perceptual intuition (the particular) under the concept of a villa (the general); and in "Villas are houses," the concept of a villa (the particular) is subsumed under the concept of a house (the general). See "power of judgment," "reflecting," "rule," "determining."

supersensible (*übersinnlich*)   Those things that we can think but not experience or comprehend, for instance, God, freedom, or immortality. There is no cognition of the supersensible, but reflecting about morality, for instance, we have good reasons to demand its existence. Trying to imagine the supersensible, we make use of symbols. In the third *Critique* Kant shows how beauty can be a symbol of morality and indicates a possible link between theoretical and practical (moral) reason and the supersensible.

synthetic (*synthetisch*)   Means combining (*verknüpfend*); said of judgment, proposition, principle, or method; opposite to "analytic." See "analytic."

teleology (*Teleologie*)   From the Greek *telos* (aim or purpose). The study of goals, aims, intentions, and purposes, especially those that we (seem to) find in nature. The general idea, going back to Aristotle, is to explain phenomena and processes not from their causes but from the goals toward which they seem to be directed. The second half of the *Critique of the Power of Judgment* is about this teleology. There Kant argues that (and why) teleological considerations can be useful in regulating and guiding our scientific investigations but that by themselves they cannot provide any knowledge of nature. Instead they tell us something about ourselves and about our power of judgment. For Kant, the principles of teleology thus belong to the power of judgment. See "purposiveness," "reflecting," and "power of judgment."

transcendental (*transzendental*)   Said with respect to the a priori conditions and elements of our experience; more specifically, said of our knowledge, or investigation, of these a priori elements and their application in experience. "Transcendental" is not to be confused with "transcendent": Transcendent is what lies beyond the limits of our experience, whereas the transcendental spells out what makes our (everyday) experience possible. There is transcen-

ing cooperates with sensibility, the faculty of intuitions. The pure understanding is the source of the categories. See "sensibility," "concept," "rule,"
and "reflecting."

universal (*universal*)   To be distinguished from "general" (*general*); a rule or
judgment is universal (universally valid) if it allows for no exception, whereas
it is merely general if no exception has been encountered so far. In German
there is a third word, *allgemein*, which can mean either: the universal or the
general. Universality (*universale Allgemeinheit*) is a sign of necessity, and there
must be a higher reason from which it follows. Generality (*generale Allgemeinheit*), on the other hand, is merely empirical. Universality and necessity point
to a priori justifying grounds. For more on "universality," see the section
"Subjective Universality" in chapter 2.

Bibliography

Works by Kant

In German, the standard edition is *Kants Gesammelte Schriften*, edited by the Deutsche Akademie der Wissenschaften (Walter de Gruyter, 1902). This is a rather expensive edition. But there is also a very inexpensive edition of the main works, available in paperback in 10 volumes, which has been edited by Wilhelm Weischedel and is also widely used. This edition even has an advantage over the Akademie Ausgabe: it is sometimes closer to the original and in such cases always indicates the tacit changes made by the Akademie Ausgabe.

In English we now luckily have, for the first time, a complete and uniform set of translations: *The Cambridge Edition of the Works of Immanuel Kant*. In particular, there is the *Critique of the Power of Judgment*, translated by Paul Guyer and Eric Matthews (Cambridge University Press, 2000), which I have been following; and the *Critique of Pure Reason*, translated by Paul Guyer and Allen W. Wood (Cambridge University Press, 1998).

Other primary works

Addison, Joseph. Several essays published in the *Spectator*, 1711–12.

Baumgarten, Alexander Gottlieb. *Meditationes philosophicae de nonnullis ad poema pertinentibus*, 1735. (*Reflections on Poetry*. Trans. Karl Aschenbrenner and W. B. Holther, Berkeley and Los Angeles: University of California Press, 1954.)

——*Metaphysica*. Halle, 1739.

——*Aesthetica*, 2 vols. Frankfurt an der Oder, 1750–8.

Burke, Edmund. *A Philosophical Enquiry into the Origin of our Ideas of the Sublime and the Beautiful*. London: R. & J. Dodsley, 1757, revised edition 1759.

Gerard, Alexander. *An Essay on Taste*. London and Edinburgh, 1759.

Gottsched, Johann Christoph. *Versuch einer Critischen Dichtkunst*. Leipzig, 1730.

——*Erste Gründe der gesamten Weltweisheit*. 2 vols. Leipzig, 1733–4.

——*Auszug aus der Herrn Batteux schönen Künsten*. Leipzig, 1754.

Hamann, J. G. *Sokratische Denkwürdigkeiten*. Amsteram 1759. (*Hamann's Socratic Memorabilia. A Translation and Commentary*. Trans. James C. O'Flaherty, Baltimore: John Hopkins University Press, 1967.)

——*Aesthetica in Nuce*. 1762.

Hume, David. "Of the Standard of Taste," in his *Four Dissertations*, London, 1757.

——*Essays, Moral, Political, and Literary*. Edinburgh, 1741–2.

——*A Treatise of Human Nature*. London, 1739–40.

——*An Enquiry Concerning the Principles of Morals*. 1751.

——*Dialogues Concerning Natural Religion*. London, 1779.

Hutcheson, Francis. *An Inquiry into the Original of our Ideas of Beauty and Virtue*. London, 1725.

Kames, Lord [Henry Home]. *The Elements of Criticism*. 1762.

Meier, Georg Friedrich. *Auszug aus der Vernunftlehre*. Halle, 1752.

——*Anfangsgründe aller schönen Künste und Wissenschaften*. 3 vols. Halle, 1748–50.

Mendelssohn, Moses. *Über die Empfindungen*. Berlin, 1755.

——"Über das Erhabene und das Naïve in den schönen Wissenschaften." Leipzig, 1758.

——"Philosophische Untersuchungen des Ursprungs unserer Ideen vom Erhabenen und Schönen." Leipzig, 1758. (*Philosophical Writings*, edited by Daniel O. Dahlstrom, Cambridge Texts in the History of Philosophy. Cambridge: Cambridge University Press, 1997.)

Shaftesbury, third earl of [Anthony Ashley Cooper]. *Characteristics of Men, Manners, Opinions, Times*. 1711.

Sulzer, Johann Georg. *Unterredungen über die Schönheit der Natur*. Berlin, 1770.

Tetens, Johann Nicolas. *Philosophische Versuche über die menschliche Natur und ihre Entwicklung*. 2 vols. Leipzig, 1776–7.

Wolff, Chrisitan. *Vernünfftige Gedancken von Gott, der Welt, und der Seele des Menschen, Auch allen Dingen überhaupt*. Halle, 1720.

Winckelmann, Johann Joachim. *Gedancken über die Nachahmung der Griechischen Wercke in der Mahlerey und Bildhaue-Kunst*. 1755. Second enlarged edition, including *Sendschreiben* and *Erläuterungen*, Dresden, Leipzig, 1756. (*Winckelmann: Writings on Art*. Edited by David Irwin. London: Phaidon, 1972.)

Secondary works

Although this is a rather thin book on Kant and intended not primarily for specialists but also for a wider audience, including students and people working in other areas such as literature for instance, I have chosen to give a rather long list of secondary works. Anyone interested in reading more on any specific topic can find his or her way right here – or at least the first steps of such a way. The suggested readings at the end of every section in this book should provide help in this.

Allison, Henry E. *Kant's Transcendental Idealism*. New Haven: Yale University Press, 1983; 2nd, much enlarged, edition 2004.

—— "Pleasure and Harmony in Kant's Theory of Taste: A Critique of the Causal Reading," in Herman Parret, ed., *Kants Ästhetik, Kant's Aestheics, L'esthétique de Kant.* Berlin and New York: Walter de Gruyter, 1998, pp. 466–83.

—— "Is the *Critique of Judgment* 'Post-Critical'?" in Sally Sedgwick, ed., *The Reception of Kant's Critical Philosophy: Fichte, Schelling, Hegel.* Cambridge: Cambridge University Press, 2000, pp. 78–92.

—— *Kant's Theory of Taste. A Reading of the "Critique of Aesthetic Judgment."* Cambridge: Cambridge University Press, 2001.

Ameriks, Karl. "How to save Kant's Deduction of Taste," *Journal of Value Inquiry* 16 (1982), pp. 295–302.

—— "Kant and the Objectivity of Taste," *British Journal of Aesthetics* 23 (1983), pp. 3–17.

—— "New Views on Kant's Judgment of Taste," in Herman Parret, ed., *Kants Ästhetik, Kant's Aesthetics, L'esthétique de Kant.* Berlin and New York: Walter de Gruyter, 1998, pp. 431–47.

Amoroso, Leonardo. *Senso e consenso. Uno studio kantiano.* Napoli: Guida, 1984.

—— "Kant et le nom de L'Esthétique," in Herman Parret, ed., *Kants Ästhetik, Kant's Aesthetics, L'esthétique de Kant.* Berlin and New York: Walter de Gruyter, 1998, pp. 701–5.

Aquila, Richard. "A New Look at Kant's Aesthetic Judgments," in Ted Cohen and Paul Guyer, eds., *Essays in Kant's Aesthetics.* Chicago and London: University of Chicago Press, 1982, pp. 87–114.

Baldacchino, Lewis. *A Study in Kant's Metaphysics of Aesthetic Experience – Reason and Feeling.* Lewiston: Edwin Mellen Press, 1992. *The History of Philosophy*, vol. 25.

Banham, Gary. *Kant and the Ends of Aesthetics.* New York: Macmillan, 2000.

Bartuschat, Wolfgang. *Zum systematischen Ort von Kants Kritik der Urteilskraft.* Frankfurt am Main: Victorio Klostermann, 1972.

Basch, Victor. *Essai critique sur l'esthétique de Kant.* Paris: F. Alcan, J. Vrin, 1896.

Baum, Manfred. "Kants Prinzip der Zweckmäßigkeit und Hegels Realisierung des Begriffs," in Hans-Friedrich Fulda and Rolf-Peter Horstmann, eds., *Hegel und die "Kritik der Urteilskraft."* Stuttgart: Klett-Cotta, 1990, pp. 158–73.

—— "Subjektivität, Allgemeingültigkeit und Apriorität des Geschmacksurteils bei Kant," *Deutsche Zeitschrift für Philosophie* 39 (1991), pp. 272–84.

Baumeister, Thomas. "Kants Geschmackskritik zwischen Transzendentalphilosophie und Psychologie," in Herman Parret, ed., *Kants Ästhetik, Kant's Aesthetics, L'esthétique de Kant.* Berlin and New York: Walter de Gruyter, 1998, pp. 158–75.

Bäumler, Alfred. *Das Problem der Allgemeigültigkeit in Kants Ästhetik.* Dissertation, München: Delpin-Verlag, 1915.

—— *Das Irrationalitätsproblem in der Ästhetik und Logik des 18. Jahrhunderts bis zur Kritik der Urteilskraft.* Halle an der Saale, 1923.

Beck, Lewis White. "Kritische Bemerkungen zur vermeintlichen Apriorität der Geschmacksurteile," in A. J. Bucher, H. Drüe, and T. M. Seebohm, eds., *Bewußt sein. Gerhard Funke zu eigen.* Bonn, 1975, pp. 369–72.

Beck, Lewis White. "On the Putative Apriority of Judgments of Taste," *Essays on Kant and Hume.* New Haven and London: Yale University Press, 1978, pp. 167–70.

Bell, David. "The Art of Judgment," *Mind* 96 (1987), pp. 221–44.

Bernstein, J. M., ed. *Classic and Romantic German Aesthetics.* Cambridge: Cambridge University Press, 2003.

Biemel, Walter. *Die Bedeutung von Kants Begründung der Ästhetik für die Philosophie der Kunst.* Kantstudien Ergänzungshefte 77, 1959.

—— "Das Wesen der Lust bei Kant," in A. J. Bucher, H. Drüe, and T. M. Seebohm, eds., *Bewußt sein. Gerhard Funke zu eigen.* Bonn: Bouvier, 1975.

Bittner, Rüdiger and Pfaff, Peter, eds. *Das ästhetische Urteil: Beiträge zur sprachanalytischen Ästhetik.* Köln: Kiepenheuer, 1977.

Blencke, Fritz. *Die Trennung des Schönen vom Angenehmen in Kants Kritik der ästhetischen Urteilskraft. Zugleich eine Verteidigung Kants gegen den Vorwurf, daß er lediglich Form-Ästhetiker im heutigen Sinne sei.* Dissertation Strassburg, Neuwied: Heusers Buchdruckerei, 1889.

Böhme, Gernot. *Kants Kritik der Urteilskraft in neuer Sicht.* Frankfurt am Main: Suhrkamp Verlag, 1999.

Bowie, Andrew. *Aesthetics and Subjectivity from Kant to Nietzsche.* Manchester: Manchester University Press, 1990.

Bradl, Beate. *Die Rationalität des Schönen bei Kant und Hegel.* München: Wilhelm Fink Verlag, 1998.

Brandt, Reinhard. "The Deductions in the *Critique of Judgment*: Comments on Hampshire and Horstmann," in Eckart Förster, ed., *Kant's Transcendental Deductions. The Three "Critiques" and the "Opus postumum."* Stanford, Calif.: Stanford University Press, 1989, pp. 177–90.

—— "Analytic/Dialectic," in Eva Schaper and Wilhelm Vossenkuhl, eds., *Reading Kant. New Perspectives on Transcendental Arguments and Critical Philosophy.* Oxford: Blackwell, 1989, pp. 179–95.

—— "Die Schönheit der Kristalle und das Spiel der Erkenntniskräfte. Zum Gegenstand und zur Logik des ästhetischen Urteils bei Kant," in R. Brandt and Werner Stark, eds., *Autographen, Dokumente und Berichte. Kant-Forschungen,* vol. 5. Hamburg: Felix Meiner, 1994, pp. 19–57.

—— *The Table of Judgments: Critique of Pure Reason A 67–76; B 92–101,* trans. Eric Watkins. Atascadero, Calif.: Ridgeview Publishing Co., 1995. *North American Kant Society Studies in Philosophy,* vol. 4.

—— "Zur Logik des ästhetischen Urteils," in Herman Parret, ed., *Kants Ästhetik, Kant's Aesthetics, L'esthétique de Kant.* Berlin and New York: Walter de Gruyter, 1998, pp. 229–45.

Bröcker, Walter. *Kants 'Kritik der ästhetischen Urteilskraft'.* Dissertation, Marburg, 1928.

Brunschwig, J. "Les multiples chemins aristotéliciens de la sensation commune," *Revue de Métaphysique et de Morale* (1991), pp. 455–74.

Bubner, Rüdiger. *Ästhetische Erfahrung.* Frankfurt am Main: Suhrkamp, 1989.

Budd, Malcolm. "Delight in the Natural World: Kant on the Aesthetic Appreciation of Nature." In three parts: "Part I: Natural Beauty," "Part II: Natural Beauty and Morality," "Part III: The Sublime in Nature," *British Journal of Aesthetics* 38 (1998) issues 1, 2, 3, pp. 1–18, 117–26, 233–50, respectively.

—— "The Pure Judgment of Taste as an Aesthetic Reflective Judgment," *British Journal of Aesthetics* 41 (2001), pp. 247–60.

Burnham, Douglas. *An Introduction to Kant's "Critique of Judgment."* Edinburgh: Edinburgh University Press, 2000.

Cassirer, Ernst. *Die Grundprobleme der Ästhetik.* Berlin: Alexander Verlag, 1989.

Cassirer, Heinrich Walter. *A Commentary of Kant's Critique of Judgment.* London: Methuen & Co, 1938, reprinted 1970.

Caygill, Howard. *Art of Judgment.* Oxford: Blackwell, 1989.

Cheetham, Mark A. *Kant, Art, and Art History. Moments of Discipline.* Cambridge: Cambridge University Press, 2001.

Chédrin, Olivier. *Sur l'esthétique de Kant et la théorie critique de la representation.* Paris: Vrin, 1982.

Cohen, Hermann. *Kants Begründung der Ästhetik.* Berlin: Dümmler, 1889.

Cohen, Ted and Guyer, Paul, eds. *Essays in Kant's Aesthetics.* Chicago and London: University of Chicago Press, 1982.

Cohen, Ted. "Why Beauty is the Symbol of Morality," in Ted Cohen and Paul Guyer, eds., *Essays in Kant's Aesthetics,* Chicago and London: University of Chicago Press, 1982, pp. 221–36.

—— "Three Problems in Kant's Aesthetics," *British Journal of Aesthetics* 42 (2002), pp. 1–12.

Coleman, Francis X. J. *The Harmony of Reason: A Study in Kant's Aesthetics.* Pittsburgh: University of Pittsburgh Press, 1974.

Cooley, Kenneth W. "Universality in Kant's Aesthetic Judgment," *Kinesis* 1 (1968), pp. 43–50.

Crawford, Donald W. *Kant's Aesthetic Theory.* Madison: The University of Wisconsin Press, 1974.

—— "Kant's Theory of Creative Imagination," in Ted Cohen and Paul Guyer, eds., *Essays in Kant's Aesthetics.* Chicago and London: University of Chicago Press 1982, pp. 151–78.

—— "The Place of the Sublime in Kant's Aesthetic Theory," in Richard Kennington, ed., *The Philosophy of Immanuel Kant.* Washington, DC: The Catholic University of America Press, 1985, pp. 161–83.

Crowther, Paul. *The Kantian Sublime: From Morality to Art.* Oxford: Clarendon Press, 1989.

Danto, Arthur. *After the End of Art: Contemporary Art and the Pale of History.* Princeton: Princeton University Press, 1997.

Derrida, Jacques. *The Truth in Painting,* trans. Geoff Bennington and Ian McLeod. Chicago and London: The University of Chicago Press, 1987. (*La vérité en peinture.* Paris: Flammarion, 1978.)

Dickie, George. *The Century of Taste: The Philosophical Odyssey of Taste in the Eighteenth Century.* New York and Oxford: Oxford University Press, 1996.

Dörflinger, Bernhard. *Die Realität des Schönen in Kants Theorie rein ästhetischer Urteilskraft. Zur Gegenstandsbedeutung subjektiver und formaler Ästhetik.* Bonn: Bouvier 1988.

Dumouchel, Daniel. "Esthétique et moralité selon Kant. Le cas du sublime," *Dialogue* 32 (1993), pp. 329–46.

162   BIBLIOGRAPHY

Dumouchel, Daniel. "Genèse de la *Troisième Critique*, le rôle de l'esthétique dans l'achève- ment du système critique," in Herman Parret, ed., *Kants Ästhetik, Kant's Aesthetics, l'esthétique de Kant.* Berlin and New York: Walter de Gruyter, 1998, pp. 18–40.

——*Kant et la genèse de la subjectivité esthétique. Esthétique et philosophie avant la critique de la faculté de juger.* Paris: Vrin, 2000.

Dunham, Barrows. "Kant's Theory of Aesthetic Form," in George T. Whitney and David F. Bowers, eds., *The Heritage of Kant.* Princeton: Princeton University Press, 1939, pp. 359–75.

Düsing, Klaus. "Beauty as the Transition from Nature to Freedom in Kant's *Critique of Judgment*," *Noûs* 24 (1990), pp. 79–92.

Elliott, R. K. "The Unity of Kant's *Critique of Aesthetic Judgment*," *British Journal of Aes- thetics* 8 (1968), pp. 244–59.

Falk, Barry. "The Communicability of Feeling," in Eva Schaper, ed., *Pleasure, Preference and Value: Studies in Philosophical Aesthetics.* Cambridge: Cambridge University Press, 1983, pp. 57–85.

Feger, Hans. *Die Macht der Einbildungskraft in der Ästhetik Kants und Schillers.* Heidelberg: Universitätsverlag C. Winter, 1995.

Ferguson, Francis. "The Sublime from Burke to the Present," in Michael Kelly, ed., *Encyclopedia of Aesthetics*, vol. 4, pp. 326–31.

Ferry, Luc. *Homo Aestheticus. L'invention du gout à l'âge démocratique.* Paris: Grasset, 1990.

Fisher, John. "Universalizability and Judgments of Taste," *American Philosophical Quarterly* 11 (1974), pp. 219–25.

Fisher, J. and Maitland, J. "The Subjectivist turn in Aesthetics: A Critical Analysis of Kant's Theory of Appreciation," *Review of Metaphysics* 27 (1974), pp. 726–51.

Floyd, Juliet. "Heautonomy: Kant on Reflective Judgment and Systematicity," in Herman Parret, ed., *Kants Ästhetik, Kant's Aesthetics, L'esthétique de Kant.* Berlin and New York: Walter de Gruyter, 1998, pp. 192–218.

Foisy, Suzanne. "L'ambiguité du sens esthétique transcendental," *Dialogue* 23 (1993), pp. 659–79.

Forrest, Williams. "Philosophical Anthropology and the Critique of Aesthetic Judgment," *Kant-Studien* 46 (1954/5), pp. 170–88.

Förster, Eckart. "Die Bedeutung von §§76, 77 der *Kritik der Urteilskraft* für die Entwick- lung der nachkantischen Philosophie," *Zeitschrift für Philosophische Forschung* 56 (2002), part I, pp. 169–90; part II, pp. 321–45.

——ed. *Kant's Transcendental Deductions. The Three "Critiques" and the "Opus postumum."* Stanford: Stanford University Press, 1989.

Frank, Manfred and Larthomas, Jean-Paul and Philonenko, Alexis. *Sur la troisième Critique.* Combas: Eclat, 1994.

——"Kants 'Reflexionen zur Ästhetik'. Zur Werkgeschichte der 'Kritik der ästhetischen Urteilskraft'," *Revue Internationale de la Philosophie* 44 (1990), pp. 552–80.

Fricke, Christel. *Kants Theorie des reinen Geschmacksurteils.* Berlin and New York: Walter de Gruyter, 1990.

——"Explaining the Inexplicable. The Hypothesis of the Faculty of Reflective Judgment in Kant's Third Critique," *Noûs* 24 (1990), pp. 45–62.

—— "Kants Theorie der schönen Form," *Akten des 7. Internationalen Kant-Kongress, II. 1.* Bonn: Bouvier, 1991, pp. 623–32.

Gadamer, Hans-Georg. *Truth and Method,* Joel Winsheimer and Donald G. Marshall, trans. New York: The Continuum Publishing Company, 1999. (*Wahrheit und Methode,* Tübingen, 1960.)

Gaiger, Jason. "Constraints and Conventions: Kant and Greenberg on Aesthetic Judgment," *British Journal of Aesthetics,* 39 (1999), pp. 376–99.

Gammon, Martin. "'Exemplary Originality': Kant on Genius and Imitation," *Journal of the History of Philosophy* 35 (1997), pp. 563–92.

—— "*Parerga* and *Pulchritudo adhaerens*: A Reading of the Third Moment of the 'Analytic of the Beautiful'," *Kant-Studien* 90 (1999), pp. 148–67.

Genova, Anthony C. "Kant's Transcendental Deduction of Aesthetic Judgments," *Journal of Aesthetics and Art Criticism* 30 (1971/72), pp. 459–75.

—— "Aesthetic Justification and Systematic Unity in Kant's Third Critique," in Gerhard Funke and Thomas M. Seebohm, eds., *Proceedings of the Sixth International Kant Congress,* Washington, DC: Center for Advanced Research in Phenomenology and University Press of America, 1989, vol. 2, pt. 2, pp. 293–309.

Gibbons, Sarah. *Kant's Theory of Imagination, Bridging Gaps in Judgment and Experience.* Oxford: Clarendon Press, 1994.

Ginsborg, Hannah. *The Role of Taste in Kant's Theory of Cognition.* New York and London: Garland Publishing Company, 1990.

—— "Reflective Judgment and Taste," *Noûs* 24 (1990), pp. 63–78.

—— "On the Key to Kant's Critique of Taste," *Pacific Philosophical Quarterly* 72 (1991), pp. 290–313.

—— "Lawfulness without a Law: Kant on the Free Play of Imagination and Understanding," *Philosophical Topics,* vol. 25 (1997), pp. 37–81.

—— "Kant on the Subjectivity of Taste," in Herman Parret, ed., *Kants Ästhetik, Kant's Aesthetics, L'esthétique de Kant.* Berlin and New York: Walter de Gruyter, 1998, pp. 448–65.

—— "Lawfulness without a Law: Kant on the Free Play of Imagination and Understanding," *Philosophical Topics* 25 (1997), pp. 37–81.

Giordanetti, Piero. "Das Verhältnis von Genie, Künstler und Wissenschaftler in der Kantischen Philosophie. Entwicklungsgeschichtliche Beobachtungen," *Kant-Studien* 86 (1995), pp. 406–30.

Gotshalk, D. W. "Form and Expression in Kant's Aesthetics," *British Journal of Aesthetics* 7 (1967), pp. 250–60.

Gould, Timothy. "The Audience of Originality: Kant and Wordsworth on the Reception of Genius," in Ted Cohen and Paul Guyer, eds., *Essays in Kant's Aesthetics.* Chicago: University of Chicago Press, 1982.

Gracyk, Theodore A. "Sublimity, Ugliness, and Formlessness in Kant's Aesthetic Theory," *Journal of Aesthetics and Art Criticism* 45 (1986), pp. 49–56.

Gregor, Mary J. "Aesthetic Form and Sensory Content in the Critique of Judgment: Can Kant's 'Critique of Aesthetic Judgment' Provide a Philosophical Basis for Modern Formalism?" in Richard Kennington, ed., *The Philosophy of Immanuel Kant,* Washington, DC: The Catholic University of America Press, 1985, pp. 185–99.

Guyer, Paul. "Formalism and the Theory of Expression in Kant's Aesthetics," *Kant-Studien* 68 (1977), pp. 46–70.

—— "Disinterestedness and Desire in Kant's Aesthetics," *Journal of Aesthetics and Art Criticism* 36 (1977/78), pp. 449–60.

—— *Kant and the Claims of Taste.* 1st edition: Harvard University Press, 1979; 2nd edition (with an additional chapter on fine art): Cambridge University Press, 1997.

—— "Kant's Distinction between the Beautiful and the Sublime," *Review of Metaphysics* 35 (1982/83), pp. 753–83.

—— "Nature, Art and Autonomy: A Copernican Revolution in Kant's Aesthetics," *Theorie der Subjektivität. Dieter Henrich zum 60. Geburtstag.* Frankfurt am Main: Suhrkamp, 1987, pp. 299–343. (Reprinted in *Kant and the Experience.*)

—— "Pleasure and Society in Kant's Theory of Taste," in Ted Cohen and Paul Guyer, eds., *Essays in Kant's Aesthetics.* Chicago and London: University of Chicago Press, 1982, pp. 21–54.

—— "Autonomy and Integrity in Kant's Aesthetics," *The Monist* 66 (1985).

—— "Reason and Reflective Judgment: Kant on the Significance of Systematicity," *Noûs* 24 (1990), pp. 17–43.

—— *Kant and the Experience of Freedom: Essays on Aesthetics and Morality.* Cambridge and New York: Cambridge University Press, 1993.

—— "Kant's Conception of Fine Art," *Journal of Aesthetics and Art Criticism* 52, 1994, pp. 275–85.

—— "Free and Adherent Beauty: A Modest Proposal," *British Journal of Aesthetics* 42 (2002), pp. 357–66.

——, ed. *The Cambridge Companion to Kant.* Cambridge: Cambridge University Press, 1992.

Hampshire, Stuart. "The Social Spirit of Mankind," in Eckart Förster, ed., *Kant's Transcendental Deductions. The Three "Critiques" and the "Opus postumum."* Stanford, Calif.: Stanford University Press, 1989, pp. 145–56.

Harper, Albert. *Essays on Kant's Third "Critique".* London: Mekler & Deahl Pub. 1989.

Heidemann, Ingeborg. *Der Begriff des Spiels und das ästhetische Weltbild in der Philosophie der Gegenwart.* Berlin: Walter de Gruyter, 1968.

Heintel, Peter. *Die Bedeutung der Kritik der ästhetischen Urteilskraft für die transzendentale Systematik.* Bonn: Bouvier, 1972.

Henckmann, Wolfahrt. "Über das Problem der Allgemeingültigkeit des ästhetischen Urteils in Kants Kritik der Urteilskraft," in Lewis White Beck, ed., *Proceedings of the 3rd International Kant Congress.* Dordrecht: Reidel, 1972, pp. 295–306.

Henrich, Dieter. *Aesthetic Judgment and the Moral Image of the World. Studies in Kant.* Stanford, Calif.: Stanford University Press, 1992.

Horkheimer, Max. *Über Kants Kritik der Urteilskraft als Bindeglied zwischen theoretischer und praktischer Philosophie.* Frankfurt am Main, 1925.

Horstmann, Rolf-Peter. "Why Must There Be a Transcendental Deduction in Kant's *Critique of Judgment?*" in Eckart Förster, ed., *Kant's Transcendental Deductions. The Three "Critiques" and the "Opus postumum."* Stanford, Calif.: Stanford University Press, 1989, pp. 157–76.

Hudson, Hud. "The Significance of an Analytic of the Ugly in Kant's Deduction of Pure Judgments of Taste," in Ralf Meerbote, ed., *Kant's Aesthetics*. Atascadero, Calif.: Ridgeview Publishing Company, 1991, pp. 87–103.

Jeng, Jyh-Jong. *Natur und Freiheit. Eine Untersuchung zu Kants Theorie der Urteilskraft.* Amsterdam and New York: Rodopi, 2004

Juchem, Hans-Georg. *Die Entwicklung des Begriffs des Schönen bei Kant.* Bonn: Bouvier, 1970.

Kaehler, Klaus Erich. "Zweckmäßigkeit ohne Zweck: Die systematischen Voraussetzungen und Rahmenbedingungen des dritten Moments des Geschmacksurteils in Kants "Kritik der Urteilskraft," in Jürgen-Eckardt Pleines, ed., *Zum teleologischen Argument in der Philosophie: Aristoteles, Kant, Hegel.* Würzburg: Königshausen und Neumann, 1991.

Kaminsky, Jack. "Kant's Analysis of Aesthetics," *Kant-Studien* 50 (1958/59), pp. 77–88.

Kaulbach, Friedrich. *Ästhetische Welterkenntnis bei Kant.* Würzburg: Königshausen und Neumann, 1984.

Kemal, Salim. "Aesthetic Necessity, Culture, and Epistemology," *Kant-Studien* 74 (1983), pp. 176–205.

——*Kant and Fine Art: An Essay on Kant and Philosophy of Fine Art and Culture.* Oxford: Clarendon Press, 1986.

——*Kant's Aesthetic Theory: An Introduction.* London: Macmillan, 1992.

Kinnaman, Ted. "Symbolism and Cognition in General in Kant's *Critique of Judgment*," *Archiv für Geschichte der Philosophie* 82 (2000), pp. 266–96.

Kivy, Peter. "Kant and the *Affektenlehre*: What He Said, and What I Wish He Had Said," in Ralf Meerbote, ed., *Kant's Aesthetics*. Atascadero, Calif.: Ridgeview Publishing Company, 1991, pp. 63–73.

Kneller, Jane. "Kant's Concept of Beauty," *History of Philosophy Quarterly* 3 (1986), pp. 311–24.

——"The Interests of Disinterest," in Hoke Robinson, ed., *Proceedings of the Eighth International Kant Congress Memphis 1995.* Milwaukee: Marquette University Press, 1996, vol. 1, part 2, pp. 777–86.

Kohler, Georg. *Geschmacksurteil und ästhetische Erfahrung; Beiträge zur Auslegung von Kants 'Kritik der ästhetischen Urteilskraft'.* Kantstudien Ergänzungsheft 111. Berlin and New York: Walter de Gruyter, 1980.

Kong, Byung-Hye. *Die ästhetische Idee in der Philosophie Kants.* Frankfurt am Main, Berlin, Bern, New York, Paris, and Vienna: Peter Lang, 1995.

Kotzin, Rhoda H. and Lansing, East and Baumgärtner, Jörg. "Sensations and Judgments of Perceptions. Diagnosis and Rehabilitation of some of Kant's Misleading Examples," *Kant-Studien* 81 (1990), pp. 401–12.

Krämling, Gerhard. *Die systembildende Rolle von Ästhetik und Kulturphilosophie bei Kant.* Freiburg-München: Alber, 1985.

Kroner, Richard. *Über logische und ästhetische Allgemeingültigkeit.* Leipzig: F. Eckardt, 1908.

Kulenkampff, Jens. "The Objective of Taste: Hume and Kant," *Noûs* 24 (1990), pp. 93–110.

——"Vom Geschmack als einer Art von sensus communis – Versuch einer Neubestimmung des Geschmacksurteils," *Autonomie der Kunst? Zur Aktualität von Kants Ästhetik.* Berlin: Akademie Verlag, 1994.

BIBLIOGRAPHY

Kulenkampff, Jens. *Kants Logik des ästhetischen Urteils*. Frankfurt am Main: Vitorio Klostermann, 1978; 2nd, enlarged edition 1994.

——, ed. *Materialien zu Kants 'Kritik der Urteilskraft'*. Frankfurt am Main: Suhrkamp, 1974.

Kuypers, K. *Kants Kunsttheorie und die Einheit der Kritik der Urteilskraft*. Amsterdam and London: North Holland Publishing Company, 1972.

Lang, Berel. "Kant and the Subjective Objects of Taste," *Journal of Aesthetics and Art Criticism* 25 (1967), pp. 247–53.

Lebrun, Gérard. *Kant et la fin de la métaphysique. Essai sur la "Critique de la faculté de Juger."* Paris: Librairie Armand Colin, 1970.

Lee Ming-Hui. *Das Problem des Moralischen Gefühls in der Entwicklung der Kantischen Ethik*. *Literary and Philosophical Studies Series 2*. Taiwan, ROC: Institute of Chinese Literature and Philosophy, Academia Sinica, 1994.

Lehmann, Gerhard. *Kants Nachlasswerk und die Kritik der Urteilskraft*. Berlin: Junker und Dünnhaupt, 1939.

Liedtke, Max. *Der Begriff der reflektierenden Urteilskraft in Kants Kritik der reinen Vernunft*. Diss. Hamburg, 1964.

Lohmar, Dieter. "Das Geschmacksurteil über das faszinierend Häßliche," in Herman Parret, ed., *Kants Ästhetik, Kant's Aesthetics, L'esthétique de Kant*. Berlin and New York: Walter de Gruyter, 1998, pp. 498–512.

Longuenesse, Béatrice. "Kant et les jugements empiriques. Jugements de perception et jugements d'expérience," *Kant-Studien* 86 (1995), pp. 278–307.

——*Kant and the Capacity to Judge: Sensibility and Discursivity in the Transcendental Analytic of the Critique of Pure Reason*, trans. Charles T. Wolfe. Princeton: Princeton University Press, 1998.

Lories, Danielle. "Génie et goût: complicité ou conflit? Autour du Par. 50 de la Troisième Critique," in Herman Parret, ed., *Kants Ästhetik, Kant's Aesthetics, L'esthétique de Kant*. Berlin and New York: Walter de Gruyter, 1998, pp. 564–93.

Lüthe, Rudolf. "Kants Lehre von den ästhetischen Ideen," *Kant-Studien* 75 (1984), pp. 65–74.

Lyotard, Jean-François. "Sensus Communis," *Cahiers du Collège International de Philosophie* 3 (1987), pp. 67–87.

——*Lessons on the Analytic of the Sublime*, trans. Elizabeth Rottenberg. Stanford, Calif.: Stanford University Press, 1994. (*Leçons sur l'Analytique du sublime*. Paris: Galilée, 1991.)

MacMillan, Claude. "Kant's Deduction of Pure Aesthetic Judgments," *Kant-Studien* 76 (1985), pp. 43–54.

Maitland, Jeffrey. "Two Senses of Necessity in Kant's Aesthetic Theory," *British Journal of Aesthetics* 16 (1976), pp. 347–53.

Makkreel, Rudolf A. *Imagination and Interpretation in Kant, The Hermeneutical Import of the Critique of Judgment*. Chicago and London: The University of Chicago Press, 1990.

Marc-Wogau, Konrad. *Vier Studien zu Kants Kritik der Urteilskraft*. Uppsala, 1938.

Matthews, Patricia. "Kant's Sublime: A Form of Pure Aesthetic Reflective Judgment," *Journal of Aesthetics and Art Criticism* 54 (1996), pp. 165–79.

McCloskey, Mary A. *Kant's Aesthetic*. Albany: State University of New York Press, 1987.

Meerbote, Ralf. "Reflection on Beauty," in Ted Cohen and Paul Guyer, eds., *Essays in Kant's Aesthetics*, Chicago and London: University of Chicago Press, 1982, pp. 55–86.

—— "The Singularity of Pure Judgments of Taste," in Herman Parret, ed., *Kants Ästhetik, Kant's Aesthetics, l'esthétique de Kant*. Berlin and New York: Walter de Gruyter, 1998, pp. 415–430.

Meerbote, Ralf and Hudson, Hud, eds. *Kant's Aesthetics*. Atascadero, Calif.: Ridgeview Publishing Company, 1991. *North American Kant Society Studies in Philosophy*, vol. 1.

Menzer, Paul. *Kants Ästhetik in ihrer Entwicklung*. Berlin: Akademie Verlag, 1952.

Mertens, Helga. *Kommentar zur Ersten Einleitung in Kants Kritik der Urteilskraft*. München: Johannes Berchmans Verlag, 1973.

Model, Anselm. *Metaphysik und Reflektierende Urteilskraft bei Kant. Untersuchungen zur Transformierung des Leibnizschen Monadenbegriffs in der "Kritik der Urteilskraft."* Frankfurt am Main: Athenäum, 1987.

Monk, Samuel. *The Sublime. A Study of Critical Theories in XVIII-Century England*. Ann Arbor: University of Michigan Press, 1960.

Mörchen, Hermann. *Die Einbildungskraft bei Kant* (Dissertation 1928). Tübingen: Max Niemeyer Verlag, 1970.

Mothersill, Mary. *Beauty Restored*. Oxford: Clarendon, 1984.

—— "The Antinomy of Taste," in Ralf Meerbote, ed., *Kant's Aesthetics*, Atascadero, Calif.: Ridgeview Publishing Company, 1991, pp. 75–86.

Müller, Ulrich. "Objektivität und Fiktionalität. Einige Überlegungen zu Kants Kritik der ästhetichen Urteilskraft," *Kant-Studien* 77 (1986), pp. 203–23.

Munzel, G. Felicitas. "'The Beautiful Is the Symbol of the Morally-Good': Kant's Philosophical Basis of Proof for the Idea of the Morally-Good," *Journal of the History of Philosophy* 33 (1995), pp. 301–29.

—— "The Privileged Status of Interest in Nature's Beautiful Forms: A Response to Jane Kneller," in Hoke Robinson, ed., *Proceedings of the Eighth International Kant Congress Memphis 1995*. Milwaukee: Marquette University Press, 1996, vol. 1, part 2, pp. 787–92.

Myskja, Bjørn K. *The Sublime in Kant and Beckett*. Berlin: Walter de Gruyter, 2002. *Kant-Studien Ergänzungshefte* 140.

Naum, Manfred. "Kants Prinzip der Zweckmässigkeit und Hegels Realisierung des Begriffs," in Hans-Friedrich Fulda and Rolf-Peter Horstmann, eds., *Hegel und die Kritik der Urteilskraft*, Stuttgart: Klett-Cotta, 1990, pp. 158–73.

Nenon, Thomas. *Objektivität und endliche Erkenntnis – Kants transzendentalphilosophische Korrespondenztheorie der Wahrheit*. Freiburg und München: Verlag Karl Alber, 1986.

Neumann, Karl. *Gegenständlichkeit und Existenzbedeutung des Schönen*. Bonn: Bouvier, 1973.

Neville, Michael R. "Kant's Characterization of Aesthetic Experience," *Journal of Aesthetics and Art Criticism* 33 (1984), pp. 193–202.

Nuyen, A. T. "The Kantian Theory of Metaphor," *Philosophy of Rhetoric* 22 (1989), pp. 95–109.

Otto, Marcus. *Ästhetische Wertschätzung. Bausteine zu einer Theorie des Ästhetischen*. Berlin: Akademie Verlag, 1993.

Parret, Herman. "De Baumgarten à Kant: sur la beauté," *Revue Philosophique de Louvain* 90 (1992), pp. 318–43.

Parret, Herman. "Zur Logik des Ästhetischen Urteils," in Herman Parret, ed., *Kants Ästhetik, Kant's Aesthetics, l'esthétique de Kant*. Berlin and New York: Walter de Gruyter, 1998, pp. 229–45.

Parret, Herman ed. *Kants Ästhetik, Kant's Aesthetics, L'esthétique de Kant*. Berlin and New York: Walter de Gruyter, 1998.

Pätzold, Heinz. *Ästhetik des deutschen Idealismus. Zur Idee ästhetischer Rationalität bei Baumgarten, Kant, Schelling, Hegel und Schopenhauer*. Wiesbaden: F. Steiner, 1983.

Peter, Joachim. *Das transzendentale Prinzip der Urteilskraft. Eine Untersuchung zur Funktion und Struktur der reflektierenden Urteilskraft bei Kant*. Berlin and New York: Walter de Gruyter, 1992. *Kantstudien Ergänzungshefte* 126.

Pippin, Robert B. "The Significance of Taste: Kant, Aesthetic and Reflective Judgment," *Journal of the History of Philosophy* 34 (1996), pp. 549–69.

——*Kant's Theory of Form. An Essay on the Critique of Pure Reason*. New Haven and London: Yale University Press, 1982.

Posy, Carl J. in Ralf Meerbote, ed., "Imagination and Judgment in the Critical Philosophy," *Kant's Aesthetics*. Atascadero, Calif.: Ridgeview Publishing Company, 1991, pp. 27–48.

Prauss, Gerold. "Kants Theorie der ästhetischen Einstellung," *Dialectica* 35 (1981), pp. 265–81.

Rind, Miles. "Kant's Beautiful Roses: A Response to Cohen's 'Second Problem'," *British Journal of Aesthetics* 43 (2003), pp. 65–74.

Rogerson, Kenneth R. *Kant's Aesthetics: The Roles of Form and Expression*. Lanham, Md., New York, and London: University Press of America, 1986.

Rohs, Peter. "Die Vermittlung von Natur und Freiheit in Kants Kritik der Urteilskraft," *Akten des 7. Internationalen Kant-Kongresses* I, 1990, pp. 213–34.

Saint-Girons, Baldine. *Fiat lux, une philosophie du sublime*. Paris: Quai Voltaire, 1993.

Savile, Anthony. "Objectivity in Aesthetic Judgment: Eva Schaper on Kant," *British Journal of Aesthetics* 21 (1981), pp. 364–69.

——*Aesthetic Reconstruction: The Seminal Writings of Lessing, Kant, and Schiller*. Oxford: Blackwell, 1987.

Schaeffer, Jean-Marie. *Art of the Modern Age, Philosophy of Art from Kant to Heidegger*, trans. Steven Rendall. Princeton: Princeton University Press, 2000.

Schaper, Eva. "The Kantian 'As-if' and its Relevance for Aesthetics," *Proceedings of the Aristotelian Society* 65 (1965), pp. 219–34.

——"Free and Dependent Beauty," *Kant-Studien* 65, Sonderheft (1974), pp. 247–62.

——*Studies in Kant's Aesthetics*. Edinburgh: Edinburgh University Press, 1979.

——"Zur Problematik des ästhetischen Urteils," *Akten des 7. Internationalen Kant-Kongresses* I, 1990, pp. 15–30.

——"Taste, Sublimity, and Genius: The Aesthetics of Nature and Art," in Paul Guyer, ed., *The Cambridge Companion to Kant*. Cambridge: Cambridge University Press, 1992, pp. 367–93.

——, ed. *Pleasure, Preference and Value, Studies in Philosophical Aesthetics*. Cambridge: Cambridge University Press, 1983.

——and Vossenkuhl, Wilhelm, eds. *Reading Kant. New Perspectives on Transcendental and Critical Philosophy*, Oxford: Blackwell, 1989.

Scheffer, T. *Kants Kritik der Wahrheit*. Berlin and New York: Walter de Gruyter, 1993.

Schlapp, Otto. *Kants Lehre vom Genie und die Enstehung der "Kritik der Urteilskraft."* Göttingen: Vandenhoedt & Ruprecht, 1901.

Schott, Rolin. "Kant and the Objectification of Aesthetic Pleasure," *Kant-Studien* 80, 1989, pp. 83–92.

Sedgwick, Sally, ed. *The Reception of Kant's Critical Philosophy: Fichte, Schelling, Hegel*. Cambridge, Cambridge University Press, 2000.

Seel, Gerhard. "Über den Grund der Lust an schönen Gegenständen. Kritische Fragen an die Ästhetik Kants," in H. Oberer, G. Seel, eds., *Kant. Analysen-Probleme-Kritik*. Würzburg: Königshausen & Neumann, 1988.

Shier, David. "Why Kant Finds Nothing Ugly," *British Journal of Aesthetics* 38 (1988), pp. 412–18.

Sibley, Frank. "Aesthetic Concepts," *The Philosophical Review* 68 (1959), pp. 421–50.

Simon, Josef. "Intersubjektivität bei Kant und Hegel," in Lothar Eley, ed., *Hegels Theorie des subjektiven Geistes*. Stuttgart: Bad Cannstatt, 1990.

Souriau, Michel. *Le judgment refléchissant dans la philosophie critique de Kant*. Paris: Librairie Félix Alcan, 1926.

Strasser, S. *Das Gemüt*. Freiburg-Utrecht: Herder-Spectrum, 1956.

Strub, Christian. "Das Hässliche und die 'Kritik der ästhetischen Urteilskraft,' Überlegungen zu einer systematischen Lücke," *Kant-Studien* 80 (1989), pp. 416–46.

Strube, Werner. "'Interesselosigkeit.' Zur Geschichte eines Grundbegriffs der Ästhetik," *Archiv für Begriffsgeschichte* 23 (1979), pp. 148–74.

Tassin, E. "Sens commun et communauté: la lecture arendienne de Kant," *Les Cahiers de Philosophie (Hannah Arendt Confrontations)*. Lille, 1987, pp. 81–112.

Ternay, Henri de. "Relation du sensus communis du jugement esthétique avec le contrat originaire de l'humanité," in Herman Parret, ed., *Kants Ästhetik, Kant's Aesthetic, l'esthétique de Kant*. Berlin and New York: Walter de Gruyter, 1998, pp. 557–63.

Thompson, Garrett. "Kant's Problems with Ugliness," *Journal of Aesthetics and Art Criticism* 50 (1992), pp. 107–15.

Tonelli, Giorgio. "Kant's Early Theory of Genius (1770–1779)," *Journal of the History of Philosophy* 4 (1966), part I, pp. 109–31; part II, pp. 209–24.

——"La formazione del testo della *Kritik der Urteilskraft*," *Revue Internationale de Philosophie* 8 (1954), pp. 423–48.

——"Von den verschiedenen Bedeutungen des Wortes 'Zweckmäßigkeit' in der Kritik der Urteilskraft," *Kant-Studien* 49 (1957/58), pp. 154–66.

Trebels, Andreas Heinrich. *Einbildungskraft und Spiel. Untersuchungen zur Kantischen Ästhetik*. Bonn: Walter de Gruyter, 1967. *Kantstudien Ergänzungshefte* 93.

Tschurenev, Eva-Maria. *Kant und Burke. Kants Ästhetik als Theorie des Gemeinsinns*. Frankfurt am Main, Bern and New York: Peter Lang, 1992.

Tumarkin, Anna. "Zur Transzendentalen Methode der Kantischen Ästhetik," *Kant-Studien* 11 (1906), pp. 348–78.

Tuschling, Burkhard. "The System of Transcendental Idealism: Questions Raised and Left Open in the Kritik der Urteilskraft," in Hoke Robinson, ed., *System and Teleology in Kant's Critique of Judgment* (Spindel Conference 1991), *Southern Journal of Philosophy* 30 (1992), supp. vol., pp. 109–27.

Uehling, Theodore E. *The Notion of Form in Kant's Critique of Aesthetic Judgment.* The Hague-Paris: Mouton, 1971.

Vaihinger, Hans. *Die Philosophie des Als Ob.* Berlin: Reuther & Reichard, 1911.

Verhaegh, Marcus. "The Truth of the Beautiful in the *Critique of Judgment*," *British Journal of Aesthetics* 41 (2001), pp. 371–94.

Weatherston, Martin. "Kant's Assessment of Music in the *Critique of Judgment*," *British Journal of Aesthetics* 36 (1996), pp. 56–65.

Wenzel, Christian Helmut. "Kant Finds Nothing Ugly?," *British Journal of Aesthetics* 39 (1999), pp. 416–22.

——*Das Problem der subjektiven Allgemeingültigkeit des Geschmacksurteils bei Kant.* Kantstudien-Ergänzungshefte 137, Walter de Gruyter, 2000.

——"Kann aus dem Urteil über das Angenehme ein Geschmacksurteil ähnlich wie aus dem Wahrnehmungsurteil ein Erfahrungsurteil werden?" *Akten des Neunten Internationalen Kant-Kongresses Berlin 2000,* vol. 3, Walter de Gruyter, 2001, pp. 468–476.

——"Beauty, Genius, and Mathematics. Why Did Kant Change His Mind?" *History of Philosophy Quarterly* 18 (2001), pp. 415–432.

Wettstein, Ronald H. *Kants Prinzip der Urteilskraft.* Königstein/Ts.: Forum Academicum in der Verlagsgruppe Athenäum, Hain, Scriptor, Hanstein, 1981.

Wilbur, J. B. "Kant's Critique of Art and the Good Will," *Kant-Studien* 61 (1970).

Winterbourne, A. T. "Art and Mathematics in Kant's Critical Philosophy," *British Journal of Aesthetics* 28 (1988), pp. 266–77.

Wohlfart, Günter. "Transzendentale Ästhetik und Ästhetische Reflexion," *Zeitschrift für Philosophische Forschung* 36 (1982), pp. 64–76.

——"Zum Problem der transzendentalen Affinität in der Philosophie Kants," *Akten des 5. Internationalen Kant-Kongresses,* I.1 (1981), pp. 313–22.

——*Metakritik der Ästhetischen Urteilskraft.* Diss: Frankfurt am Main, 1970.

Wolff, Michael. *Die Vollständigkeit der kantischen Urteilstafel. Mit einem Essay über Freges "Begriffsschrift."* Frankfurt am Main: Vittorio Klostermann, 1995.

Wood, Allan W., ed. *Self and Nature in Kant's Philosophy.* Ithaca and London: Cornell University Press, 1984.

Zammito, John H. *The Genesis of Kant's "Critique of Judgment."* Chicago and London: The University of Chicago Press, 1992.

Zimmermann, Jörg. *Sprachanalytische Ästhetik. Ein Überblick.* Stuttgart, 1980.

Zimmermann, Robert L. "Kant: The Aesthetic Judgment," in R. P. Wolff, ed., *Kant. A Collection of Critical Essays.* Garden City, NY: Doubleday & Co., 1967, pp. 385–406.

Zöller, Günther. "Toward the Pleasure Principle. Kant's Transcendental Psychology of the Feeling of Pleasure and Displeasure," *Akten des 7. Internationalen Kant-Kongresses* II.1 (1991), pp. 812–19.

Index

Numbers in italics, like *26*, indicate a reference to an entry from a Further Reading section; numbers in bold, like **26**, indicate a reference to an entry in the Glossary.